From Databases to Hypermedia

Springer-Verlag Berlin Heidelberg GmbH

Springer-Verlag Berlin Heidelberg GmbH

Hermann Maurer   Nick Scherbakov
Zahran Halim   Zaidah Razak

From Databases to Hypermedia

With 26 CAI Lessons

With 261 Figures
Including CD-ROM

 Springer

Hermann Maurer
Nick Scherbakov

IICM, Graz University of Technology
Schiessstattgasse 4a
A-8010 Graz, Austria

Zahran Halim
KUB Teknologi Sdn Bdh
Pekeliling Business Centre
Jalan 65C Off Jalan Pahang Barat
53000 Kuala Lumpur, Malaysia

Zaidah Razak
KUB Research Sdn Bhd
Lot 1-2, Incubator 3
Technology Park Malaysia
Bukit Jalil
57000 Kuala Lumpur, Malaysia

Additional material to this book can be downloaded from http://extras.springer.com.

ISBN 978-3-540-63754-7

```
Library of Congress Cataloging-in-Publication Data
From databases to hypermedia: with 26 CAI lessons / Hermann
Maurer ... (et al.). p. cm.
  Includes bibliographical references.
  ISBN 978-3-540-63754-7       ISBN 978-3-642-58763-4 (eBook)
  DOI 10.1007/978-3-642-58763-4
  1. Database management.  2. Interactive multimedia.
I. Maurer, Hermann A., 1941-
QA76.9.D3.F78   1998    005.74--dc21     98-36068   CIP
```

© Springer-Verlag Berlin Heidelberg 1998
Originally published by Springer-Verlag Berlin Heidelberg New York in 1998

Cover Design: Künkel & Lopka, Heidelberg
Typesetting: Camera ready by authors
Printed on acid-free paper SPIN 10552009 45/3142 5 4 3 2 1 0

Preface

The number of books on databases is very large. Thus, our decision to yet add another book to the body of literature requires some justification. However, even a cursory glance through this book will show that we have taken a rather different approach indeed when compared to monographs on databases.

First, material ties together the well-known relational model with the newer and not yet as solidly established object oriented one and leads to data models for hypermedia system. This is unique and timely: the chaos on the World Wide Web is getting out of hand, and one of the main reasons is that the underlying data model is too weak.

Second, the book is full of illustrations. And those illustrations are not only available in printed form, but also on a CD ROM. Actually, much more is true: for each of the 26 chapters, electronic courseware is available, one lesson per chapter.

Third, the lessons described contain explanations that are easier or better to understand than those provided in the printed chapter, since a number of dynamic and interactive features are used.

Fourth, the lessons can be used in a variety of modes: as complement for the book; as stand-alone material instead of the book; as slides for the lecturer; and as help for the student. And, as explained below they can be easily modified.

Fifth, existing books tend to describe database technology but do not take into consideration either the teaching process lecturers have to go through or the learning process required from the students. Thus, in order to deliver a course on databases, instructors usually have to prepare material including transparencies to illustrate the main points graphically; they have to produce material to hand out or describe in detail which sections of which book are going to be relevant; they have to think about examination questions and other supporting material. Much of this is taken care of by the book and the CD ROM. From a student point of view, the courseware provided is a better substitute than just printed material alone if a lecture has been missed, or some points have not been understood. In this fashion the combination book / courseware helps both teachers and students: teachers find nicely pre-packaged material that is quite modular (see below), with the courseware or the diagrams in it suitable for direct presentation in the classroom.

Sixth, the material is modular, so it is also possible to use only parts of it. For example, some instructors may decide to just use Lesson 4: "Relational Data Model: Normalization" and Lesson 19: "Introduction to Multimedia". They can make those two lessons available on floppies or on a suitable server; see, e.g., the Hyperwave server *http://www.iicm.edu/hmcard/courseware/courseware.htm*. Actually, the modularity goes deeper. Suppose a teacher does not want to use all the courseware, but wants to use some of the hundreds of diagrams: well, all diagrams can be copied individually, resized, collected on a server or printed out as desired.

Seventh, the book comes with a complete version of the editing software: to modify a particular lesson it is sufficient to install the "HM-Card Editor" from the CD ROM and look into the "Help" files to understand how to operate the editor.

Finally, the book covers the basic concepts usually taught in all undergraduate university level courses, without going into too much technical detail. Hence the book should have a rather wide appeal.

This book is written by teachers for teachers and their students. It makes it easier to teach an introductory course on databases without restricting the freedom of instructors to go deeper with respect to issues they consider particularly important. Students have found the combination of book and courseware very useful, as a number of anonymous evaluations has shown.

Thus, this book is not just an ordinary book on databases, but a comprehensive set of tools for teaching and for learning the subject matter.

Despite of the broad appeal of this book, it also does have its limitations. First, the software runs only on Windows platforms, i.e., it cannot be used under UNIX or on Macs (sorry, folks!); and second, important topics such as the Network (CODASYL) Data Model, deductive databases, and functional databases are not included.

We thus pose this challenge to you: if you like the book and the courseware, but if you find that the last mentioned topics are crucial for you, or that a more platform-independent form is needed, let us know. If we get enough encouragement, two of us (Nick and Hermann) have decided to go ahead and use a Java based approach within a GEneral Networked Training and Learning Environment (GENTLE: see

http://www.iicm.edu/gentle.htm)

and to produce a second follow-up volume for the topics mentioned.

We now hope that you will enjoy book and courseware. Both have been tested by students in Europe and Asia with good success. I hope you will find that our material also works for you.

As the co-author who mainly co-ordinated production of the book with Springer, I also feel obliged to tell you a bit about the role of the four authors of the book. *The* main author (and we have debated for a long time whether we should not deviate from the alphabetical order and list him first) is Nick Scherbakov. Nick is professor for Computer Science at my institute in Graz, Austria. He was the one who developed and tested most of the courseware, with just occasional inputs from me. Zahran Halim and Zaidah Razak are professors for Computer Science at Universiti Malaysia Sarawak (UNIMAS), have been instrumental in checking the material and transcribing the lessons into independently readable chapters. Particularly the part on relational databases was very much influenced by them. Most of the diagrams in the book were drawn by Nick's wife Irina.

At this point it is also appropriate to thank Dr. Hans Woessner from Springer for his continued encouragement and infinite patience: the book took much longer to complete than we all had expected!

Happy reading is what we all wish you now,

Hermann Maurer,

Graz University of Technology/Austria.

hmaurer@iicm.edu

P.S. Please direct all questions concerning the courseware and its editor to the person who was the real driving force and main author, Nick Scherbakov, at *nsherbak@iicm.edu*

Table of Contents

Part I
Databases and the Relational Data Model

1. Introduction to Databases

1.1. Introduction

We live in an information age. By this we mean that, first, we accept the universal fact that information is required in practically all aspects of human enterprise. The term 'enterprise' is used broadly here to mean any organisation of activities to achieve a stated purpose, including socio-economic activities. Second, we recognise further the importance of efficiently providing timely relevant information to an enterprise and of the importance of the proper use of technology to achieve that. Finally, we recognise that the unparallelled development in the technology to handle information has and will continue to change the way we work and live, ie. not only does the technology support existing enterprises but it changes them and makes possible new enterprises that would not have otherwise been viable.

The impact is perhaps most visible in business enterprises where there are strong elements of competition. This is especially so as businesses become more globalised. The ability to coordinate activities, for example, across national borders and time zones clearly depends on the timeliness and quality of information made available. More important perhaps, strategic decisions made by top management in response to perceived opportunities or threats will decide the future viability of an enterprise, one way or the other. In other words, in order to manage a business (or any) enterprise, future development must be properly estimated. Information is a *vital* ingredient in this regard.

Information must therefore be collected and analysed in order to make decisions. It is here that the proper use of technology will prove to be crucial to an enterprise. Up-to-date management techniques should include computers, since they are very powerful tools for processing large quantities of information. Collecting and analysing information using computers is facilitated by current Database Technology, a relatively mature technology which is the subject of this book.

1.2. Information Model

Information stored in computer memory is called *data*. In current computer systems, such data can (persistently) reside on a number of memory devices, most common of which are floppy disks, CD-ROMs, and hard disks.

Data that we store and manipulate using computers are meaningful only to the extent that they are associated with some real world object in a given context. Take, for example, the number '23'. This is a piece of data, but by itself a meaningless quantity. If it was associated with, say, a person and interpreted to denote that person's age (in years), then it begins to be more meaningful. Or, if it was associated with, say, an organisation that sells electronic goods and interpreted to mean the number of television sets sold in a given month, then again it becomes more meaningful. Notice that in both preceding examples, other pieces of data had to be brought into context - a person, a person's age, a shop, television sets, a given month, etc.

If the data is a collection of related facts about some enterprise (eg. a business, an organisation, an activity, etc), then it is called a database. The data stored need not include every conceivable piece of fact about that enterprise. Usually, only facts relevant to some area of an enterprise are captured and organised, typically to provide information to support decision making at various levels (operational, management, etc). Such a constrained area of focus is also often referred to as the *problem domain* or *domain of interest*, and is typical of databases. In this sense, a database is an *information model* of some (real-world) problem domain.

1.2.1. Entities

Information models operate on so-called entities and entity relationships. In this section we will clarify what an entity is. Entity relationships are described in 1.2.2.

An *entity* is a particular object in the problem domain. For example, we can extend the electronics organisation above to identify three distinct entities: products, customers and sales representatives (see Figure 1-1). They are distinct from one another in the sense that each has characteristic *properties* or *attributes* that distinguish it from the others. Thus a product has properties such as type, function, dimensions, weight, brand name, cost and price; a customer has properties such as name, city of residence, age, credit rating, etc.; and a sales representative has properties such as name, address, sales region, basic salary, etc. Each entity is thus *modelled* in the database as a collection of data items corresponding to its relevant attributes. (Note that we distinguish between entities even if in the real world they are from the same class of objects. For example, a customer and a sales representative are both people, but a customer is a person who purchases goods while a sales representative is one who sells goods. The different 'roles' played distinguishes each from the other)

Note also the point made earlier that an information model captures only what is relevant in the given problem domain. Certainly, there are other entities in the organisation - regional offices, warehouses, store keepers, distributors, etc - but these may be irrelevant in the context of, say, analysing sales transactions and are thus omitted from the information model. Even at the level of entity attributes, not all conceivable properties need be captured as data items. A customer's height, weight, hair colour, hobby, formal qualification, favourite foods, etc, are probably irrelevant and can thus omitted from the model.

Strictly speaking, the objects we referred to above as entities are perhaps more accurately called entity classes because they each denote a set of objects (individual entities), each of which exhibits the properties/attributes described for the class. Thus the entity class 'customer' is made up of individual entities, each of which has attributes 'name', 'city of residence', 'age', etc. Every individual entity will then have these attributes but one individual will differ from another in the *values* (data items) associated with attributes. For example, one customer entity might have the value 'Smith' as its 'name' attribute, while another might have the value 'Jones'.

Figure 1-1 Problem domain entities and their attributes

Notice now that in our information model an attribute is really a pair: an attribute description or name (such as 'age') and an attribute value (such as '56'), or simply, an 'attribute–value' pair. An individual entity is completely modelled only when all its attribute descriptions have been associated with appropriate attribute values. The collection of attribute–value pairs that model a particular individual entity is termed a *data object*. Figure 1-2 illustrates three data objects in the database, each being a complete model of an individual from its corresponding entity class.

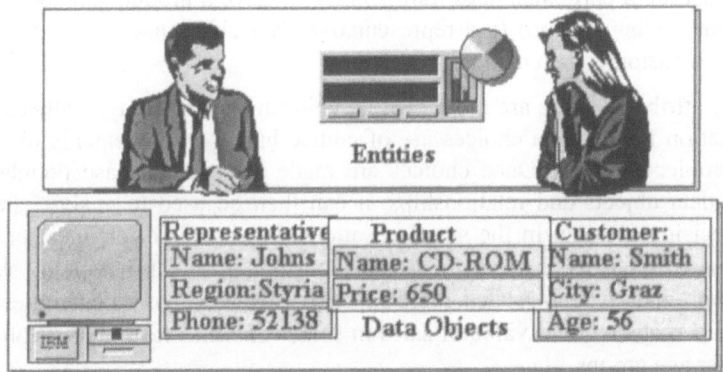

Figure 1-2. Data objects model particular entities in the real world

1.2.2. Entity Relationships

An entity by itself is often not as interesting or as informative as when it relates in some way to some other entity or entities. A particular product, say a CD-ROM drive, itself only tells us about its intrinsic properties as recorded in its associated data object. A database, however, models more than individual entities in the problem domain. It also models *relationships* between entities.

In the real world, entities do not stand alone. A CD-ROM drive is supplied by a supplier, is stored in a warehouse, is bought by a customer, is sold by a sales representative, is serviced by a technician, etc. Each of these is an example of a relationship, a logical association between two or more entities.

Figure 1-3. Relationships between entities

Figure 1-3 illustrates such relationships by using links labelled with the type of association between entities. In the figure, a representative sells a product and a customer buys a product. Taken together, these links and the entities they link model a sales transaction: a particular sales transaction will have a product data object related (through the 'sells' relation) to a representative data object and (through the 'buys' relation) to a customer data object.

Like entity attributes, there are many more relationships than are typically captured in an information model. The choices are of course based on judgements of relevance given a problem domain. Once choices are made and the database populated with particular data objects and relationships, it can then be used to analyse the data to support decision making. In the simple example developed so far, there are already many types of analysis that can be carried out, eg. the distribution of sales of a particular product type by sales region, the performance of sales representatives (measured perhaps by total value of sales in some time interval), product preferences by customer age groups, etc.

1.3. Database Management

The real world is dynamic. As an organisation goes about its business, entities are created, modified or destroyed. Similarly with entity relationships. This is easy to see even for the simple problem domain above, eg. when a sales is made, the product sold is then logically linked to the customer that bought it and to the representative that sold it. Many sales transactions could take place each day and thus many new logical links created between many individual entities. New entities can also be introduced, eg. a new customer arrives on the scene, a new product is offered, or a new salesperson is hired. Likewise, some entities may no longer be of concern to the organisation, eg. a product is discontinued, a salesperson quits or is fired, etc (these entities may still exist in the real world but have become irrelevant for the problem domain). Clearly, an information model must also change to reflect the changes in the problem domain that it models.

If the problem domain is small, involving only a few entities and relationship, and the dynamic changes are relatively few or infrequent, manual methods may be sufficient to maintain an accurate record of the state of the business. But if hundreds or thousands of entities are involved and the business is very dynamic, then maintaining accurate records of its state becomes more of a problem. This is when computers with their immense power to handle large amounts of information become crucial to an organisation. Frequently, it is not just a question of efficiency, but of survival, especially in intensely competitive business sectors.

The need to use computers to efficiently and effectively store databases and to keep them current has developed over the years special software packages called *Database Management Systems* (DBMS). A DBMS enables users to create, modify, access and protect their databases (Figure 1-4).

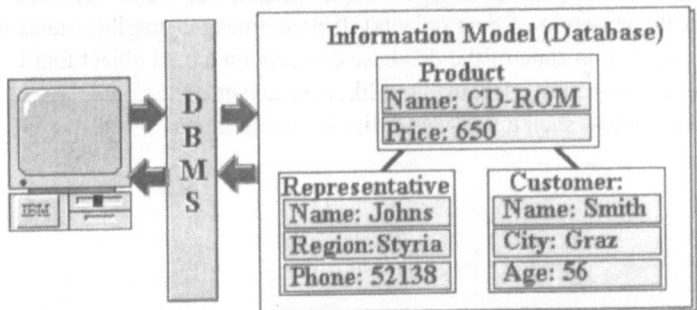

Figure 1-4 A DBMS is a tool to create and use databases

In other words, a DBMS is a *tool* to be applied by users to build an accurate and useful information model of their enterprise.

Conceptually, database management is based on the idea of separating a database *structure* from its *contents*. Quite simply, a database structure is a collection of static descriptions of entity classes and relationships between them. At this point, it is perhaps simplest to think of an entity class description as a collection of attribute labels. Entity contents can then be thought of as the values that get associated with attribute labels, creating data objects. In other words, the distinction between structure and content is little more than the distinction made earlier between attribute label and attribute value.

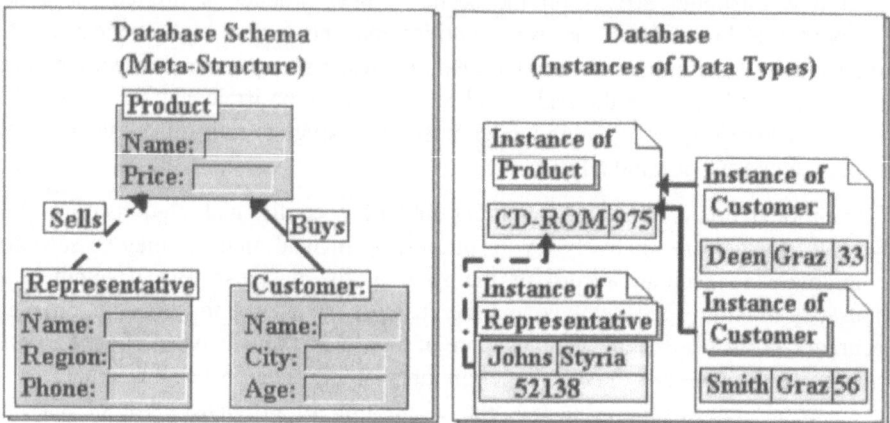

Figure 1-5 Separation of structure from content

Relationship descriptions likewise are simply labelled links between entity descriptions. They specify possible links between data objects, ie. two data objects can be linked only if the database structure describes a link between their respective entity classes. Figure 1-5 illustrates this separation of structure from content.

The database structure is also called a *schema* (or *meta-structure* - because it describes the structure of data objects). It predefines all possible states of a database, in the sense that no state of the database can contain a data object that is not the result of instantiating an entity schema, and likewise no state can contain a link between two data objects unless such a link was defined in the schema.

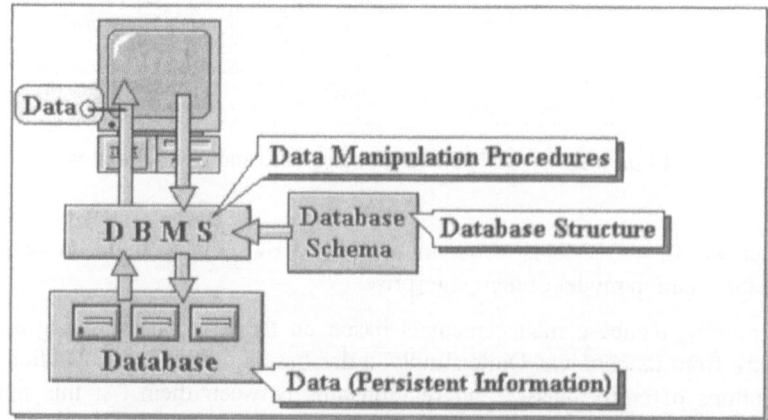

Figure 1-6 Architecture of database systems

Moreover, data manipulation procedures can be separated from the data as well! Thus the architecture of database systems may be portrayed as in Figure 1-6.

1.4. Database Languages

We see from the foregoing that to build a database, a user must

1. Define the Database Schema
2. Apply a collection of operators supported by the DBMS to create, store, retrieve and modify data of interest

A typical DBMS would provide tools to facilitate the above tasks. At the heart of these tools, a DBMS typically maintains two closely related *languages*:

1. A Data Description Language (DDL), which is used to define database schemas, and
2. A Data Manipulation Language (DML), which allows the user to manipulate data objects and relationships between them in the context of given database schemas

These languages may vary from one DBMS to another, in their underlying data model, complexity, functionality, and ease of use (user interface).

So far, we have talked about 'users' as if they were all equal in interacting with a DBMS. In actual fact, though, there may be several types of users distinguished by their role (a division of labour, often necessary because of highly technical aspects of DBMSs). For example, an organisation that uses a DBMS will normally have a Database Administrator (DBA) whose job is to create and maintain a consistent set of database schemas to satisfy the needs of different parts of the organisation. The DBA is the principal user of the DDL. Then there are application developers who develop specific functions around the database (eg. product inventory, customer information, point-of-sale transaction handling, etc). They are the principal users of the DML. And finally, there are the end-users who use the applications developed to support their work in the organisation. They normally don't see (and don't care to know about!) the DDL or the DML.

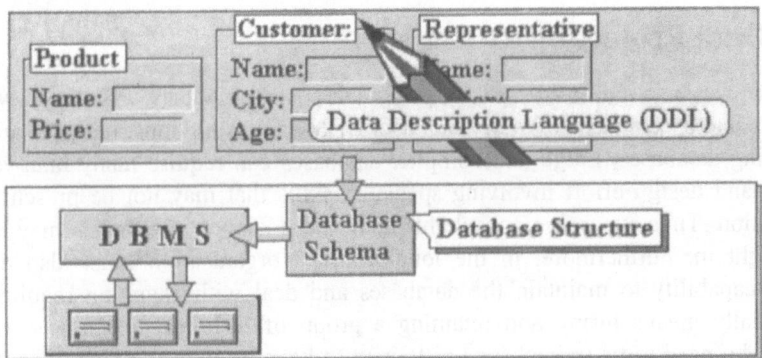

Figure 1-7 (notional) DDL definition

The DDL is a collection of statements for the description of data types. The DBA must define the target database structure in terms of these data types.

For instance, the data object, attribute and link mentioned above are data types, and hence may be perceived as a simple DDL. Thus the data structures in Figure 1-5 are notionally DDL descriptions of a database schema, as illustrated in Figure 1-7 ('notional' because the actual language will have specific syntactical constructs that may differ from one DBMS to another).

A DML is a collection of operators that can be applied to valid instances (ie. data objects) of the data types in the schema. As illustrated in Figure 1-8, the DML is used to manipulate instances, including the creation, modification and retrieval of instances. (Like the DDL above, the illustration here is notional; more concrete forms of these languages will be covered in later sections of this book).

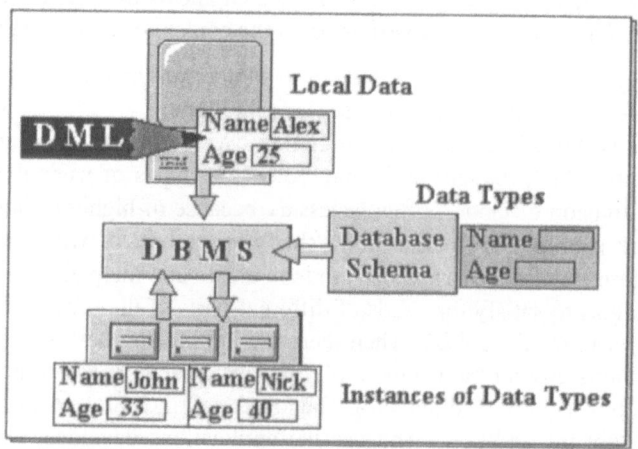

Figure 1-8 DML manipulations of instances

1.5. Data Protection

Databases can be a major investment. There are costs, obviously, associated with the hardware and specialised software such as a DBMS. Less obvious, perhaps, are costs of creating databases. Large and complex databases can require many man-years of analysis and design effort involving specialist skills that may not be present in the organisation. Thus expensive consultants and other technical specialists may have to be brought in. Furthermore, in the long-term, an organisation must also develop internal capability to maintain the databases and deal with changing requirements. This usually means hiring and retaining a group of technical specialists, such as DBAs, who need to be trained (and re-trained to keep up with the technology). End-users too will need to be trained to use the system properly. In other words, there are considerable running costs as well. In all, databases can be *very* expensive.

Aside from the expenses above, databases often are crucial to a business. Imagine what would happen, say, if databases of customer accounts maintained by a bank were (accidently or maliciously) destroyed! Because of these actual and potential costs, databases must be deliberately protected against any conceivable harm.

Generally, there are three types of security that must be put in place:

1. *Physical Protection*: these are protective measures to guard against natural disasters (eg. fire, floods, earthquakes, etc), theft, accidental damage to equipment and other threats that can cause the physical loss of data. This is generally the area of physical installation management and is outside the scope of this book.

2. *Operational Protection*: these are measures to minimise or even eliminate the impact of human errors on the databases' integrity. Errors can occur, for example, in assigning values to attributes - a value may be unreasonable (eg. an age of 213!) or of the wrong type (eg. the value 'Smith' assigned to the age attribute). These measures are typically embodied in a set of *integrity constraints* (a set of assertions) that must be enforced (ie. the truth of the assertions must be preserved across all database transactions). An example of an assertion might be 'the price of a product must be a positive number'. Any operation then is invalid if it violates a stated constraint, eg. "Store ... Price= -9.99". These constraints are typically specified by a DBA in the database schema.

3. *Authorisational Protection*: these are measures to ensure that access to the databases are by authorised users only, and then only for specific modes of access (eg. some users may only be allowed to read while others can modify database contents). They are necessary to ensure that confidentiality and correctness of information is preserved. Access control can be applied at various levels in the system. At the installation level, access through computer terminals may be controlled using special access cards or passwords. At successively lower levels, control may be applied to an entire database, to its physical devices (or parts thereof), or to its logical parts (parts of the schema). In extremely sensitive problem domains, access control may even be applied to individual instances or data objects in the database.

2. Basic Relational Data Model

2.1 Introduction

Basic concepts of information models, their realisation in databases comprising data objects and object relationships, and their management by DBMS's that separate structure (schema) from content, were introduced in the last chapter. The need for a DDL to define the structure of entities and their relationships, and for a DML to specify manipulation of database contents were also established. These concepts, however, were presented in quite abstract terms, with no commitment to any particular data structure for entities or links nor to any particular function to manipulate data objects.

There is no single method for organising data in a database, and many methods have in fact been proposed and used as the basis of commercial DBMS's. A method must fully specify:

1. the rules according to which data are structured, and

2. the associated operations permitted

The first is typically expressed and encapsulated in a DDL, while the second, in an associated DML. Any such method is termed a *Logical Data Model* (often simply referred to as a *Data Model*). In short,

$$\boxed{\text{Data Model} = \text{DDL} + \text{DML}}$$

and may be seen as a technique for the formal description of data structure, usage constraints and allowable operations. The facilities available typically vary from one Data Model to another.

Each DBMS may therefore be said to maintain a particular Data Model (see Figure 2-1).

More formally, a Data Model is a combination of at least three components:

(1) A collection of data structure *types*

(2) A collection of *operators* or *rules of inference*, which can be applied to any valid instance of data types in (1)

(3) A collection of general *integrity rules*, which implicitly or explicitly define the set of consistent database states or change of state or both

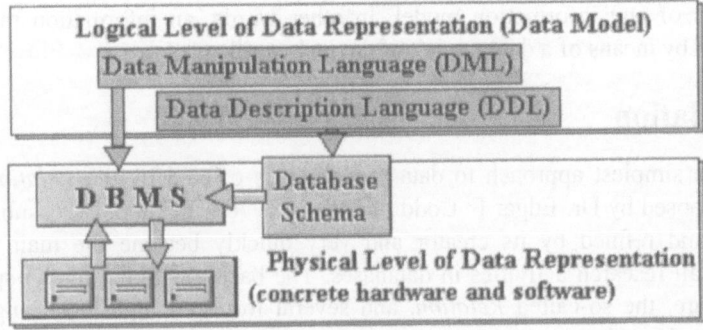

Figure 2-1 Logical data model

It is important to note at this point that a Data Model is a *logical representation* of data which is then realised on specific hardware and software platforms (its *implementation*, or *physical representation* as illustrated in Figure 2-1). In fact, there can be many different implementations of a given model, running on different hardware and operating systems and differing perhaps in their efficiency, performance, reliability, user interface, additional utilities and tools, physical limitations (eg. maximum size of databases), costs, etc. (see Figure 2-2). All of them, however, will support a mandatory minimal set of facilities defined for that data model. This is analogous to programming languages and their implementations, eg. there are many C compilers and many of them implement an agreed set of standard features regardless of the hardware and software platforms they run on. But as with programming languages, we need not concern ourselves with the variety of implementations when developing database applications - knowledge of the basic logical data model is sufficient for us to do that.

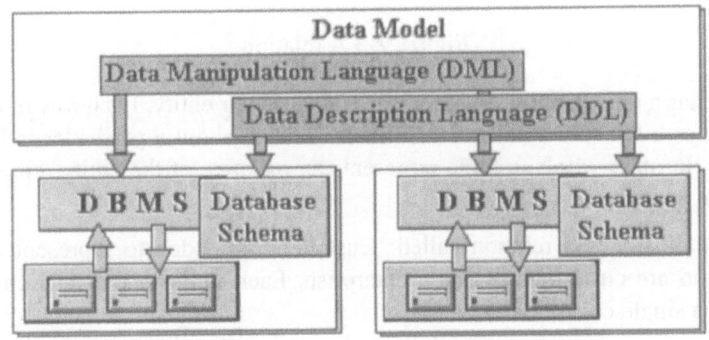

Figure 2-2 Multiple realisations of a single data model

It is also important not to confuse the terms *information model* and *data model*. The former is an abstraction of a real world problem domain and talks of entities, relationships and instances (data objects) specific to that domain. The latter provides a domain independent formal framework for expressing and manipulating the abstractions of any information model. In other words, an information model is a description, by means of a data model, of the real world.

2.2   Relation

Perhaps the simplest approach to data modelling is offered by the *Relational Data Model*, proposed by Dr. Edgar F. Codd of IBM in 1970. The model was subsequently expanded and refined by its creator and very quickly became the main focus of practically all research activities in databases. The basic relational model specifies a data structure, the so-called *Relation*, and several forms of high-level languages to manipulate relations.

The term *relation* in this model refers to a two-dimensional table of data. In other words, according to the model, information is arranged in columns and rows. The term *relation*, rather than matrix, is used here because data values in the table are not necessarily homogenous (ie. not all of the same type as, for example, in matrices of integers or real numbers). More specifically, the values in any row are not homogenous. Values in any given column, however, are all of the same type (see Figure 2-3).

Customer			
C#	Cname	Ccity	Cphone
1	Codd	London	2263035
2	Martin	Paris	5555910
3	Deen	London	2234391

Figure 2-3 A relation

A relation has a unique name and represents a particular entity. Each row of a relation, referred to as a *tuple*, is a collection of facts (values) about a particular individual of that entity. In other words, a tuple represents an *instance* of the entity represented by the relation.

Figure 2-4 illustrates a relation called 'Customer', intended to represent the set of persons who are customers of some enterprise. Each tuple in the relation therefore represents a single customer.

The columns of a relation hold values of attributes that we wish to associate with each entity instance, and each is labelled with a distinct attribute name at the top of the column. This name, of course, provides a unique reference to the entire column or to a particular value of a tuple in the relation. But more than that, it denotes a *domain* of values that is defined *over all relations* in the database.

The term *domain* is used to refer to a set of values of the same kind or type. It should be clearly understood, however, that while a domain comprises values of a given type, it is *not* necessarily the same as that type. For example, the column 'Cname' and 'Ccity' in Figure 2-4 both have values of type string (ie. valid values are any string). But they denote different domains, ie. 'Cname' denotes the domain of customer names while 'Ccity' denotes the domain of city names. They are different domains even if they share common values. For example, the string 'Paris' can conceivably occur in the Column 'Cname' (a person named Paris). Its meaning, however, is quite different to the occurrence of the string 'Paris' in the column 'Ccity' (a city named Paris)! Thus it is quite meaningless to compare values from different domains even if they are of the same type.

Customer			
C#	Cname	Ccity	Cphone
1	Codd	London	2263035
2	Martin	Paris	5555910
3	Deen	London	2234391

Tuple →

Customer Number 2 (C#);
Name: Martin (Cname)
Lives in Paris (Ccity)
Phone: 5555910 (Cphone)

Figure 2-4 Relation and entity

Moreover, in the relational model, the term domain refers to the *current set* of values found under an attribute name. Thus, if the relation in Figure 2-4 is the only relation in the database, the domain of 'Cname' is the set {Codd, Martin, Deen}, while that of 'Ccity' is {London, Paris}. But if there were other relations and an attribute name occurs in more than one of them, then its domain is the *union* of values in all columns with that name.

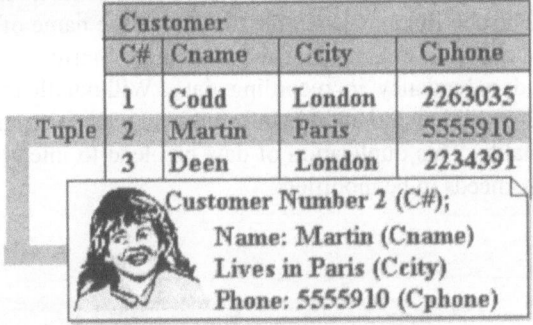

Figure 2-5 Domain of an attribute

This is illustrated in Figure 2-5 where two relations each have a column labelled 'C#'. It also clarifies the statement above that a domain is defined over all relations, ie. an attribute name always denotes the same domain in whatever relation in occurs.

This property of domains allows us to represent relationships between entities. That is, when two relations share a domain, identical domain values act as a *link* between tuples that contain them (because such values mean the same thing). As an example, consider a database comprising three relations as shown in Figure 2-6. It highlights a Transaction tuple and a Customer tuple linked through the C# domain value '2', and the same Transaction tuple and a Product tuple linked through the P# domain value '1'. The Transaction tuple is a record of a purchase by customer number '2' of product number '1'. Through such links, we are able to retrieve the name of the customer and the product, ie. we are able to state that the customer 'Martin' bought a 'Camera'. They help to avoid redundancy in recording data. Without them, the Transaction relation in Figure 2-6 will have to include information about the appropriate Customer and Product in its table. This duplication of data can lead to integrity problems later, especially when data needs to be modified.

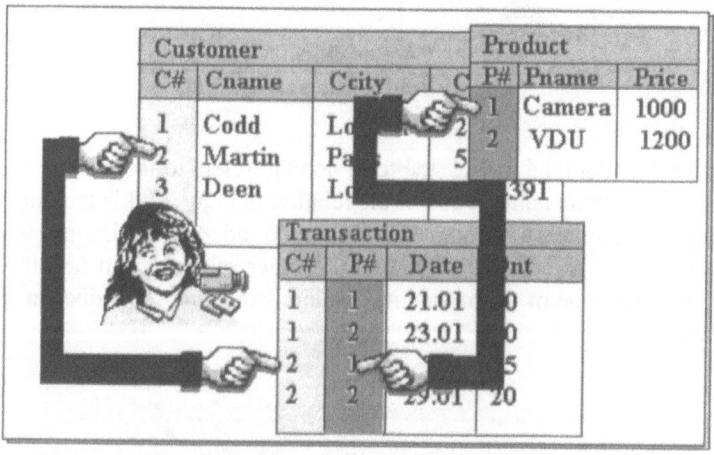

Figure 2-6 Links through domain sharing

2.3   Properties of a Relation

A relation with N columns and M rows (tuples) is said to be of *degree* N and *cardinality* M. This is illustrated in Figure 2-7 which shows the Customer relation of degree four and cardinality three. The product of a relation's degree and cardinality is the number of attribute values it contains.

Customer			
C#	Cname	Ccity	Cphone
1	Codd	London	2263035
2	Martin	Paris	5555910
3	Deen	London	2234391

Cardinality 3

Degree 4

Figure 2-7 Degree and cardinality of a relation

The characteristic properties of a relation are as follows:

1. All entries in a given column are of the same kind or type

2. The ordering of columns is immaterial. This is illustrated in Figure 2-8 where the two tables shown are identical in every respect except for the ordering of their columns. In the relational model, column values (or the value of an attribute of a given tuple) are not referenced by their position in the table but by name. Thus the display of a relation in tabular form is free to arrange columns in any order. Of course, once an order is chosen, it is good practice to use it everytime the relation (or a tuple from it) is displayed to avoid confusion.

Customer				Customer			
C#	Cname	Ccity	Cphone	C#	Cname	Ccity	Cphone
1	Codd	London	2263035	3	Deen	London	2234391
2	Martin	Paris	5555910	1	Codd	London	2263035
3	Deen	London	2234391	2	Martin	Paris	5555910

These relations are exactly the same.

Figure 2-8 Column ordering is unimportant

3. No two tuples are exactly the same. A relation is a *set* of tuples. Thus a table that contains duplicate tuples is not a relation and cannot be stored in a relational database.

4. There is only one value for each attribute of a tuple. Thus a table such as in Figure 2-9 is not allowed in the relational model, despite the clear intended representation, ie. that of customers with two abodes (eg. Codd has one in London and one in Madras). In situations like this, the multiple values must be split into multiple tuples to be a valid relation.

This is not a relation !			
Customer			
C#	Cname	Ccity	Cphone
1	Codd	London Madras	2263035 52176
2	Martin	Paris Graz	5555910 825146

Figure 2-9 A tuple attribute may only have one value

5. The ordering of tuples is immaterial. This follows directly from defining a relation as a *set* of tuples, rather than a sequence or list. One is free therefore to display a relation in any convenient way, eg. sorted on some attribute.

The *extension* of a relation refers to the current set of tuples in it (see Figure 2-10). This will of course vary with time as the database changes, ie. as we insert new tuples, or modify or delete existing ones. Such changes are effected through a DML, or put another way, a DML operates on the extensions of relations.

The more permanent parts of a relation, viz. the relation name and attribute names, are collectively referred to as its *intension* or *schema*. A relation's schema effectively describes (and constrains) the structure of tuples it is permitted to contain. DML operations on tuples are allowed only if they observe the expressed intensions of the affected relations (this partially addresses database integrity concerns raised in the last chapter). Any given database will have a database schema which records the intensions of every relation in it. Schemas are defined using a DDL.

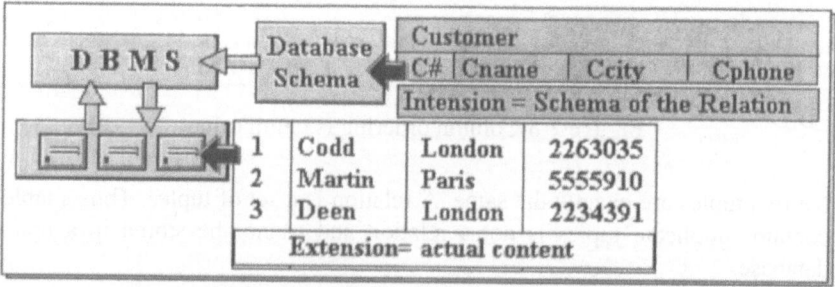

Figure 2-10 The Intension and extension of a relation

2.4   Keys of a Relation

A *key* is a part of a tuple (one or more attributes) that uniquely distinguishes it from other tuples in a given relation. Of course, in the extreme, the entire tuple is the key since each tuple in the relation is guaranteed to be unique. However, we are interested in smaller keys if they exist, for a number of practical reasons. First, keys will typically be used as links, ie. key values will appear in other relations to represent their associated tuples (as in Figure 2-6 above). Thus keys should be as small as possible and comprise only nonredundant attributes to avoid unnecessary duplication of data across relations. Second, keys form the basis for constructing indexes to speed up retrieval of tuples from a relation. Small keys will decrease the size of indexes and the time to look up an index.

Consider Figure 2-11 below. The customer number (C#) attribute is clearly designed to uniquely identify a customer. Thus we would not find two or more tuples in the relation having the same customer number and it can therefore serve as a unique key to tuples in the relation.

However, there may be more than one such key in any relation, and these keys may arise from natural attributes of the entity represented (rather than a contrived one, like customer number). Examining again Figure 2-11, no two or more tuples have the same value combination of Ccity and Cphone. If we can safely assume that no customer will share a residence and phone number with any other customer, then this combination is one such key. Note that Cphone alone is not - there are two tuples with the same Cphone value (telephone numbers in different cities that happen to be the same). And neither is Ccity alone as we may expect many customers to live in a given city.

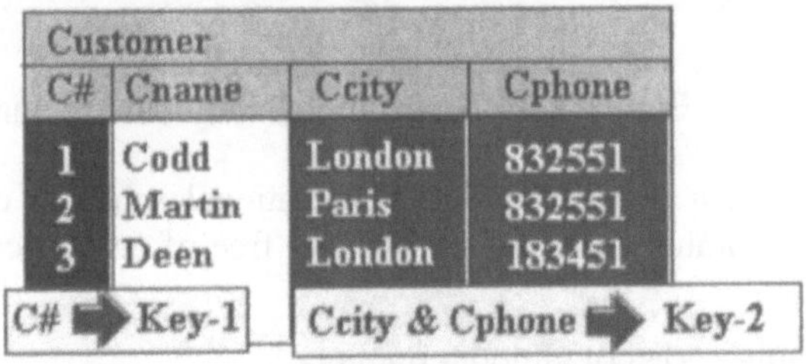

Customer			
C#	Cname	Ccity	Cphone
1	Codd	London	832551
2	Martin	Paris	832551
3	Deen	London	183451

C# ➡ Key-1	Ccity & Cphone ➡ Key-2

Figure 2-11 Candidate keys

While a relation may have two or more *candidate keys*, one must be selected and designated as the *primary key* in the database schema. For the example above, C# is the obvious choice as a primary key for the reasons stated earlier. When the primary key values of one relation appear in other relations, they are termed *foreign keys*. Note that foreign keys may have duplicate occurrences in a relation, while primary keys may not.

For example, in Figure 2-6, the C# in Transaction is a foreign key and the key value '1' occurs in two different tuples. This is allowed because a foreign key is only a reference to a tuple in another relation, unlike a primary key value, which must uniquely identify a tuple in the relation.

2.5   Relational Schema

A Relational Database Schema comprises

1. the definition of all domains

2. the definition of all relations, specifying for each

   a) its intension (all attribute names), and

   b) a primary key

Figure 2-12 shows an example of such a schema which has all the components mentioned above. The primary keys are designated by shading the component attribute names. Of course, this is only an informal view of a schema. Its formal definition must rely on the use of a specific DDL whose syntax may vary from one DBMS to another.

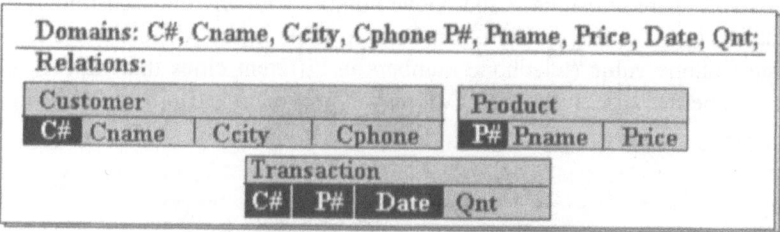

Figure 2-12 An example relational schema

There is, however, a useful notation for relational schemas commonly adopted to document and communicate database designs free of any specific DDL. It takes the simple form:

   <relation name>: <list of attribute names>

Additionally, attributes that are part of the primary key are underlined.

Thus, for the example in Figure 2-12, the schema would be written as follows:

   Customer: (C#, Cname, Ccity, Cphone)

   Transaction: (C#, P#, Date, Qnt)

   Product: (P#, Pname, Price)

This notation is useful in clarifying the overall organisation of the database but omits some details, particularly the properties of domains. As an example of a more complete definition using a more concrete DDL, we rewrite some the schema above using Codd's original notation. The principal components of his notation are annotated alongside.

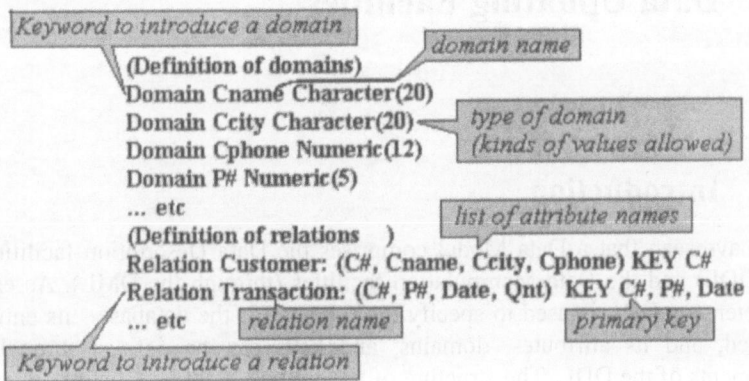

3. Data Updating Facilities

3.1 Introduction

We have seen that a Data Model comprises the Data Description facilities (through the DDL) and the Data Manipulation facilities (through the DML). As explained in Chapter 2, a DDL is used to specify the schema for the database - its entities can be created, and its attributes, domains, and keys can be defined through language statements of the DDL. The structure of the entities is defined, but not the data within them. DDL thus supports only the declaration of the database structure.

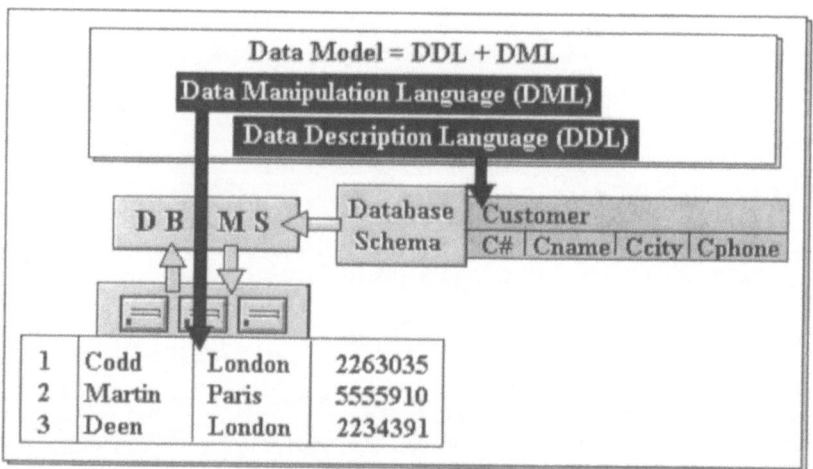

Figure 3-1: Data definition and manipulation facilities of a data model

In this chapter, we shall see how the second component, the DML, can be used to support the manipulation or processing of the data within the database structures defined by the DDL. Manipulation begins with the placement of data values into the structures. When the data values have been stored, the end user should be able to get at the data. The user would have a specific purpose for the piece of data he/she wants to get - perhaps to display the data on the screen in order to know the value, to write the data to an output report file to be printed, to use the data as part of a computation, or to make changes to it.

3.2   Data Manipulation Facilities

The manipulative part of the relational model comprises the DML which contains commands to put new data, delete and modify the existing data. These facilities of a Database Management System are known as Updating Facilities or Data Update Functions, because unlike the DDL which executes operations on the structure of the database's entities, the DML performs operations on the data within those structures.

Given a relation declared in a database schema, the main update functions of a DML are:

1. To insert or add new tuples into a particular relation

2. To delete or erase existing tuples from a relation

3. To modify or change data in an existing relation

Examples:

1. To insert a new tuple
The company receives a new customer. To ensure that its database is up-to-date, a new tuple containing the data that is normally kept about customers must be created and inserted.

Step1. A user (through an application program) chooses a relation, say the Customer relation. It has 4 attributes, and 3 existing tuples.

Customer

C#	Cname	Ccity	Cphone
1	Codd	London	2263035
2	Martin	Paris	5555910
3	Deen	London	2234391

Step 2. The user prepares a new tuple of the relation (database) on the screen or in the computer's memory

4	Lampl	Graz	832551

Step 3. Through a DML command specified by the user, the DBMS puts a new tuple into the relation of the database according to the definition of the DDL to place data in that row. The Customer relation now has 4 tuples.

Customer

C#	Cname	Ccity	Cphone
1	Codd	London	2263035
2	Martin	Paris	5555910
3	Deen	London	2234391
4	Lampl	Graz	832551

This is thus a way to load data into the database.

2. To delete an existing tuple

An existing customer no longer does any business with the company, in which case, the corresponding tuple must be erased from the customer database.

Step1. The user chooses the relation, Customer.	Customer			
	C#	Cname	Ccity	Cphone
Step 2. The user issues a DML command to retrieve the tuple to be deleted.	1	Codd	London	2263035
	2	Martin	Paris	5555910
	3	Deen	London	2234391
	4	Lampl	Graz	832551
Step 3. The DBMS deletes the tuple from the relation.	Customer			
The updated relation now has one less tuple.	C#	Cname	Ccity	Cphone
	1	Codd	London	2263035
	2	Martin	Paris	5555910
	4	Lampl	Graz	832551

3. To modify an existing tuple

An existing customer has moved to a new location (or that the current value in the data field is incorrect). He has new values for the city and telephone number. These new values must replace the previous values.

Step1. The user chooses the relation.	Customer			
	C#	Cname	Ccity	Cphone
Step 2. The user issues a DML retrieval command to get the tuple to be changed.	1	Codd	London	2263035
	2	Martin	Paris	5555910
	4	Lampl	Graz	832551
Step 3. The user modifies one or more data items.	4	Lampl	Graz	832551
Step 4. The DBMS inserts the modified tuple into the relation.	4	Lampl	Paris	242149
	Customer			
	C#	Cname	Ccity	Cphone
	1	Codd	London	2263035
	2	Martin	Paris	5555910
	4	Lampl	Paris	242149

Two types of modifications are normally done:

1. Assigned - an assigned modification entails the simple assignment of a new value into the data field (as in the example above)
2. Computed - in computed modification, the existing value is retrieved, then some computation is done on it before restoring the updated value into the field (e.g. all Cphone numbers beginning with the digit 5 are to be changed to begin with the digits 58).

Additionally, it is possible to insert new tuples into a relation with one or more unknown values. Such unknown values, called NULL-VALUEs, are denoted by **?**

4. To insert a tuple with unknown values

A new customer, Deen, is created.
But Deen has yet to notify the company of
his living place and telephone number.

At a later point in time, when Deen has
confirmed his living place and telephone, the
tuple with his details can be modified by
replacing the ?s with the appropriate values.

Customer

C#	Cname	Ccity	Cphone
1	Codd	London	2263035
2	Martin	Paris	5555910
3	Deen	?	?

At this stage, we only mention these update functions via logical definitions such as above. In the implementation of DMLs, there exist many RDBMS systems with wide variations in the actual language notations . We shall not discuss these update functions of concrete data manipulation languages yet.

3.3 User Interface

3.3.1 Users

Now that data values are stored in the database, we shall look at how users can communicate with the database system in order to access the data for further manipulation. First let us take a look at the characteristics of users and the processing and inquiries they tend to make.

There are essentially two types of users:

1. End Users: End users are those who directly use the information obtained from the database. They are likely to be computer novices or neophytes, using the computer system as an extended tool to assist them with their main job function (which may be to do financial analysis or to register students). End users may feel uncomfortable with computers or may simply be not interested in the technical details, but their lack of knowledge should not be a handicap to the main job which they have to do.

End users should be able to retrieve the data in the database in any manner they wish, which are likely to be in the form of:

- casual, unanticipated or *ad hoc* queries which often must be satisfied within a short space of time, if not immediately (e.g. "How many students over the age of 30 are taught by professors below the age of 30?")

- standard or predictable queries that need to be executed on a routine basis (e.g. "Produce the monthly cash flow analysis report")

2. Database specialists: Specialist users are knowledgeable about the technicalities of the database management system. They are likely to hold positions such as the database administrator, database programmer, database support person, systems analyst or the like. They are likely to be responsible for tasks like:

- defining the database schema

- handling complex queries, reports or tailored software applications

- defining data security and ensuring data integrity

- performing database backups and recoveries

- monitoring database performance

3.3.2 Interface

Interactions with the database would require some form of *interface* with the users. There are two basic ways in which the User-Database interface may be organized, i.e. the database may be accessed from a:

1. purpose-built, non-procedural *Self-Contained Language*, or a

2. *Host Language* (such as C, C++, COBOL, Pascal, etc.)

The Self -Contained Language tend to be the tool favored by end-users to access the database, whereas access through a host language is a tool of the technical experts and skilled programmers who use it to develop specialised software or database applications,

In either case, the access is still through the database schema and using the DML.

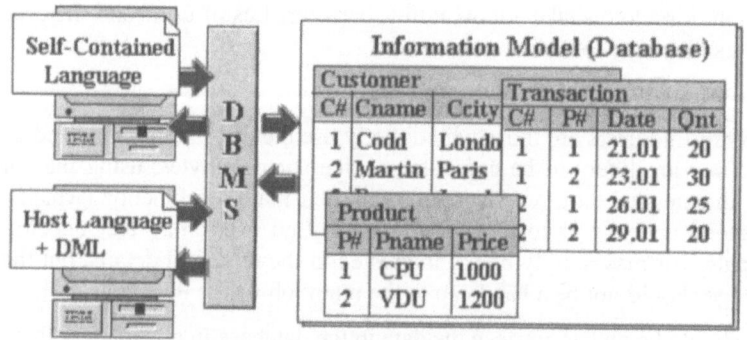

Figure 3-2: Two different interfaces to the database

3.3.3 Self-Contained Language

Let us first take a look at the tool favored by the end users:
Here we have a collection of DML statements (e.g. GET, SELECT) to access the database. These statements can be expanded with other statements that are capable of doing arithmetic operations, computing statistical functions, and so on. The DML

statements, as we have seen, are dependent on the database schema. However, the additional statements for statistical functions etc. are not, and thus add a form of independence from the schema. This is illustrated in the Figure 3-3. Hence the name "Self-Contained" language for such a database language.

Figure 3-3: Expanding DML with additional functions

The self-contained language is most suitable for end users to gain rapid or online access to the data. It is often used to make *ad hoc* inquiries into the database, involving mainly the retrieval operation. It is often described as being user friendly, and can be learnt quite quickly. Instead of waiting for the database specialists or some technical whiz to program their requests, end users can now by themselves create queries and format the resulting data into reports.

The language is usually non-procedural and command-oriented where the user specifies English-like text. To get a flavor of such a language, let us look at some simple examples which uses a popular command-oriented data-sublanguage, SQL. (More will covered in Chapter 9).

Suppose we take the 3 relations introduced earlier:

Customer (C#, Cname, Ccity, Cphone)

Product (P#, Pname, Price)

Transaction (C#, P#, Date, Qnt)

with the following sample values in the tuples:

Customer				Transaction				Product		
C#	Cname	Ccity	Cphone	C#	P#	Date	Qnt	P#	Pname	Price
1	Codd	London	2263035	1	1	21.01	20	1	CPU	1000
2	Martin	Paris	5555910	1	2	23.01	30	2	VDU	1200
3	Deen	London	2234391	2	1	26.01	25			
				2	2	29.01	20			

Figure 3-4: Sample database

We shall illustrate the use of some simple commands:

- SELECT * FROM CUSTOMER

This will retrieve all data values of the Customer relation, with the following resulting relation:

C#	Cname	Ccity	Cphone
1	Codd	London	2263035
2	Martin	Paris	5555910
3	Deen	London	2234391

- SELECT CNAME
     FROM CUSTOMER
        WHERE CCITY="London"

This will retrieve, from the Customers relation, the names of all customers whose city is London:

Cname
Codd
Deen

- SELECT CNAME, P#
     FROM CUSTOMER, TRANSACTION
        WHERE CUSTOMER.C# = TRANSACTION.C#

This will access the two relations, Customer and Transaction, and in effect, retrieve from them the Names of customers who have transactions and the Part numbers supplied to them (note, customers with no transactions will not be retrieved).

The resultant relation is:

Cname	P#
Codd	1
Codd	2
Martin	1
Martin	2

- SELECT COUNT (*), AVG (PRICE) FROM PRODUCT

Here, the DML/SELECT statement is expanded with additional arithmetic/statistical functions. This will access the Product relation and perform functions to

(1) count the total number of products and

(2) get the average of the Price values:

Count	Avg
2	1100

Once end users know how to define queries in terms of a particular language, it would seem that they can quite easily do the their own queries like the above. It is a matter of a few lines of commands which may be quickly formulated to get the desired information. However if the query is too involved or complex, like the following example, then the end-users will have to be quite expert database users or will have to rely on help from the technical specialists.

```
SELECT  DISTINCT P# FROM  PRODUCT, TRANSACTION
WHERE  NOT EXISTS
    (SELECT * FROM  PRODUCT, TRANSACTION
    WHERE PRODUCT.P# = TRANSACTION.P#
    AND NOT EXISTS
        ( SELECT * FROM  PRODUCT, CUSTOMER
        WHERE PRODUCT.P# = TRANSACTION.P#
        AND   CUSTOMER.C# = "3"  ) )
```

Can you figure what this query statement does?

3.3.4 Host Language

Apart from simple queries, end users need specialised reports that require technical specialists to write computer programs to process them.

The interface for the skilled programmers is usually in the form a database command language and a programming language with utilities to support other data operations. Here in the second case, the DML statements are embedded into the text of an application program written in a general purpose host programming language. Thus SQL statements to access the relational database, for example, are embedded in C, C++ or Cobol programs.

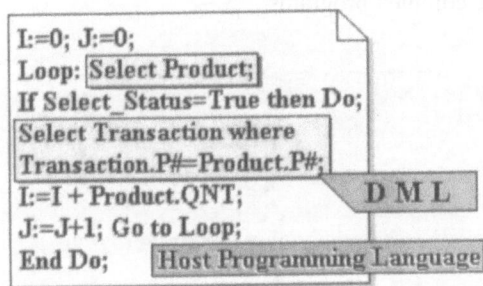

```
I:=0; J:=0;
Loop: Select Product;
If Select_Status=True then Do;
Select Transaction where
Transaction.P#=Product.P#;
I:=I + Product.QNT;           D M L
J:=J+1; Go to Loop;
End Do;        Host Programming Language
```

Figure 3-5: Embedding DML in a host language

Embedded host language programs provide the application with full access to the databases to:

- manipulate data structures (such as to create, destroy or update the database tables),
- manipulate the data (such as to retrieve, delete, append or update the data items in the database tables),
- manage groups of statements as a single transaction (such as to abort a group of statements), and
- perform a host of other database management functions as well (such as to create access permits on database tables).

The DML/SQL statements embedded in the program code is usually placed between delimiters such as

EXEC SQL
      SELECT ..../*Embedded DML Statement*/
END-EXEC

The program is then pre-compiled to convert the DML into the host source code that can subsequently be compiled into object code for running.

Compared to the command lines of queries written in self-contained languages, an application program such as the above takes more effort and time. Good programming abilities are required. Applications are written in an embedded host language for various reasons, including for:

- large or complex databases which contain a hundred million characters or more
- a well known set of applications transactions, perhaps running hundreds of times a day (e.g. to make airline seat reservations) or standard/predictable queries that need to be executed on a routine basis (e.g. "generate the weekly payroll")
- unskilled end-users or if the query becomes too involved or complicated for the end-user.

However, for end-users, again special interfaces may be designed to facilitate the access to these more complex programs.

Figure 3-6: Easy-to-use end user interface

Such interfaces are usually in the form of simple, user-friendly screens comprising easy-to-learn languages, a series of menus, fill-in-the-blank data-entry panels or report screens - sufficient for the user to check, edit and format data, make queries, or see the results, and without much technical staff intervention.

In this section we have seen that user interfaces are important to provide contact with the underlying database. One of the advantages of relational databases is the use of languages that are standardized, such as SQL and the availability of interface products that are easy-to-use. Often it takes just a few minutes to define a query in terms of a Self-Contained language (but the realization of such a query may take much more time). End users can thus create queries and generate their own reports without having to rely heavily on the programming staff to respond to their requests. More importantly, they can also be made more responsible for their own data, information retrieval and report generation. The technical staff must thus ensure that good communication exists between them and the end-users, that sufficient training is always given, and that good coordination all around is vital to ensure that these users know what they are doing.

These are the things that give relational databases their true flexibility and power (compared to the other models such as the hierarchical or network databases).

3.4   Integrity

Having seen what and how data can be manipulated in a database, we shall next see the importance of assuring the reliability of data and how this can be achieved through the imposition of constraints during data manipulation operations.

Apart from providing data access to the user who wishes to retrieve or update the data, a database management system must also provide its users with other utilities to assure them of the proper maintenance, protection and reliability of the system. For example, in single-user systems, where the entire database is used, owned and maintained by a single user, the problems associated with data sharing do not arise. But when an enterprise-wide database is used by many users, often at the same time, the problems of who can access what, when and how - confidentiality and update - become a very big concern. Thus *data security* and *data integrity* are crucial.

People should not see what is not intended for them (e.g. individuals must have privacy rights on their medical or criminal records, businesses must safeguard their commercially sensitive information, and the military must secure their operation plans). Additionally, people who are not authorized to update data, must not be allowed to change them (e.g. an electronic bank transfer must have the proper authorization).

While the issue of data security concerns itself with the protection of the database against unauthorized users who may disclose, alter or destroy data they are not supposed to have access to, data integrity concerns itself with protecting the database against authorized users. In this section, we shall focus on the latter (the former will be covered in greater detail in Chapter 11).

Thus integrity protection is an important part of the data model. By integrity we mean the correctness and reliability of the data maintained in the database. One must be confident that the data accessed is accurate, correct, relevant and valid. The protection can be viewed as a set of constraints that prevents any undesirable updates on the database. Two types of constraints may be applied:

- Implicit Integrity Constraints

- Explicit Integrity Constraints

3.4.1 Implicit Integrity Constraints

The term "Implicit Integrity Constraints" means that a user need not explicitly define these Integrity Constraints in a database schema. They are a property of the relational data model as such. The Relational Data Model provides two types of Implicit Integrity Constraints:

1. Entity Integrity

Recall that an attribute is usually chosen from a relation to be its primary key. The primary key is used to identify the tuple and is useful when one wishes to sort or access the tuples efficiently. It is a unique identifier for a given tuple. As such, no two tuples can have the same key values, and nor can the values be null. Otherwise, uniqueness cannot be guaranteed.

Customer			
C#	Cname	Ccity	Cphone
1	Codd	London	2263035
2	Martin	Paris	5555910
?	Deen	London	2234391	Entity Integrity Violation !

Figure 3-7: Entity integrity violation

A primary key that is null would be a contradiction in terms, for it would effectively state that there is an entity that has no known identity. Hence, the term entity integrity.

Note that whilst the primary key cannot be null, (which in this case, C# cannot have a null value), the other attributes, may be so (for example, Cname, Ccity or Cphone may have null values).

Thus the rule for the "Entity Integrity" constraint asserts that no attribute participating in the primary key of a relation is permitted to accept null values.

2. Referential Integrity

We have seen earlier how a primary or secondary key in one relation may be used by another relation to handle many-to-many relationships. For example, the Transaction relation has the attribute C# which is also an attribute in the Customer relation. But C# is a primary key of Customer, thus making C# a foreign key in Transaction.

The foreign key in the Transaction relation cross-references data in the Customer relation, e.g. using the value of C# in Transaction to get details on Cname which is not found directly in it but in Customer. When relations make references to another relation via foreign keys, the database management system must ensure that data between the relations are valid. For example, Transaction cannot have a tuple with a C# value that is not found in the Customer relation for the tuple would then be referring to a customer that does not exist.

Thus, for referential integrity a foreign key can have only two possible values - either the relevant primary key or a null value. No other values are allowed.

Customer			
C#	Cname	Ccity	Cphone
1	Codd	London	2263035
2	Martin	Paris	5555910
3	Deen	London	2234391

Transaction			
C#	P#	Date	Qnt
1	1	21.01	20
1	2	23.01	30
2	1	26.01	25
4	2	29.01	20	Referential Integrity Violation !

Figure 3-8: Referential integrity violation

Figure 3-8 above shows that by adding a tuple with C# 4 means that we have a foreign key that does not reference a valid key in the parent Customer relation. Thus a violation by an insert operation. Likewise, if we were to delete C# 2 from the Customer relation, we would again have a foreign key that no longer references a matching key in the base or parent relation.

Also note that the foreign key here, C# is not allowed to have a null value either since it is a part of Transaction's primary key (which is the combined attributes of C#, P#, Date). But if the foreign key is a simple attribute, and not a combined/compound one, then it may have null values. In other words, a foreign key cannot be partially null, it must be wholly null if it does not refer to any particular key in the base relation. Unlike primary keys which are not permitted to accept null values, there may be instances when foreign keys have to be null. For example, a database about employees and departments would have a foreign key, say Dept# in the Employee relation which indicates the department to which the employee is assigned. But when a new employee joins the company, it is possible that the employee is not assigned to any department yet. Her Employee tuple may then have a null Dept#.

Thus the rule for the "Referential Integrity" constraint asserts that if a relation R2 includes a foreign key that matches the primary key of another relation R1, then every attribute value of the foreign key in R2 must either (i) be equal to the value of the primary key in some tuple of R1 or (ii) be wholly null.

3.4.2 Explicit Integrity Constraints

In addition to the general, implicit constraints of the relational model, any specific database will often have its own set of local rules that apply to it alone. This is again to ensure that the data values maintained are reliable. Specific validity checks are done on them, for otherwise unexpected or erroneous data may be created. Occasionally, one hears for example, of the case of the telephone subscriber getting an unreasonably large bill.

Various kinds of checks can be imposed. Amongst the usual constraints practised in data processing are tests on:
- class or data type, e.g. alphabetic or numeric type
- sign e.g. positive or negative number
- presence or absence of data, e.g. if spaces or null
- value, e.g. if value > 100
- range or limit, e.g. $-10 \le x \le +10$
- reasonableness, e.g. if y positive and < 10000
- the consistency, e.g. if x < y and y < 100

In a Relational Data Model, explicit integrity constraints may be declared to handle the above cases as follows:

1. Domain Constraints

Such constraints characterize the constraints that can be defined on domains, such as value set restriction, upper and lower limits, etc. For example:

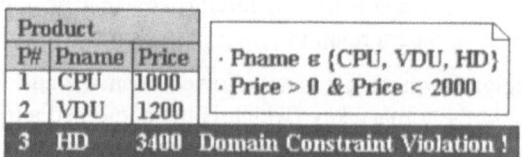

Figure 3-9: Domain constraint violation

Whilst the Pname of the third tuple in Figure 3-9 complied with the allowable values, its Price should have been less than 2000. An error message is flagged and the tuple cannot be inserted into the relation.

2. Tuple Constraints

The second type of explicit constraint characterizes the rules that can be defined on tuples, such as inter-attribute restrictions. For example:

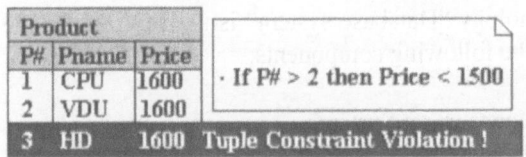

Figure 3-10: Tuple constraint violation

With such a declaration, then the above tuple with P# 3 cannot have a Price value that is greater or equal to 1500.

3. Relation Constraints

Relation constraints characterize the constraints that can be defined on a relation structure, such as alternate keys or inter-relation restrictions. For example,

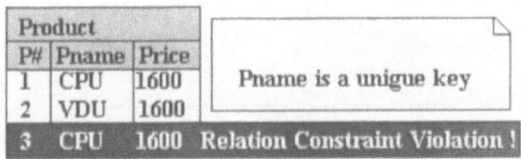

Figure 3-11: Relational constraint violation

Pname, being an alternate key to the primary key, P#, should have unique values. However, Pname may be null (unlike P# which if null, would violate the entity integrity).

Product		
P#	Pname	Price
1	CPU	1600
2	VDU	1600
3	?	1500

Figure 3-12: Allowable Null foreign key

Other attributes too may have null or duplicate values without violating any integrity constraint.

3.5 Database Transactions

All these data manipulation operations are part of the fundamental purpose of any database system, which is to carry out database "transactions" (not to be confused with the relation named "Transaction" that has been used in many of the earlier examples). A database transaction is a logical unit of work. It consists of the execution of an application-specified sequence of data manipulation operations.

Recall that the terminology "Database system" is used to refer to the special system that includes at least the following components:

- the database
- the Database Management System
- the particular database schema, and
- a set of special-purpose application programs

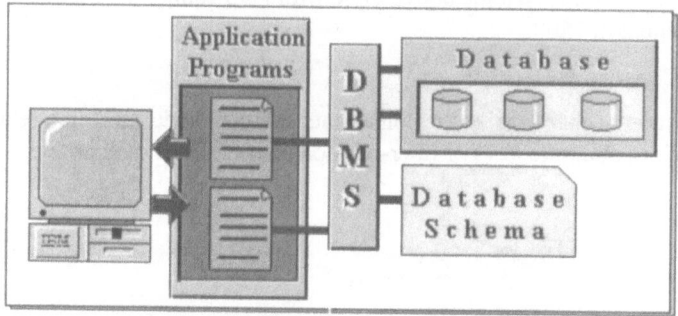

Figure 3-13: Database system components

Normally one database transaction invokes a number of DML operators. Each DML operator, in turn, invokes a number of data updating operations on a physical level, as illustrated in Figure 3-14 below.

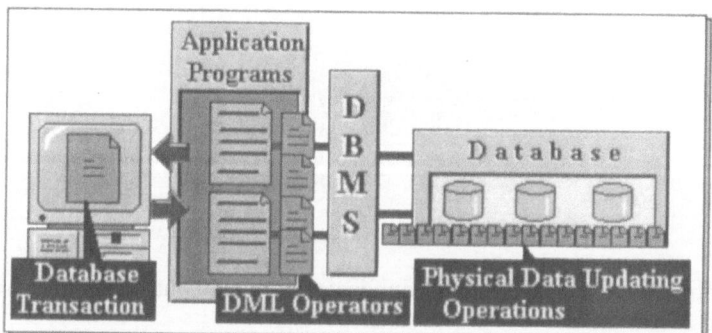

Figure 3-14: Correspondance between transaction, DML and physical operations

If the "self contained language" is used, the data manipulation operators and database transactions have a "one-to-one" correspondence. For example, a transaction to put data values into the database entails a single DML INSERT operator command.

However, in other instances, especially where embedded language programs are used, a single transaction may in fact comprise several operations.

Suppose we have an additional attribute, TotalQnt, in the Product relation, i.e. our database will contain the following relations:

Customer (<u>C#,</u> Cname, Ccity, Cphone)

Product (<u>P#,</u> Pname, Price, TotalQnt)

Transaction (<u>C#, P#, Date,</u> Qnt)

TotalQnt will hold the running total of Qnt of the same P# found in the Transaction relation. TotalQnt is in fact a value that is computed as follows:

$$\text{Product.TotalQnt} \leftarrow \sum_{\text{P\#}} \text{Transaction.Qnt}$$

Consider for example if we wish to add a new **Transaction** tuple. With this single task, the system will effectively perform the following 2 sequential operations:

- insert a new tuple into the Transaction relation

- update the Product relation such that the new Transaction.Qnt is added on to the value of Product.TotalQnt for that same P#

A transaction must be executed as an intact unit, for otherwise if a failure happens after the insert but before the update operation, then the database will left in an inconsistent state with the new value inserted but the total quantity not updated. But with transaction management and processing support, if an unplanned error or system crash occurs before normal termination, then those earlier operations will be undone - a transaction is executed in its entirety or totally aborted. It is this support to group operations into a transaction that helps guarantee that a database would be in a "consistent" state in the event of any system failure during its data manipulation operations.

And finally, it must be noted that as far as the end-user is concerned, he/she "can see" database transactions as undivided portions of information sent to the system, or received from the system. It is also not important how the data is actually physically stored, only how it is logically available. This flexibility of data access is readily achieved with relational database management systems.

4. Normalisation

4.1 Introduction

Suppose we are now given the task of designing and creating a database. How do we produce a good design? What relations should we have in the database? What attributes should these relations have? Good database design needless to say, is important. Careless design can lead to uncontrolled data redundancies that will lead to problems with data anomalies.

In this chapter we will examine a process known as *Normalisation* - a rigorous design tool that is based on the mathematical theory of relations which will result in very practical operational implementations. A properly normalised set of relations actually simplifies the retrieval and maintenance processes and the effort spent in ensuring good structures is certainly a worthwhile investment. Furthermore, if database relations were simply seen as file structures of some vague file system, then the power and flexibility of RDBMS cannot be exploited to the full.

For us to appreciate good design, let us begin by examining some bad ones.

4.1.1 A Bad Design

E.Codd has identified certain structural features in a relation which create retrieval and update problems. Suppose we start off with a relation with a structure and details like:

Customer details				Transaction details							
C#	Cname	Ccity	..	P1#	Date1	Qnt1	P2#	Date2		P9#	Date9
1	Codd	London	..	1	21.01	20	2	23.01			
2	Martin	Paris	..	1	26.10	25					
3	Deen	London	..	2	29.01	20					

Figure 4-1: Simple structure

This is a simple and straightforward design. It consists of one relation where we have a single tuple for every customer and under that customer we keep all his transaction records about parts, up to a possible maximum of 9 transactions. For every new transaction, we need not repeat the customer details (of name, city and telephone), we simply add on a transaction detail.

However, we note the following disadvantages:

- The relation is wide and clumsy

- We have set a limit of 9 (or whatever reasonable value) transactions per customer. What if a customer has more than 9 transactions?

- For customers with less than 9 transactions, it appears that we have to store null values in the remaining spaces. What a waste of space!

- The transactions appear to be kept in ascending order of P#s. What if we have to delete, for customer Codd, the part numbered 1- should we move the part numbered 2 up (or rather, left)? If we did, what if we decide later to re-insert part 2? The additions and deletions can cause awkward data shuffling.

- Let us try to construct a query to "Find which customer(s) bought P# 2" ? The query would have to access every customer tuple and for each tuple, examine every of its transaction looking for

$$(P1\# = 2) \; OR \; (P2\# = 2) \; OR \; (P3\# = 2) \; \dots \; OR \; (P9\# = 2)$$

A comparatively simple query seems to require a clumsy retrieval formulation!

4.1.2 Another Bad Design

Alternatively, why don't we re-structure our relation such that we do not restrict the number of transactions per customer. We can do this with the following structure:

Transaction						
C#	Cname	Ccity	Cphone	P#	Date	Qnt
1	Codd	London	2263035	1	21.01	20
1	Codd	London	2263035	2	23.01	30
2	Martin	Paris	5555910	1	26.01	25
3	Deen	London	2234391	2	29.01	20

This way, a customer can have just any number of Part transactions without worrying about any upper limit or wasted space through null values (as it was with the previous structure). Constructing a query to "Find which customer(s) bought P# 2" is not as cumbersome as before as one can now simply state: P# = 2.

But again, this structure is not without its faults:

- It seems a waste of storage to keep repeated values of Cname, Ccity and Cphone.

- If C# 1 were to change his telephone number, we would have to ensure that we update ALL occurrences of C# 1's Cphone values. This means updating tuple 1, tuple 2 and all other tuples where there is an occurrence of C# 1. Otherwise, our database would be left in an inconsistent state.

- Suppose we now have a new customer with C# 4. However, there is no part transaction yet with the customer as he has not ordered anything yet. We may find that we cannot insert this new information because we do not have a P# which serves as part of the 'primary key' of a tuple. (A primary key cannot have null values).

- Suppose the third transaction has been canceled, i.e. we no longer need information about 25 of P# 1 being ordered on 26 Jan. We thus delete the third tuple. We are then left with the following relation:

Transaction						
C#	Cname	Ccity	Cphone	P#	Date	Qnt
1	Codd	London	2263035	1	21.01	20
1	Codd	London	2263035	2	23.01	30
3	Deen	London	2234391	2	29.01	20

But then, suppose we need information about the customer "Martin", say the city he is located in. Unfortunately as information about Martin was held in only that tuple and having the entire tuple deleted because of its P# transaction, meant also that we have lost all information about Martin from the relation.

As illustrated in the above instances, we note that badly designed, unnormalised relations waste storage space. Worse, they give rise to the following storage irregularities:

1. *Update anomaly*
   Data inconsistency or loss of data integrity can arise from data redundancy/repetition and partial update.

2. *Insertion anomaly*
   Data cannot be added because some other data is absent.

3. *Deletion anomaly*
   Data maybe unintentionally lost through the deletion of other data.

4.1.3 The Need for Normalisation

Intuitively, it would seem that these undesirable features can be removed by breaking a relation into other relations with desirable structures. We shall attempt by splitting the above Transaction relation into the following two relations, Customer and Transaction, which can be viewed as entities with a one to many relationship.

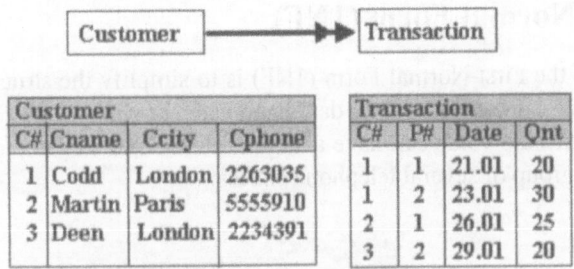

Figure 4-2: 1:M data relationships

Let us see if this new design will alleviate the above storage anomalies:

1. *Update anomaly*
If C# 1 were to change his telephone number, as there is only one occurrence of the tuple in the Customer relation, we need to update only that one tuple as there are no redundant/duplicate tuples.

2. *Addition anomaly*
Adding a new customer with C# 4 can be easily done in the Customer relation of which C# serves as the primary key. With no P# yet, a tuple in Transaction need not be created.

3. *Deletion anomaly*
Canceling the third transaction about 25 of P# 1 being ordered on 26 Jan would now mean deleting only the third tuple of the new Transaction relation above. This leaves information about Martin still intact in the new Customer relation.

This process of reducing a relation into simpler structures is the process of *Normalisation*. Normalisation may be defined as a step by step reversible process of transforming an unnormalised relation into relations with progressively simpler structures. Since the process is reversible, no information is lost in the transformation.

Normalisation removes (or more accurately, minimises) the undesirable properties by working through a series of stages called *Normal Forms*. Originally, Codd defined three types of undesirable properties:
1. Data aggregates
2. Partial key dependency
3. Indirect key dependency
and the three stages of normalisation that remove the associated problems are known, respectively, as the:
  • First Normal Form (1NF)
  • Second Normal Form (2NF), and
  • Third Normal Form (3NF)

We shall now show a more formal process on how we can decompose relations into multiple relations by using the Normal Form rules for structuring.

4.2   First Normal Form (1NF)

The purpose of the First Normal Form (1NF) is to simplify the structure of a relation by ensuring that it does *not* contain data aggregates or *repeating groups*. By this we mean that no attribute value can have a set of values. In the example below, any one customer has a group of several telephone entries:

Customer			
C#	Cname	Ccity	Cphone
1	Codd	London	2263035
			5555910
2	Deen	London	2234391
			832551

Figure 4-3. Presence of repeating groups

This is thus not in 1NF. It must be "flattened". This can be achieved by ensuring that every tuple defines a single entity by containing only *atomic* values. One can either re-organise into one relation as in:

Customer			
C#	Cname	Ccity	Cphone
1	Codd	London	2263035
1	Codd	London	5555910
2	Deen	London	2234391
2	Deen	London	832551

Figure 4-4: Atomic values in tuples

or split into multiple relations as in:

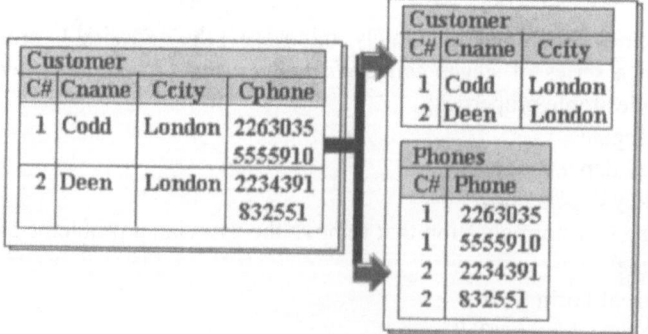

Figure 4-4: Reduction to 1NF

Note that earlier we defined 1NF as one of the characteristics of a relation (Lesson 2). Thus we consider that *every* relation is at least in the *first normal form* (thus the

Figure 4-3 is not even a relation). The Transaction relation of Figure 4-2 is however a 1NF relation.

We may thus generalise by saying that "A relation is in the 1NF if the values in the relation are atomic for every single attribute of the relation".

Before we can look into the next two normal forms, 2NF and 3NF, we need to first explain the notion of 'functional dependency' as these two forms are constrained by functional dependencies.

4.3   Functional Dependencies

4.3.1 Determinant

The value of an attribute can uniquely determine the value in another attribute. For example, in every tuple of the Transaction relation in Figure 4-2:

- C# uniquely determines Cname
- C# also uniquely determines Ccity as well as Cphone

Given C# 1, we will know that its Cname is 'Codd' and no other. On the other hand, we cannot say that given Ccity 'London', we will know that its Cname is 'Codd' because Ccity 'London' will also give Cname of 'Deen'. Thus Ccity cannot uniquely determine Cname (in the same way that C# can).

Additionally, we see that:

- (C#, P#, Date) uniquely determines Qnt

We can now introduce the definition of a "determinant" as being an attribute (or a set of non-redundant) attributes which can act as a unique identifier of another attribute (or another set of attributes) of a given relation.

We may thus say that:

- C# is a unique key for Cname, Ccity and Cphone.
- (C#, P#, Date) is a unique key for Qnt.

These keys are non-redundant keys as no member of the composite attribute can be left out of the set. Hence, C# is a determinant of Cname, Ccity, and Cphone. (C#, P#, Date) is a determinant of Qnt.

A determinant is written as:

$$A \rightarrow B$$

and can be read as "A determines B" (or A is a determinant of B). If any two tuples in the relation R have the same value for the A attribute, then they must also have the same value for their B attribute.

Applying this to the Transaction relation above, we may then say:

C# → Cname

C# → Ccity

C# → Cphone

(C#, P#, Date) → Qnt

The value of the attribute on the left-hand side of the arrow is the determinant because its value uniquely determines the value of the attribute on the right.

Note also that:

(Ccity, Cphone) → Cname

(Ccity, Cphone) → C#

The converse notation

$$A \;\; \xrightarrow{\; \text{x} \;}\!\!\!\!\!\rightarrow B$$

can be read as A "does not determine" B.

Taking again the Transaction relation, we may say therefore that Ccity cannot uniquely determine Cname

Ccity $\xrightarrow{\; \text{x} \;}\!\!\!\!\!\rightarrow$ Cname

because there exists a number of customers living in the same city.

Likewise:

Cname $\xrightarrow{\; \text{x} \;}\!\!\!\!\!\rightarrow$ (Ccity, Cphone)

Cname $\xrightarrow{\; \text{x} \;}\!\!\!\!\!\rightarrow$ C#

as there may exist customers with the same name.

4.3.2 Functional Dependence

The role of determinants is also expressed as "functional dependencies" whereby we can say:

"If an attribute A is a determinant of an attribute B, then B is said to be functionally dependent on A"

and likewise

"Given a relation R, attribute B of R is functionally dependent on attribute A if and only if each A-value in R has associated with it one B-value in R at any one time".

"C# is a determinant of Cname, Ccity and Cphone" is thus also "Cname, Ccity and Cphone are functionally dependent on C#". Given a particular value of Cname value, there exists precisely one corresponding value for each of Cname, Ccity and Cphone. This is more clearly seen via the following functional dependency diagram:

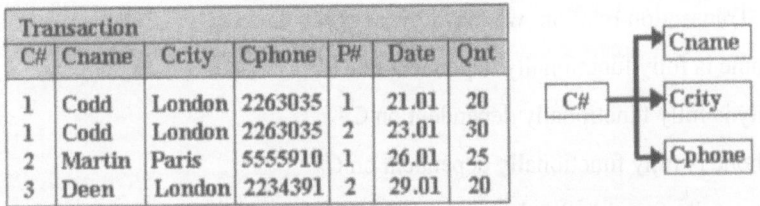

Figure 4-5: Functional dependencies in the Transaction relation

Similarly, "(C#, P#, Date) is a determinant of Qnt" is thus also "Qnt is functionally dependent on the set of attributes (C#, P#, Date)". The set of attributes is also known as a composite attribute.

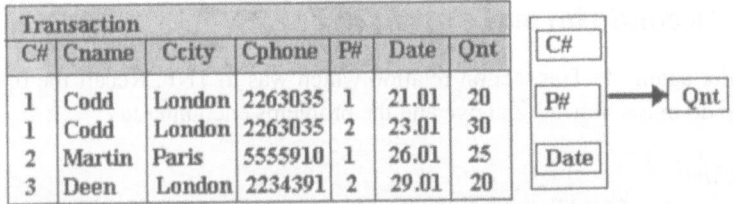

Figure 4-6: Functional dependency on a composite attribute

4.3.3 Full Functional Dependence

"If an attribute (or a set of attributes) *A* is a determinant of an attribute (or a set of attributes) *B*, then *B* is said to be fully functionally dependent on *A*"

and likewise

"Given a relation *R*, attribute *B* of *R* is *fully functionally* dependent on attribute *A* of *R* if it is functionally dependent on *A* and not functionally dependent on any subset of *A* (*A* must be composite)".

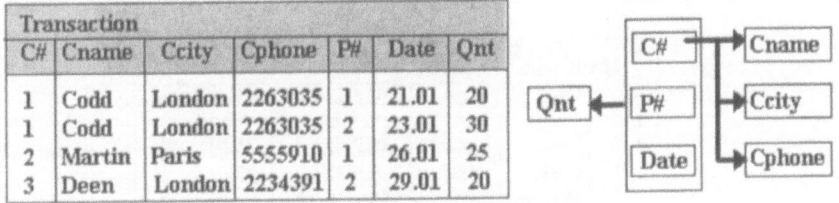

Figure 4-7: Functional dependencies in the Transaction relation

For the Transaction relation, we may now say that:

- Cname is fully functionally dependent on C#

- Ccity is fully functionally dependent on C#

- Cphone is fully functionally dependent on C#

- Qnt is fully functionally dependent on (C#, P#, Date)

- Cname is not fully functionally dependent on (C#, P#, Date), it is only *partially* dependent on it (and similarly for Ccity and Cphone).

Having understood about determinants and functional dependencies, we are now in a position to explain the rules of the second and third normal forms.

4.4   Second Normal Form (2NF)

Consider again the Transaction relation which was in 1NF. Recall the operations we tried to do in Section 4.1.2 above and the problems encountered:

1. Update
What happens if Codd's telephone number changes and we update only the first tuple (but not the second)?

| Transaction | | | | | | |
C#	Cname	Ccity	Cphone	P#	Date	Qnt
1	Codd	London	2263035	1	21.01	20
1	Codd	London	2263035	2	23.01	30
2	Martin	Paris	5555910	1	26.01	25
3	Deen	London	2234391	2	29.01	20

2. Insertion
If we wish to introduce a new customer, we cannot do so unless an appropriate transaction is effected.

| Transaction | | | | | | |
C#	Cname	Ccity	Cphone	P#	Date	Qnt
1	Codd	London	2263035	1	21.01	20
1	Codd	London	2263035	2	23.01	30
2	Martin	Paris	5555910	1	26.01	25
3	Deen	London	2234391	2	29.01	20
4	Smith	Vienna	?	?	?	?

Entity Integrity Violation: P# is a part of primary key !

3. Deletion

If the data about a transaction is deleted, the information about the customer is also deleted. If this happens to the last transaction for that customer the information about the customer will be lost.

Transaction						
C#	Cname	Ccity	Cphone	P#	Date	Qnt
1	Codd	London	2263035	1	21.01	20
1	Codd	London	2263035	2	23.01	30
2	Martin	Paris	5555910	1	26.01	25
3	Deen	London	2234391	2	29.01	20

(Delete →) points to row: 2 Martin Paris 5555910 1 26.01 25

Clearly, the Transaction relation although it is normalised to 1NF still have storage anomalies. The reason for such violations to the database's integrity and consistency rules is because of the *partial dependency on the primary key*.

Recall, the functional dependencies as shown in Figure 4-7. The determinant (C#, P#, Date) is the composite key of the Transaction relation - its value will uniquely determine the value of every other non-key attribute in a tuple of the relation. Note that whilst Qnt is fully functionally dependent on all of (C#, P#, Date), Cname, Ccity and Cphone are only partially functionally dependent on the composite key (as they each depend only on the C# part of the key only but not on P# or Date).

The problems are avoided by eliminating partial key dependence in favour of full functional dependence, and we can do so by separating the dependencies as follows:

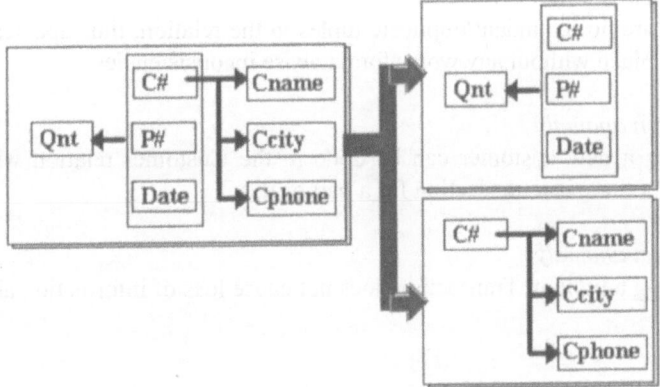

The source relation is thus split into two (or more) relations whereby each resultant relation no longer has any partial key dependencies:

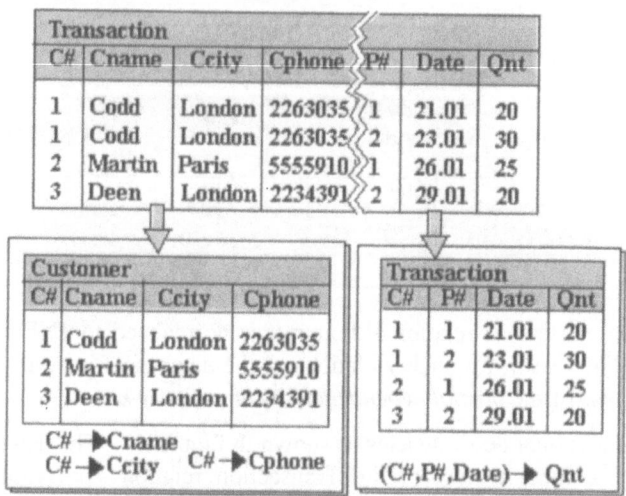

Figure 4-8: Relations in 2NF

We now have two relations, both of which are in the second normal form. These are the same relations of Figure 4-2 above, and the discussion we had earlier clearly shows that the storage anomalies caused by the 1NF relation have now been eliminated:

1. *Update anomaly*
   There are no redundant/duplicate tuples in the relation, thus updates are done just at one place without any worry for database inconsistencies.

2. *Addition anomaly*
   Adding a new customer can be done in the Customer relation without concern whether there is a transaction for a part or not

3. *Deletion anomaly*
   Deleting a tuple in Transaction does not cause loss of information about Customer details.

More generally, we shall summarise by stating the following:

1. Suppose, there is a relation **R**

R: (K1	K2	I1	I2)
1	1	a	x
1	2	b	y
2	1	c	x
2	2	d	y

where the composite attribute (K1, K2) is the Primary Key. Suppose also that there exist the following functional dependencies:

(K1, K2) →   I1

i.e. a full functional dependency on the composite key (K1, K2)..

K2 →   I2

i.e. a partial functional dependency on the composite key (K1, K2).

The partial dependencies on the primary key must be eliminated. The reduction of 1NF into 2NF consists of replacing the 1NF relation by appropriate "projections" such that every non-key attribute in the relations are fully functionally dependent on the primary key of the respective relation. The steps are:

1. Create a new relation R2 from R. Because of the functional dependency **K2 →
    I2,** R2 will contain K2 and I2 as attributes. The determinant, K2, becomes the key of R2.

2. Reduce the original relation R by removing from it the attribute on the right hand side of **K2 → I2**. The reduced relation R1 thus contain all the original attributes but without I2.

3. Repeat steps 1. and 2. if more than one functional dependency prevents the relation from becoming a 2NF.

4. If a relation has the same determinant as another relation, place the dependent attributes of the relation to be non-key attributes in the other relation for which the determinant is a key.

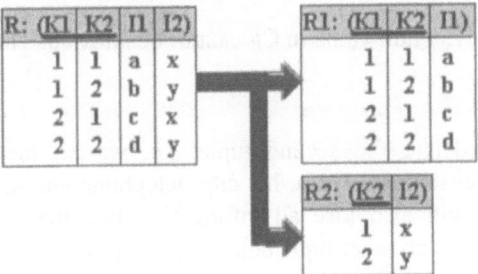

Figure 4-9: Reduction of 1NF into 2NF

Thus, "A relation R is in 2NF if it is in 1NF and every non-key attribute is fully functionally dependent on the primary key".

4.5   Third Normal Form (3NF)

A relation in the Second Normal Form can still be unsatisfactory and show further update anomalies. Suppose we add another attribute, Salesperson, to the Customer relation who attends to the needs of the customer.

Customer				
C#	Cname	Ccity	Cphone	Salesperson
1	Codd	London	2263035	Smith
2	Martin	Paris	5555910	Ducruer
3	Deen	London	2234391	Smith

Its associated functional dependencies are:

C# → Cname, Ccity, Cphone, Salesperson

Consider again operations that we may want to do on the data

1. *Update*
Can we change the salesperson servicing customers in London? Here, we find that there are several occurrences of London customers (e.g. Codd and Deen). Thus we must ensure that we update all tuples such that 'Smith' is now replaced by the new salesperson, say 'Jones', otherwise we end up with a database inconsistency problem again.

2. *Insertion*
Can we enter data that 'Fatimah' is the salesperson for the city of 'Sarawak' although no customer exists there yet?

Customer				
C#	Cname	Ccity	Cphone	Salesperson
1	Codd	London	2263035	Smith
2	Martin	Paris	5555910	Ducruer
3	Deen	London	2234391	Smith
?	?	Sarawak	?	Fatimah

As C# is the primary key, a null value in C# cannot be allowed. Thus the tuple cannot be created.

3. *Deletion*
What happens if we delete the second tuple, i.e. we no longer need to keep information about the customer Martin, his city, telephone and salesperson ? If this tuple is removed, we will also lose all information that the salesperson Ducruet services the city of Paris as no other tuple holds this information.

As another, more complex example, consider keeping information about parts that are being kept in bins, where the following relation called Stock

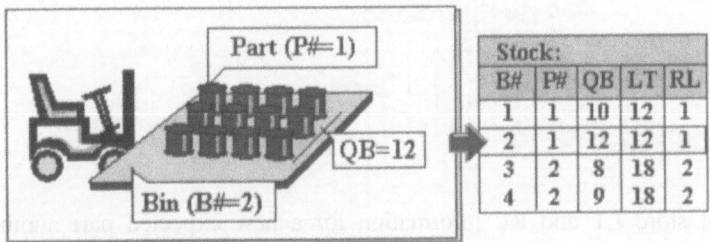

which contains information on:
- the bin number (B#)
- the part number (P#) of the part kept inside a given bin
- the quantity of pieces of the part in a given bin (QB)
- the lead time (LT) taken to deliver a part after an order has been placed for it
- the re-order level (RL) of the part number which indicates the an order must be placed to re-order new stock of that part whenever the existing stock quantity gets too low, i.e. when QB ≤ RL

We further assume that:
- parts of a given part number may be stored in several bins
- the same bin holds only one type of part, i.e. it does not hold parts of more than one part number
- the lead time and re-order level are fixed for each part number

The only candidate key for this relation is B#, hence it must be selected as the primary key. Since the B# is a single attribute, the question of partial dependency does not arise (the relation is in Second Normal Form).

Its associated functional dependencies (which are *full* functional dependencies) are:

B# → P#, QB, LT, RL

But in this case, we also have data anomalies:

1. *Update*
Suppose the re-order level for part number 1 is updated, i.e. RL for P# 1 must be changed from 1 to 4. We must ensure that we update all tuples containing P#1, i.e. tuples 1 and 2; any partial updates will lead to an inconsistent database inconsistency.

2. *Insertion*

Stock:				
B#	P#	QB	LT	RL
1	1	10	12	1
2	1	12	12	1
3	2	8	18	2
4	2	9	18	2
?	3	?	24	3

Null Value is not permitted since B# is a primary key

We cannot store LT and RL information for a new expected part number in the database unless we actually have a bin number allocated to it.

3. *Deletion*

If the data (tuple) about a particular bin is deleted, the information about the part is also deleted. If this happens to the last bin containing that part, the information about the concrete part (LT, RL) will also be lost.

From the two examples above, it is still evident that despite having relations in 2NF, problems can still arise and we should now try to eliminate them. It would seem we need to further normalise them, i.e. we need a third normal form to eliminate these anomalies.

Scrutinising the functional dependencies of these examples, we notice the existence of "other" dependencies:

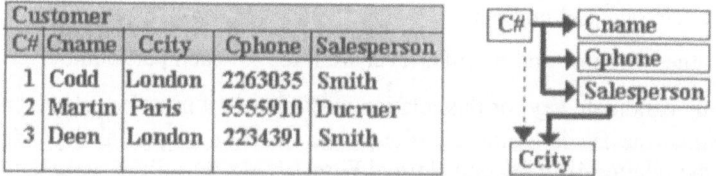

Customer				
C#	Cname	Ccity	Cphone	Salesperson
1	Codd	London	2263035	Smith
2	Martin	Paris	5555910	Ducruer
3	Deen	London	2234391	Smith

Figure 4-10: All functional dependencies in the Customer relation

Notice for example that the dependency of the attribute Salesperson on the key C#, i.e.

C# → Salesperson

is only an *indirect* or *transitive* dependency, which is also indicated in the diagram as a dotted arrow ┈┈▶ .

This is considered indirect because **C# → Ccity** and **Ccity → Salesperson**, and thus **C# → Salesperson**.

Thus for the Stock relation:

B# → **P#, QB**   and   **P#** → **LT, RL**

then   **B#** → **P#, QB, LT, RL**

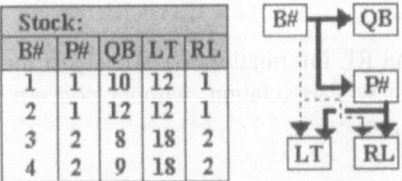

Figure 4-11: All functional dependencies in the Stock relation

The Indirect Dependency obviously causes data duplication (e.g. note the two occurrences of P#1 and LT 12 in the first two tuples of Stock). which leads to the above anomalies. This can be eliminated by *removing all indirect/transitive dependencies*. We do this by splitting the source relation into two or more other relations, as illustrated in the following example:

where we can then get

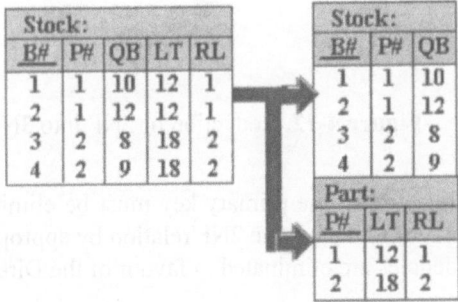

We can say that the storage anomalies caused by the 2NF relation can now be eliminated:

1. *Update anomaly*

To update the re-order level for part number 1, we need only change one (the first) tuple in the new Part relation without concern for other duplicates that used to exist before.

2. *Addition anomaly*

We can now store LT and RL information for a new part number in the database by creating a tuple in the new Part relation, without concern whether there is a bin number allocated to it or not.

3. *Deletion anomaly*

Deleting the tuple about a particular bin will remove a tuple form the new Stock relation. Should the part that was deleted from that bin be the only bin where it could be found, however does not mean the loss of data about that part. Information on the LT and RL of the part is still in the new Part relation.

More generally, we shall summarise by stating the following:

Suppose there is a relation R with attributes A, B and C. A is the determinant.
If $A \rightarrow B$ and $B \rightarrow C$
then
$A \rightarrow C$ is the 'Indirect Dependency'
(Of course, if $A \rightarrow C$ and B does not exist, then $A \rightarrow C$ is a 'Direct Dependency')

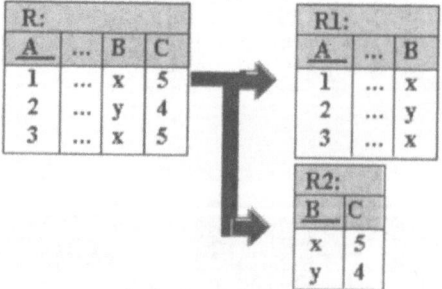

Figure 4-12. Reduction of 2NF into 3NF

The Indirect Dependencies on the primary key must be eliminated. The reduction of 2NF into 3NF consists of replacing the 2NF relation by appropriate "projections" such Indirect Key Dependencies are eliminated in favour of the Direct Key Dependencies.

The steps are:

1. Reduce the original relation R by removing from it the attribute on the right hand side of any indirect dependencies **A** → **C**. The reduced relation R1 thus contain all the original attributes but without **C**.

2. Form a new relation R2 that contains all attributes that are in the dependency **B** → **C**.

3. Repeat steps 1. and 2. if more than one indirect dependency prevents the relation from becoming a 3NF.

4. Verify that every determinant in every relation is a key in that relation

Thus, "A relation R is in 3NF if it is in 2NF and every non-key attribute is fully and directly dependent on the primary key".

There is another definition of 3NF which states that "A relation is in third normal form if every data item outside the primary key is identifiable by the primary key, the whole primary key and by nothing but the primary key".

In order to avoid certain update anomalies, each relation declared in the data base schema, should be at least in the Third Normal Form. Structurally, 2NF is better than 1NF, and 3NF is better than 2NF. There are of course other higher normal forms like the Boyce-Codd Normal Form (BCNF), the Fourth Normal Form (4NF) and the Fifth Normal Form (5NF).

However, the Third Normal Form is quite sufficient for most business database design purposes, although some very specialised applications may require the higher-level normalisation.

It must be noted that although normalisation is a very important database design component, we should not always design in the highest level of normalisation, thinking that it is the best. Often at the physical implementation level, the decomposition of relations into higher normal form mean more pointer movements are required to access and the thus slower the response time of the database system. This may conflict with the end-user demand for fast performance. The designer may sometimes have to "denormalise" some portions of a database design in order to meet performance requirements at the expense of data redundancy and its associated storage anomalies.

5. Relational Algebra I

5.1. Relational Algebra and Relational Calculus

Many different DMLs can be designed to express database manipulations. Different DMLs will probably differ in syntax, but more importantly they can differ in the basic operations provided. For those familiar with programming, these differences are not unlike that found in different programming languages. There, the basic constructs provided can greatly differ in syntax and in their underlying approach to specifying computations. The latter can be very contrasting indeed - look at, for example, the differences between procedural (eg. C) and declarative (eg. Prolog) approaches to specifying computations.

Relational Algebra and Relational Calculus are two approaches to specifying manipulations on relational databases. The distinction between them is somewhat analogous to that between procedural and declarative programming. Thus, before looking at the details of these approaches, it is instructive to briefly digress and look at procedural and declarative programming a little more closely. We will then try to put into context how the algebra and calculus help in the design and implementation of DMLs.

Briefly, the procedural approach specifies a computation to be performed as *explicit sequences* of *operations*. The operations themselves are built from a basic set of primitive operations and structuring/control primitives that build higher level operations. An operation can determine the flow of control (ie. determines the next operation to be executed) and/or cause data to be transformed. Thus programming in the procedural style involves working out the operations and their appropriate order of execution to effect the desired transformation(s) on input data.

The declarative approach, in contrast, would specify the same computation as a description of the logical relationship between input and output data. These relationships are typically expressed as a set of truth-valued sentences about data objects. Neither operations nor their sequences are made explicit by the programmer. Operations are instead implicit in the predetermined set of rules of inference used to derive new sentences from those given (or derived earlier).

In other words, if you used a procedural programming language, you must specify *how* input is to be transformed to desired outputs using the basic operations available in the language. However, if you used a declarative language, you must instead describe *what* relationships must be satisfied between inputs and outputs, but essentially say nothing about how a given input is to be transformed to the desired output (it is for the system to determine how, typically by some systematic application of inference rules).

Amidst such differences, users are right to raise some basic concerns. Are these differences superficial? Or do they mean that there can be computations specifiable in one but not in the other? If the latter were the case, programmers must avoid choosing languages that simply cannot express some desired computation (assuming we know exactly the limitations of each and every programming language)! Fortunately for programmers, this is not the case. It is a well-known result that every *general-purpose* programming language (whether procedural or declarative) is *equivalent* to every other. That is, if something is computable at all, it can be specified in any of these languages. Such equivalence is established by reference to a *fundamental model of computation*[1] that underlies the notion of computability.

Now what can we say about the different (existing and future) database languages? Can two different languages be said to be equivalent in some sense? To answer this question we must first ask whether, in relational databases, there is a fundamental model of database manipulation? The answer is yes - Relational Calculus defines that model!

Let us first state a fundamental definition:

A language that can define any relation definable in relational calculus is *relationally complete.*

This definition provides a benchmark by which any existing (and future) language may be judged as to its power of expression. Different languages may thus be equivalent in the sense of being relationally complete[2].

Relational Calculus, as we shall see later, provides constructs (well-formed expressions) to specify relations. These constructs are very much in a declarative style. Relational Algebra, on the other hand, also provides constructs for relational database manipulations but in a more procedural style. Moreover, it has also been established that Relational Algebra is equivalent to Relational Calculus, in that every expression in one has an equivalent expression in the other. Thus relational completeness of a database language can also be established by showing that it can define any relation expressible in Relational Algebra.

Why then should we bother with different languages and styles of expression if they are all in some sense equivalent? The answer is that besides equivalence (relational or computational), there are other valid issues that different language designs try to address including the level of abstraction, precision, comprehensibility, economy of expression, ease of writing specifications, efficiency of execution, etc. Declarative

---

[1] The Universal Turing Machine (model of computation) is accepted as defining the class of all computable functions. Every programming language shown to be equivalent to it is therefore equivalent with every other.

[2] Note however, that relational completeness is not the same as computational completeness, ie. Relational Calculus is not equivalent to general-purpose programming languages. It is a specialised calculus intended for the Relational Database Model. Thus while two languages may be relationally complete, each may have features over and above that required for relational completeness (but these need not concern us here).

constructs, by virtue of their descriptive nature (as opposed to the prescriptive nature of procedural constructs), are closer to natural language and thus easier to write and understand. Designers of declarative languages try to provide constructs that even end-users (with a little training) can use to formulate, for example, ad hoc queries. Declarative constructs, however, execute less efficiently than equivalent procedural ones. Attempts to make them more efficient typically involve first, automatic translation to equivalent procedural form, and second, optimising the resulting expressions according to some predetermined rules of optimisation. In fact, this was the original motivation for the Algebra, ie. providing a set of operations to which expressions of the Calculus could be translated and subsequently optimised for execution. But the efficency of even this approach cannot match that of carefully hand-coded procedural specifications. Thus for periodical and frequently executed manipulations, it is more efficient to use algebraic forms of database languages.

Because of the fundamental nature and role of the Relational Algebra and Calculus in relational databases, we will look at them in depth in the ensuing chapters. This will provide readers with the basic knowledge of database manipulations possible in the model. We begin in this chapter with Relational Algebra.

5.2. Overview of Relational Algebra

Relational Algebra comprises a set of basic operations. An operation is the application of an operator to one or more source (or input) relations to produce a new relation as a result. This is illustrated in Figure 5-1 below. More abstractly, we can think of such an operation as a function that maps arguments from specified domains to a result in a specified range. In this case, the domain and range happen to be the same, ie. relations.

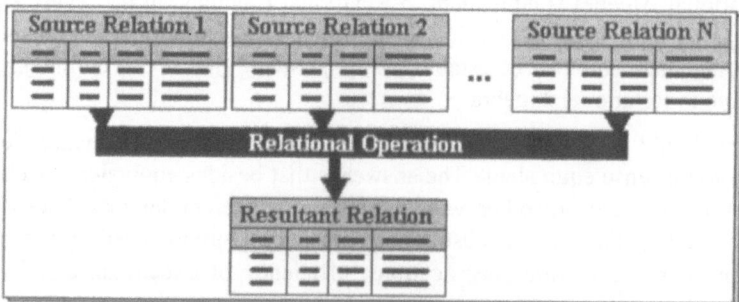

Figure 5-1 A relational algebraic operation

This is no different in principle to, say, operations in arithmetic. For example, the 'add' operation in arithmetic takes two numbers and produces a number as a result. In arithmetic, we are used to writing expressions to denote operations and their results. Thus, the 'add' operation is usually written using the '+' symbol (the operator) placed between its two aguments, eg. 145 + 168. Moreover, because an expression denotes the result of the operation (which is of the same type as its input arguments), it itself can be written as an argument in another operation, allowing us to construct complex expressions to denote one result, eg. $145 + 168 - 20 \times 3$.

Complex expressions that combine different operations are evaluated by a sequence of reductions. The sequence, in the case of arithmetic expressions, is determined by the familiar precedence of operators. Thus, the expression $145 + 168 - 20 \times 3$ would be reduced as follows:

$$145 + 168 - 20 \times 3 \;\rightarrow\; 145 + 168 - 60 \;\rightarrow\; 313 - 60 \;\rightarrow\; 253$$

This default precedence can be overridden with the explicit use of parenthesis. Thus,

$$(145 + (168 - 20)) \times 3 \;\rightarrow\; (145 + 148) \times 3 \;\rightarrow\; 393 \times 3 \;\rightarrow\; 1179$$

All these would of course be elementary to the reader! The point though is that the basic operations of relational algebra are defined to allow manipulations of relations in much the same way that arithmetic operations manipulate numbers above. With appropriately defined symbols to denote operators and syntax to denote the application of operators to arguments (relations), relational expressions combining multiple operations can be constructed to denote a resultant relation. And as with arithmetic expressions, (algebraic) relational expressions are evaluated by reduction in some specified (default or explicit) order. Thus the earlier statement that relational algebra is basically procedural in nature, ie. operations and their sequencing are explicitly specified to achieve a particular transformation of input(s) to output.

The analogy with arithmetic above has been useful to highlight the basic nature of relational algebra. However, the algebra's basic operations are much more complex than those of arithmetic. They are in fact much more related to operations on sets (viz. intersection, union, difference, etc). This is not surprising as relations are after all special kinds of sets.

As mentioned above, a relational operation maps relations to a relation. As a relation is completely defined by its intension and extension, the complete definition of a relational operation must specify both the schema of the resultant relation and the rules for generating its tuples from the input relation(s). In the following, we will do just that. Moreover, in the interest of clarity as well as precision of presentation, we will define each basic operation both informally and formally.

While notations used to denote the basic operators and operations may differ in the literature, there is no disagreement in their basic logical definitions. It will be necessary for us to use some concrete notation in what follows and, rather than introducing yet more notations, we have chosen in fact to use Codd's original notation.

5.3. Selection

Selection is used to extract tuples from a relation. A tuple from the source relation is selected (or not) based on whether it satisfies a specified predicate (condition). A predicate is a truth-valued expression involving tuple component values and their relationships. All tuples satisfying the predicate are then collected into the resultant relation. The general effect is illustrated in Figure 5-2.

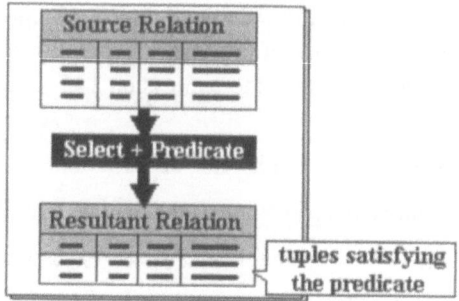

Figure 5-2 The select operation

For example, consider the 'Customer' source relation below:

Customer			
C#	Cname	Ccity	Cphone
1	Codd	London	2263035
2	Martin	Paris	5555910
3	Deen	London	2234391

The result of a selection operation applied to it with the condition that the attribute 'Ccity' must have the value "London" will be:

Result			
C#	Cname	Ccity	Cphone
1	Codd	London	2263035
3	Deen	London	2234391

because these are the only tuples that satisfy the stated condition. Procedurally, you may think of the operation as examining each tuple of the source relation in turn (say from top to bottom), checking to see if it met the specified condition before turning attention to the next tuple. If a tuple satisfies the condition, it is included in the resultant relation, otherwise it is ignored.

We shall use the following syntax to express a selection operation:

select <source-relation-name>
where <predicate>
giving <result-relation-name>

The <source-relation-name> must already have been defined in the database schema, or is the name of the result of one of previous operations.

In its simplest form, the <predicate> is a simple scalar comparison operation, ie. expressions of the form

$$\text{<value}_1\text{>} \ \text{<comparator>} \ \text{<value}_2\text{>}$$

where <comparator> is one of any comparison operator (ie. =, <, >, ≥, ≤, etc). <value$_i$> denotes a scalar value and is either a valid attribute name in the source relation, or a constant value. If an attribute name is specified, it denotes the corresponding value in the tuple under consideration. Thus, the example operation above could have been denoted by the following construct:

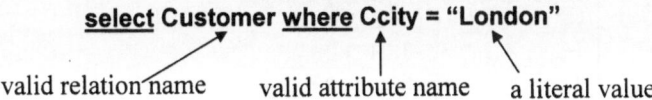

select Customer where Ccity = "London"

valid relation name   valid attribute name   a literal value

Of course, arguments to a comparator must reduce to values from the same domain.

The <predicate> may also take the more complex form of a boolean combination of simple comparison operations above, using the boolean operators 'AND', 'OR', and 'NOT'.

The <result-relation-name> is a unique name that is associated with the result relation. It can be viewed as a convenient abbreviation that can be used as <source-relation-name>s in subsequent operations. Thus, the full selection specification corresponding to the example above is:

select Customer where Ccity = "London" giving Result

Note that the intension of the resultant relation is identical to that of the source relation. In other words, the result of selection has the same number of atrributes (columns) and attribute names (column labels) as the source relation. Its overall effect, therefore, is to derive a 'horizontal' subset of the source relation.

As another example, consider the following relation. Each tuple represents a sales transaction recording the customer number of the customer purchasing the goods (C#), the product number of the goods sold (P#), the date of the transaction (Date) and the quantity sold (Qnt).

Transaction			
C#	P#	Date	Qnt
1	1	21.01	20
1	2	23.01	30
2	1	26.01	25
2	2	29.01	20

Suppose now that we are interested in looking at only those transactions which took place before January 26 with quantities of more than 25 or involving customer number 2. This need would be translated into the following selection:

select Transaction
where Date < 26.01 AND Qnt > 25 OR C# = 2
giving Result

and would yield the relation:

Result			
C#	P#	Date	Qnt
1	2	23.01	30
2	1	26.01	25
2	2	29.01	20

This example illustrates the use of boolean combinations in the <predicate>. However, formulating complex predicates is not as simple and straightforward as it may seem. The basic problem is having to deal with ambiguities at two levels.

First, the informal statement (typically in natural language) of the desired condition may itself be ambiguous. The alert reader would have noted that the phrase (in the above example)

> "...only those transactions which took place before January 26 with quantities of more than 25 or involving customer number 2..."

has two possible interpretations:

a) a transaction is selected if it is before January 26 and its quantity is more than 25, or it is selected if it involves customer number 2

b) all selected transactions must be those that are before January 26 but additionally, each must either involve a quantity of more than 25 or a customer number of 2 (or both)

Such ambiguities must be resolved first before construction of the equivalent boolean expression is attempted. In the above example, the first interpretation was assumed.

Second, the formal boolean expressions involving AND, OR and NOT may also be ambiguous. The source of ambiguity is not unlike that for natural language (ambiguity of strength or order of binding).

Thus

Cname = "Codd" AND Ccity = "London" OR Ccity = "Paris"

may be interpreted as

a) a customer Codd who either lives in London or Paris (ie. the OR binds stronger and before AND)

b) a customer Codd who lives in London, or any customer who lives in Paris (ie. the AND binds stronger and before OR)

Because of its more formal nature, however, such ambiguities are easier to overcome. It can in fact be eliminated through a convention of operator precedences and explicit (syntactical) devices to override default precedences. The conventions used are in fact as follows:

1. expressions enclosed within parentheses have greater precedence (ie. binds stronger). Thus,
   Cname = "Codd" AND (Ccity = "London" OR Ccity = "Paris")
   can only take interpretation (a) above

2. The order of precedence of the boolean connectives, unless overridden by parentheses, are (from highest to lowest) NOT, AND, OR. Thus,
   Cname = "Codd"AND Ccity = "London" OR Ccity = "Paris"
   can only take interpretation (b) above

There is no limit to the level of 'nesting' of parentheses, ie. a parenthesised expression may have within it a parenthesised subexpression, which may in turn have within it a parenthesised sub-subexpression, etc. Given any boolean expression and the above conventions, we can in fact construct a precedence tree that visually depicts its unique meaning. Figure 5-3 illustrates this. A leaf node represents a basic comparison operation, whereas a non-leaf node represents a boolean combination of its children. A node deeper in the tree binds stronger than those above it. Alternatively, the tree can be viewed as a prescription for reducing (evaluating) a boolean expression to a truth-value (**true** or **false**). To reduce a node:

a) if it is a leaf node, replace it with the result of its associated comparison operation

b) if it is a non-leaf node, reduce each of its children; then replace it with the result of applying its associated boolean operation on the truth-values of its children

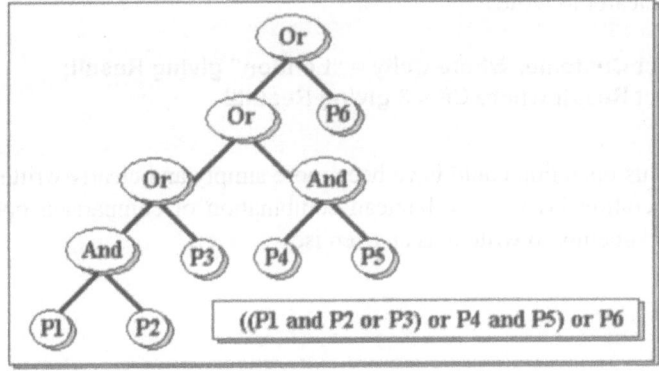

Figure 5-3 A boolean expression and its precedence tree

Using these simple conventions, we can check that expressions we construct indeed carry the intended meanings. (The reader can go back the the last example and ascertain that the intended interpretation was indeed correctly captured in the predicate of the selection statement)

At this point, we should say a few words about the notation, particularly in the context of the analogy to arithmetic expressions in the last section. Strictly speaking, the full selection syntax above is not an expression that can be used as an argument to another operation. This does not contradict the analogy, however. The selection syntax, in fact, has an expression component comprising the <u>select</u>- and <u>where</u>-clauses only, ie. without the <u>giving</u>-clause:

| <u>select</u> <source-relation-name> <u>where</u> <predicate> | <u>giving</u> <result-relation-name> |

        E x p r e s s i o n

Thus,

select Customer where Ccity = "London"

is an expression that completely specifies a selection operation while denoting also its result, in much the same way that '2+3' completely specifies an addition operation while also denoting the resultant number (ie. 5). The expression, therefore, can syntactically occur where a relation is expected and it would then be valid to write:

select (select Customer where Ccity = "London") where C# < 3

Strictly speaking, this is all we need to define the selection operation. So, of what use is the <u>giving</u>-clause? The answer, in fact, was alluded to earlier when we described the clause as allowing us to introduce a convenient *abbreviation*. It is convenient, and useful, especially in simplifying and making more readable what may otherwise be unwieldy and confusing expressions. Even the simple double selection expression above may already look unwieldy to the reader (imagine what the expression would look like if it involved 10 algebraic operations, say!).

It would be clearer to write:

select Customer where Ccity = "London" giving Result;
select Result where C# < 3 giving Result2

(of course, this operation could have been more simply and clearly written as a single selection operation involving a boolean combination of comparison operations; the reader should attempt to write it as an exercise)

Mathematical notation too have various devices to introduce abbreviations to simplify and make expressions more readable. What we are doing here with the <u>giving</u>-clause is analogous to, for example, writing:

let x = 2+3
let y = 7–2
let z = (x–y) × (x+y)

instead of the unabbreviated "((2+3)–(7–2)) × ((2+3)+(7–2))". The <u>giving</u>-clause is thus mainly a stylistic device. It is important to note that that is all it is - introducing a *temporary* abbreviation to be used in another operation. In particular, it is not to be interpreted as permanently modifying the database schema with the addition of a new relation name.

In this book, we will favour this notational style because we think it leads to a simpler and more comprehensible notation. The reader should note, however, that while other descriptions in the literature may favour and use only the expression forms, the differences are superficial.

Formal Definition

If σ denotes a relation, then let

S(σ) denote the finite set of attribute names of σ (ie. its intension)
T(σ) denote the finite set of tuples of σ (ie. its extension)
dom(α), where α ∈ S(σ), denote the set of allowable values for α
τ•α, where τ ∈ T(σ) and α ∈ S(σ), denote the value of attribute α in tuple τ

The **selection** operation takes the form

<u>**select**</u> σ <u>**where**</u> π <u>**giving**</u> ρ

where π is a predicate expression.

The syntax of a predicate expression is given by the following BNF grammar (this should be viewed as an abstract syntax not necessarily intended for an end-user language):

```
pred_exp ::= comp_exp | bool_exp | ( pred_exp )
bool_exp ::= negated_exp | binary_exp
negated_exp ::= NOT pred_exp
binary_exp ::= pred_exp bool_op pred_expr
bool_op ::= AND | OR
comp_exp ::= argument comparator argument
comparator ::= > | < | ≥ | ≤ | =
argument³ ::= attribute_name | literal
```

---

[3] The syntax of 'attribute_name' and 'literal' are unimportant in what follows and we leave it unspecified

π is well-formed iff it is syntactically correct and

- for every attribute_name α in π, $\alpha \in S(\sigma)$

- for every comp_expr $\alpha_1 * \alpha_2$ (where '*' denotes a comparator) such that $\alpha_1, \alpha_2 \in S(\sigma)$,
  either $\text{dom}(\alpha_1) \subseteq \text{dom}(\alpha_2)$ or $\text{dom}(\alpha_2) \subseteq \text{dom}(\alpha_1)$

- for every comp_expr $\alpha * \kappa$, or $\kappa * \alpha$ (where '*' denotes a comparator) such that $\alpha \in S(\sigma)$ and κ is a literal, $\kappa \in \text{dom}(\alpha)$

Further, let $\pi(\tau)$ denote the application of a well-formed predicate expression π to a tuple $\tau \in T(\sigma)$. $\pi(\tau)$ reduces π in the context of τ, ie. the occurrence of any $\alpha \in S(\sigma)$ in π is first replaced by $\tau \bullet \alpha$. The resulting expression is then reduced to a truth-value according to the accepted semantics of comparators and boolean operators.

Then ρ, the resultant relation of the selection operation, is characterised by the following:

- $S(\rho) \equiv S(\sigma)$

- $T(\rho) \equiv \{ \tau \mid \tau \in T(\sigma) \land \pi(\tau) \}$

5.4. Projection

Whereas a selection operation extracts rows of a relation meeting specified conditions, a projection operation extracts specified *columns* of a relation. The desired columns are simply specified by name. The general effect is illustrated in Figure 5-4.

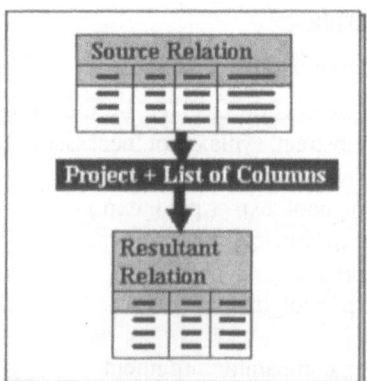

Figure 5-4: The projection operation

We could think of selection as eliminating rows (tuples) not meeting the specified conditions. In like manner, we can think of a projection as eliminating columns not named in the operation. However, an additional step is required for projection because removing columns may result in duplicate rows, which are not allowed in relations.

Quite simply, any duplicate occurrence of a row must be removed so that the result is a relation (a desired property of relational algebra operators).

For example, using again the customer relation:

Customer			
C#	Cname	Ccity	Cphone
1	Codd	London	2263035
2	Martin	Paris	5555910
3	Deen	London	2234391

its projection over the attribute 'Ccity' would yield (after eliminating all columns other than 'Ccity'):

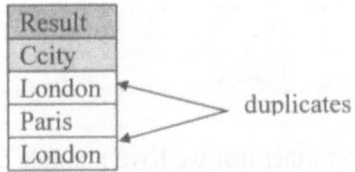

Note the duplication of row 1 in row 3. Projection can result in duplication because the resultant tuples have a smaller degree whereas the uniqueness of tuples in the source relation is only guaranteed for the original degree of the relation.

For the final result to be a relation, duplicated occurrences must be removed, ie.

Result
Ccity
London
Paris

The form of a projection operation is:

project <source-relation-name>
over <list-of-attribute-names>
giving <result-relation-name>

Thus the above operation would be written as:

project Customer
over Ccity
giving Result

As with selection, <source-relation-name> must be a valid relation - a relation name defined in the database schema or the name of the result of a previous operation. <list-of-attribute-names> is a comma-separated list of at least one identifier. Each identifier appearing in the list must be a valid attribute name of <source-relation-name>. And finally, <result-relation-name> must be a unique identifier used to name the resultant relation.

Why would we want to project a relation over some attributes and not others? Quite simply, we sometimes are interested in only a subset of an entity's attributes given a particular situation. Thus, if we needed to telephone all customers to inform them of some new product line, data about a customer's number and the city of residence are superfluous. The relevant data, and only the relevant data, can be presented using:

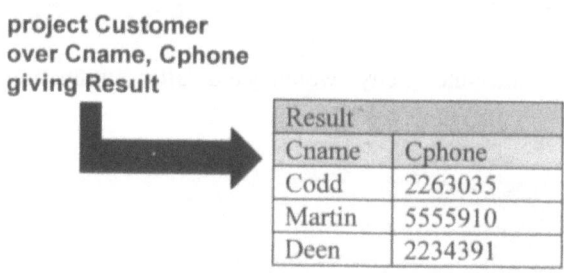

**project Customer
over Cname, Cphone
giving Result**

Result	
Cname	Cphone
Codd	2263035
Martin	5555910
Deen	2234391

Extending this example, suppose further that we have multiple offices sited in major cities and the task of calling customers is distributed amongst such offices, ie. the office in London will call up customers resident in London, etc. Now the simple projection above will not do, because it presents customer names and phone numbers without regard to their place of residence. If it was used by each office, customers will receive multiple calls and you will probably have many annoyed customers on your hands, not to mention the huge phone bills you unnecessarily incurred!

The desired relation in this case must be restricted to only customers from a given city. How can we specify this? The simple answer is that we cannot - not with just the projection operation. However, the alert reader would have realised that the requirement to restrict resultant rows to only those from a given city is exactly the sort of requirement that the selection operation is designed for! In other words, here we have an example of a situation that needs a composition of operations to compute the desired relation. Thus, for the office in London, the list of customers and phone numbers relevant to it is computed by first selecting customers from London, then projecting the result over customer names and phone numbers. This is illustrated in Figure 5-5. For offices in other cities, only the predicate of the selection needs to be appropriately modified.

Note that the order of the operations is significant, ie. a selection followed by a projection. It would not work the other way around (you can verify this by trying it out yourself).

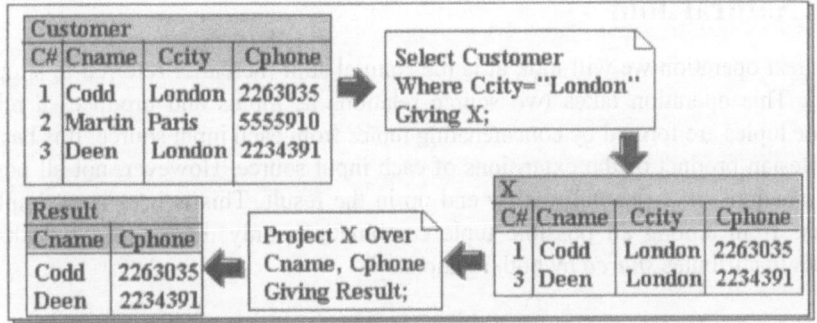

Figure 5-5 Combining operators to compute a desired relation

Formal Definition

If σ denotes a relation, then let

S(σ) denote the finite set of attribute names of σ (ie. its intension)

T(σ) denote the finite set of tuples of σ (ie. its extension)

τ•α, where τ ∈ T(σ) and α ∈ S(σ), denote the value of attribute α in tuple τ

The projection operation takes the form

project σ **over** δ **giving** ρ

where δ is a comma-separated list of attribute names. Formally, δ (as a discrete structure) may be considered a tuple, but having a concrete enumeration syntax (comma-separated list).

Let $S_{tuple}(x)$ denote the set of elements in the tuple x. Then, δ must observe the following constraint:

$$S_{tuple}(δ) \subset S(σ)$$

ie. every name occurring in δ must be a valid attribute name in the relation σ.

Furthermore, if τ ∈ T(σ) and τ' denotes a tuple, we define:

$$R(τ, δ, τ') \equiv \forall α \bullet α \in S_{tuple}(δ) \Leftrightarrow τ•α \in S_{tuple}(τ')$$

ie. a tuple element τ•α is in the tuple τ' if and only if the attribute name α occurs in δ.

Then ρ, the resultant relation of the projection, is characterised by the following:

- $S(ρ) \equiv S_{tuple}(δ)$
- $T(ρ) \equiv \{ τ' \mid τ ∈ T(σ) \wedge R(τ, δ, τ') \}$

5.5. Natural Join

The next operation we will look at is the Natural Join (hereafter referred to simply as Join). This operation takes two source relations as inputs and produces a relation whose tuples are formed by concatenating tuples from each input source. It is basically a cartesian product of the extensions of each input source. However, not all possible combinations of tuples necessarily end up in the result. This is because it implicitly selects from among all possible tuple combinations only those that have identical values in attributes *shared* by both relations.

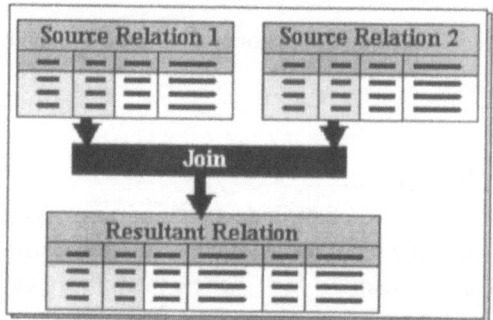

Figure 5-6 The join combines two relations over one or more common domains

Thus, in a typical application of a Join, the intensions of the input sources share at least one attribute name or domain (we assume here that attribute names are global to a schema, ie. the same name occurring in different relations denote the same attribute and value domain). The Join is said to occur over such domain(s). Figure 5-6 illustrates the general effect. The shaded left-most two columns of the inputs are notionally the shared attributes. The result comprise these and the concatenation of the other columns from each input. More precisely, if the degree of the input sources were m and n respectively, and the number of shared attributes was s, then the degree of the resultant relation is $(m+n-s)$.

As an example, consider the two relations below:

Customer

C#	Cname	Ccity	Cphone
1	Codd	London	2263035
2	Martin	Paris	5555910
3	Deen	London	2234391

Shared attribute (s = 1)

Transaction

C#	P#	Date	Qnt
1	1	21.01	20
1	2	23.01	30
2	1	26.01	25
2	2	29.01	20

These relations share the attribute 'C#', as indicated. To compute the join of these relations, consider in turn every possible pair of tuples formed by taking one tuple from each relation, and examine the values of their shared attribute. So if the pair under consideration was

<1, Codd, London, 2263035>   and   <1, 1, 21.01, 20>

we would find that the values match exactly. In such a case, we concatenate them and add the concatenation to the resultant relation. It doesn't matter if the second tuple is concatenated to the end of the first, or the first to the second, as long as we are consistent about it. By convention, we use the former. Additionally, we omit the second occurrence of the shared attribute in the result (repeated occurrence is superfluous). This gives us the tuple

<1, Codd, London, 2263035, 1, 21.01, 20>

If, on the other hand, the pair under consideration was

<3, Deen, London, 2234391>   and   <1, 1, 21.01, 20>

we would ignore it because the values of their shared attributes do not match exactly.

Thus, the resultant relation after considering all pairs would be:

Result						
C#	Cname	Ccity	Cphone	P#	Date	Qnt
1	Codd	London	2263035	1	21.01	20
1	Codd	London	2263035	2	23.01	30
2	Martin	Paris	5555910	1	26.01	25
2	Martin	Paris	5555910	2	29.01	20

The foregoing description is in fact general enough to admit operations on relations that do not share any attributes at all ($s = 0$). The join, in such a case, is simply the cartesian product of the input sources' extensions (the condition that tuple combinations have identical values over shared attributes is vacuously true since there are no shared attributes!). However, such uses of the operation are atypical.

Syntactically, we will write the Join operation as follows:

join <source-relation-name>$_1$ AND <source-relation-name>$_2$
over <attribute-name-list>
giving <result-relation-name>

where again

- <source-relation-name>$_1$ is a valid relation name (in the schema or the result of a previous operation)

- <attribute-name-list> is a comma-separated non-empty list of attribute names, each of which must occur in both input sources, and

- <result-relation-name> is a unique identifier denoting the resultant relation

With this syntax, particularly with the over-clause, we have in fact taken the liberty

(1) to insist that the join must be over at least one shared attribute, ie. we disallow expressions of pure cartesian products of two relations that do not share any attribute. This restriction is of no *practical* consequence, however, as in practice a Join is used to bring together information from different relations related through some common value.

(2) to allow a join over a subset of shared attributes, ie. we relax (generalise) the restriction that a Join is over all shared attributes.

If a Join is over a proper subset of shared attributes, then shared attributes not specified in the <u>over</u>-clause will each have its own column in the result relation. But in such cases, the respective column labels will be qualified names. We will adopt the convention of writing a qualified name as '$\rho.\alpha$', where α is the column label and ρ the relation name in which α appears. As an illustration, consider the relations below:

R1		
A1	A2	X
1	2	abc
1	3	def
2	4	ijk

R2		
A1	A2	Y
2	3	pqr
2	2	xyz

The operation

join R1 AND R2 over A1 giving Result

- will yield

Result				
A1	R1.A2	X	R2.A2	Y
2	4	ijk	3	pqr
2	4	ijk	2	xyz

To see why Join is a necessary operation in the algebra, consider the following situation (assume as context the Customer and Transaction relations above): the company decided that customers who purchased product number 1 (P# = 1) should be informed that a fault has been discovered in the product and that, as a sign of good faith and of how it values its customers, it will replace the product with a brand new fault-free one. To do this, we need to list, therefore, the names and phone numbers of all such customers.

First, we need to identify all customers who purchased product number 1. This information is in the Transaction relation and, using the following selection operation, it is easy to limit its extension to only such customers:

Transaction			
C#	P#	Date	Qnt
1	1	21.01	20
1	2	23.01	30
2	1	26.01	25
2	2	29.01	20

select Transaction
where P# = 1
giving A

A			
C#	P#	Date	Qnt
1	1	21.01	20
2	1	26.01	25

Next, we note that the resultant relation only identifies such customers by their customer numbers. What we need, though, are their names and phone numbers. In other words, we would like to extend each tuple in A with the customer name and phone number corresponding to the customer number. As such items are found in the relation Customer which shares the attribute 'C#' with A, the join is a natural operation to perform:

A			
C#	P#	Date	Qnt
1	1	21.01	20
2	1	26.01	25

Customer			
C#	Cname	Ccity	Cphone
1	Codd	London	2263035
2	Martin	Paris	5555910
3	Deen	London	2234391

join Customer And
A over C# giving B

B						
C#	Cname	...	Cphone	P#	Date	Qnt
1	Codd	...	2263035	1	21.01	20
2	Martin	...	5555910	1	26.01	25

With B, we have practically derived the information we need - in fact, more than we need, since we are interested only in the customer name (the 'Cname' column) and phone number (the 'Cphone' column). But as we've learned, the irrelevant columns may be easily removed using projection, as shown below.

B						
C#	Cname	...	Cphone	P#	Date	Qnt
1	Codd	...	2263035	1	21.01	20
2	Martin	...	5555910	1	26.01	25

project B over Cname,
Cphone giving Result

Result	
Cname	Cphone
Codd	2263035
Martin	5555910

As a final example, let us also assume we have the Product relation, in addition to the Customer and Transaction relations:

Product		
P#	Pname	Pprice
1	CPU	1000
2	VDU	1200

The task is to "get the names of products sold to customers in London". Once again, this task will require a combination of operations which must involve a Join at some point because not all the information required are contained in one relation. The sequence of operations required is shown below.

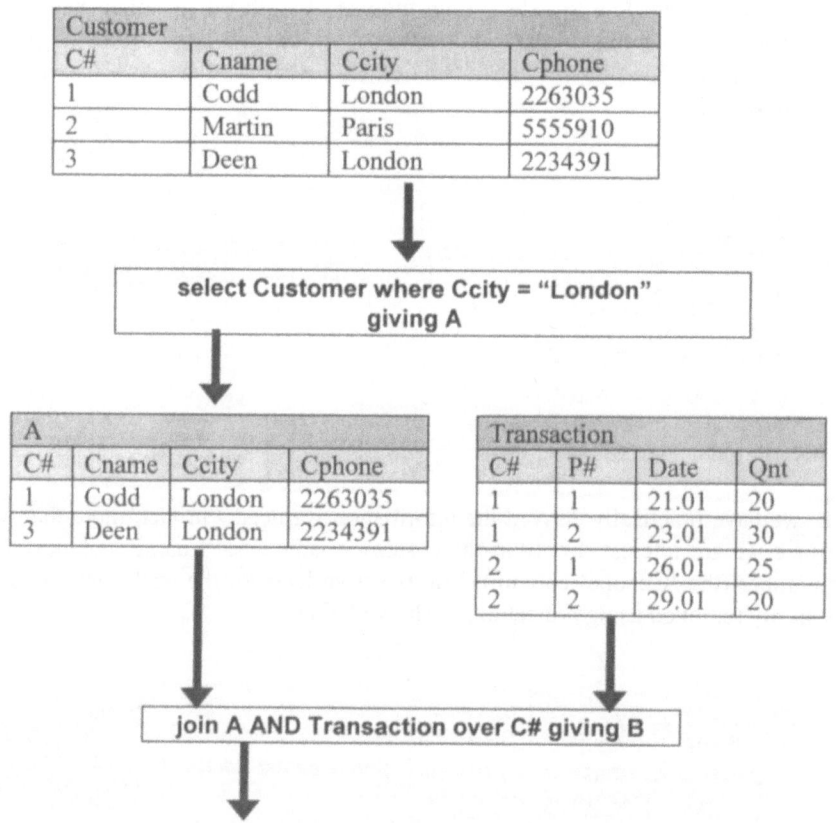

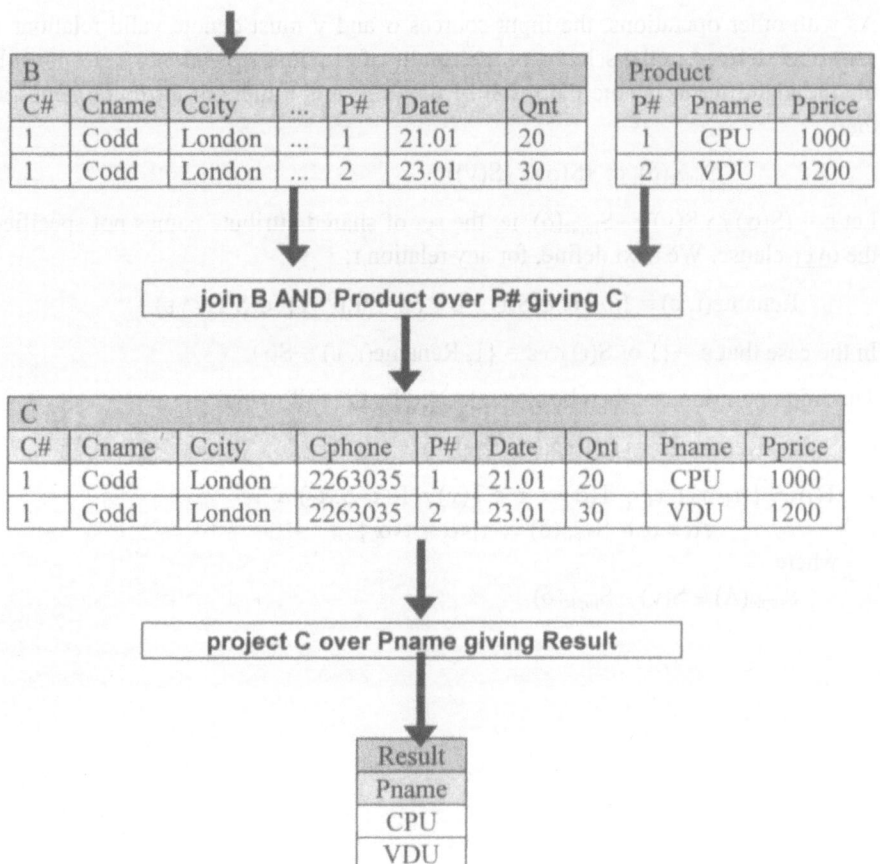

Formal Definition

As before, if σ denotes a relation, then let

       $S(\sigma)$ denote the finite set of attribute names of σ (ie. its intension)

       $T(\sigma)$ denote the finite set of tuples of σ (ie. its extension)

       $\tau\bullet\alpha$, where $\tau \in T(\sigma)$ and $\alpha \in S(\sigma)$, denote the value of attribute α in tuple τ

Further, if τ_1 and τ_2 are tuples, let $\tau_1{}^\wedge\tau_2$ denote the tuple resulting from appending τ_2 to the end of τ_1.

We will also have need to use the terminology introduced in defining projection above, in particular, S_{tuple} and the definition:

$$R(\tau, \delta, \tau') \equiv \forall\alpha \bullet \alpha \in S_{tuple}(\delta) \Leftrightarrow \tau\bullet\alpha \in S_{tuple}(\tau')$$

The (natural) join operation takes the form

    join σ **AND** v **over** δ **giving** ρ

As with other operations, the input sources σ and v must denote valid relations that are either defined in the schema or are results of previous operations, and ρ must be a unique identifier to denote the result of the join. δ is a tuple of attribute names such that:

$$S_{tuple}(\delta) \subseteq (S(\sigma) \cap S(v))$$

Let $\varepsilon = (S(\sigma) \cap S(v)) - S_{tuple}(\delta)$, ie. the set of shared attribute names not specified in the <u>over</u>-clause. We next define, for any relation r:

$$Rename(r, \varepsilon) \equiv \{ \alpha \mid \alpha \in S(r) - \varepsilon \vee (\alpha = \text{'r.p'} \wedge p \in S(r) \cap \varepsilon) \}$$

In the case that $\varepsilon = \{\}$ or $S(r) \cap \varepsilon = \{\}$, $Rename(r, \varepsilon) = S(r)$.

The Join operation can then be characterised by the following:

- $S(\rho) \equiv Rename(\sigma, \varepsilon) \cup Rename(v, \varepsilon)$

- $T(\rho) \equiv \{ \tau_1{}^\wedge\tau_2 \mid \tau_1 \in T(\sigma) \wedge \tau \in T(v) \wedge R(\tau, \Delta, \tau_2) \wedge$
  $\qquad\qquad \forall \alpha \bullet \alpha \in S_{tuple}(\delta) \Rightarrow \tau_1 \bullet \alpha = \tau \bullet \alpha \}$

  where
  $\qquad S_{tuple}(\Delta) = S(v) - S_{tuple}(\delta)$

6. Relational Algebra II

6.1. Introduction

In the previous chapter, we introduced relational algebra as a fundamental model of relational database manipulation. In particular, we defined and discussed three important operations it provides: Select, Project and Natural Join. These constitute what is called the *basic set* of operators and all relational DBMS, without exception, support them.

We have presented examples of the power of these operations to construct solutions (derived relations) to various queries. However, there are classes of practical queries for which the basic set is insufficient. This is best illustrated with an example. Using again the same example domain of customers and products they purchase, let us consider the following requirement:

> "Get the names of customers who had purchased both product number 1 and product number 2"

Customer			
C#	Cname	Ccity	Cphone
1	Codd	London	2263035
2	Martin	Paris	5555910
3	Deen	London	2234391

Transaction			
C#	P#	Date	Qnt
1	1	21.01	20
1	2	23.01	30
2	1	26.01	25
2	2	29.01	20

All the required pieces of data are in the relations shown above. It is quite easy to see what the answer is - from the Transaction relation, customers number 1 and number 2 are the ones we are interested in, and cross-referencing the Customer relation (to retrieve their names) the customers are Codd and Martin respectively. Now, how can we construct this solution using the basic operation set?

Working backwards, the final relation we wish to construct is a single-column relation with the attribute 'Cname'. Thus, the last operation needed will be a projection of some relation over that attribute. Such a relation must first be the result of joining Customer and Transaction (over 'C#'), since Customer alone does not have data on products purchased. Second, it must contain only tuples of customers who had purchased products 1 and 2, ie. some form of selection must be applied. This analysis suggests that the required sequence of operations is a Join, followed by a Select, and finally a Project.

The following then may be a possible solution:

join Customer AND Transaction over C# giving A
select A where P# = 1 AND P# = 2 giving B
project B over Cname giving Result

The join results in:

A						
C#	Cname	Ccity	Cphone	P#	Date	Qnt
1	Codd	London	2263035	1	21.01	20
1	Codd	London	2263035	2	23.01	30
2	Martin	Paris	5555910	1	26.01	25
2	Martin	Paris	5555910	2	29.01	20

At this point, however, we discover a problem: the selection on A results in an empty relation!

The problem is the selection condition: no tuple can possibly satisfy a condition that requires a *single* attribute to have *two different values* ("P# = 1 AND P# = 2"). This is obvious once it is pointed out, although it might not have been so at first glance. Thus while the selection statement is syntactically correct, its logic is erroneous. What is needed, effectively, is to select tuples of a particular customer only if there exists one with P# = 1 and another with P# = 2, ie. the form of selection needed is dependent across tuples. But the basic Select operator cannot express this because it operates on each tuple *in turn* and *independently* of one another.[1]

Thus the proposed solution above is not a solution at all. In fact, no combination of the basic operations can handle the query or other queries of this sort, for example:

"Get the names of customers who bought the product CPU but not the product VDU", or
"Get the names of customers who bought every product type that the company sells", etc.

These examples suggest that additional operations are needed. In the following, we shall present them and show how they are used.

---

[1] Some readers may have noted that if OR was used instead of AND in the selection operation, the desired result would be constructed. However, this is coincidental. The use of OR is logically erroneous—it means one or the other, but not necessarily both. To see this, change the example slightly by deleting the last tuple in Transaction and recompute the result (using OR). Your answer would still be Codd and Martin, but the correct answer should be Codd alone!

We will round up this chapter and our discussion of relational algebra with a discussion of two other important topics: how operations handle "null" values, and how sequences of operations can be optimised for performance.

A null value is inserted into a tuple field to denote an (as yet) unknown value. Clearly, this affects the evaluation of conditions involving attribute values. Exactly how will be explained in Section 6.4. Finally, we will see that there may be several different sequences of operations that derive the same result. In such cases, we may well ask which sequence is more efficient, ie. least costly or better in performance, in some sense. A more precise notion of 'efficiency' of operators and how a given operator sequence can be made more efficient will be discussed in section 6.5.

6.2. Division

As the name of this operation implies, it involves dividing one relation by another. Division is in principle a partitioning operation. Thus, $6 \div 2$ can be paraphrased as partitioning a single group of 6 into a number of groups of 2 - in this case, 3 groups of 2. The basic terminology used in arithmetic will be used here as well. Thus in an expression like $x \div y$, x is the dividend and y the divisor. Division does not always yield whole groups of the divisor, eg. $7 \div 2$ gives 3 groups of 2 and a remainder group of 1. Relational division too can leave remainders but, much like integer division, we ignore remainders and focus only on constructing whole groups of the divisor.

The manner in which a relational dividend is partitioned is a little more complex. First though, we should ask what aspect of a relation is being partitioned? The answer simply is the set of tuples in the relation. Next, we ask how we decide to group some tuples together and not others? Not surprisingly, the basis for such decisions has to do with the attribute values in the tuples. Let's take a look at an example first before we describe the process more precisely.

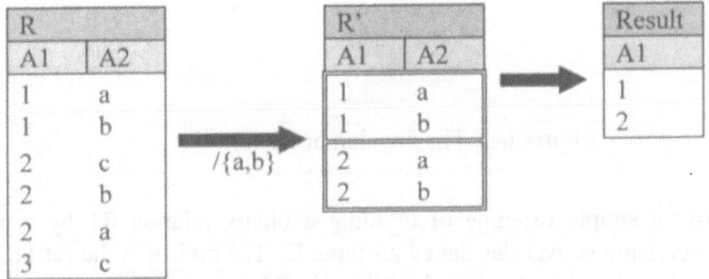

The illustration above shows how we may divide a relation R, which is a simple binary relation in this case with two attributes A1 and A2. For clarity, the values of attribute A1 have been sorted so that a given value appears in contiguous rows (where there's more than one). The question we're interested in is which of these values have *in common* an arbitrary subset of values of attribute A2.

For example,

"which values of A1 share the subset {a,b} of A2?"

By inspecting R, the reader can verify that the answer are the values 1 and 2, because only tuples with these A1 values have corresponding A2 entries of *both* 'a' and 'b'. Put another way, the tuples of R are grouped by the common denominator or divisor {a,b}. This is shown in the relation R' where we emphasise the groups formed using double-line borders. Other tuples (the remainder of the division) are ignored. Note that R' is not the final result of division - it is only an intermediate working result. The desired result are the values of attribute A1 in it, or put another way, the projection of R' over A1.

From this example, we can see that a division of a relation R is performed over some attribute of R. The divisor is a subset of values from that attribute domain and the result is a relation comprising the remaining attributes of R. In relational algebra expessions, the divisor is in fact specified by another relation D. For this to be meaningful at all, D must have at least one attribute in common with the R. The division is over the common attribute(s) and the set of values used as the actual divisor are the values found in D. The general operation is depicted in the figure below.

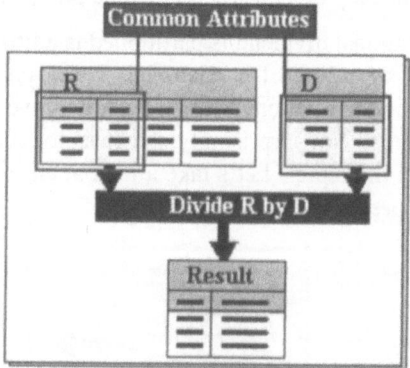

Figure 6-1. The division operation

Figure 6-2 shows a simple example of dividing a binary relation R1 by a unary relation R2. The division is over the shared attribute I2. The divisor is the set {1,2,3}, these being the values found in the shared attribute in R2. Inspecting the tuples of R1, the value 'a' occur in tuples such that their I2 values match the divisor. So 'a' is included in the result. 'b' is not, however, as there is no tuple <b,2>.

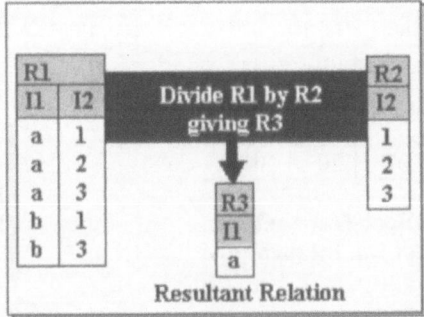

Figure 6-2 Division of a binary relation by a unary relation

We can now specify the form of the operation:

<u>divide</u> <dividend-relation-name> <u>by</u> <divisor-relation-name>
<u>giving</u> <result-relation-name>

<dividend-relation-name> and <divisor-relation-name> must be names of defined relations or results of previous operations. <result-relation-name> must be a unique name used to denote the result relation. As mentioned above, the divisor must share attributes with the dividend. In fact, we shall insist (on a stronger condition) that the intension of the divisor must be a subset of the dividend's. This is not really a restriction as any relation that shares attributes with the dividend can be turned into the required form simply by projecting over them.

We can now show how division can be used for the type of queries mentioned in the introduction. Take the query:

"Get the names of customers who bought every product type that the company sells"

The Transaction relation records customers who have ever bought anything. For this query, however, we are not interested in the dates or purchase quantities but only in the product types a customer purchased. So we project Transaction over C# and P# to give us a working relation A. This is shown on the left side of the following illustration. Next, we need all the product types the company sells, and these may be obtained by projecting the relation Product over P# to give us a working relation B. This is shown on the right side of the illustration.

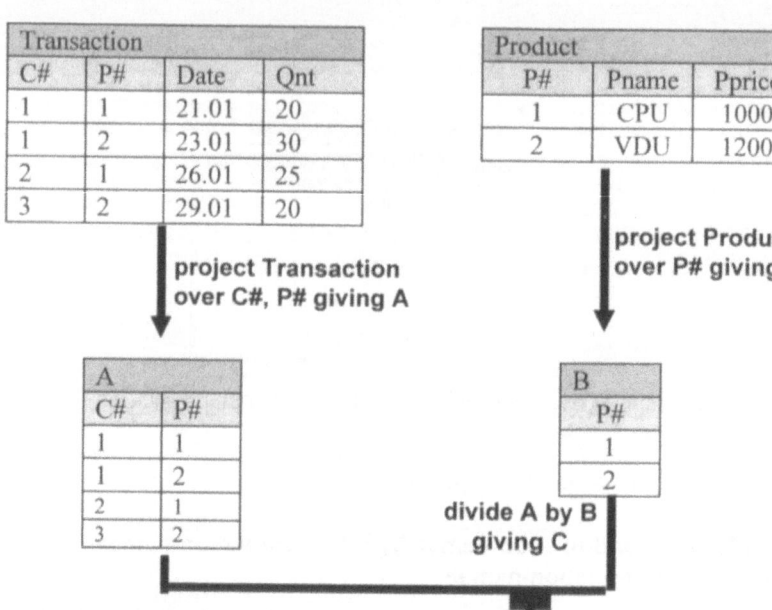

Now as we are interested in only those customers that purchased *all* products (ie. all the values in B), B is thus used to divide A to result in the working relation C. In this case, there is only one such customer. Finally, the details of the customer are obtained by joining C with the Customer relation over C#.

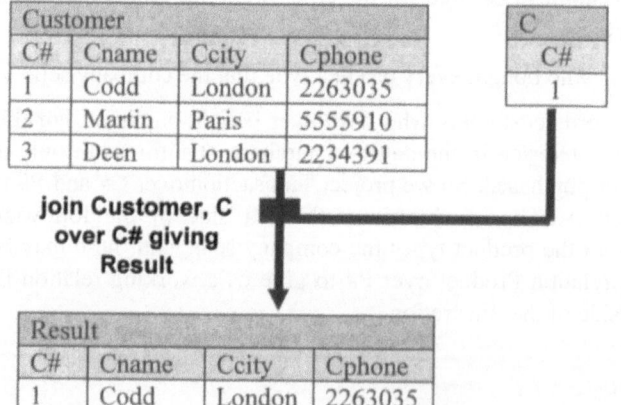

Formal Definition

To formally define the Divide operation, we will use the notation introduced and used in Chapter 5. However, for convenience, we repeat here principal definitions to be used.

If σ denotes a relation, then let

> $S(\sigma)$ denote the finite set of attribute names of σ (ie. its intension)
> $T(\sigma)$ denote the finite set of tuples of σ (ie. its extension)
> $\tau \bullet \alpha$, where $\tau \in T(\sigma)$ and $\alpha \in S(\sigma)$, denote the value of attribute α in tuple τ
> $S_{tuple}(x)$ denote the set of elements in tuple x

Furthermore, if $\tau \in T(\sigma)$, τ' denotes a tuple, and $S_{tuple}(\delta) \subseteq S(\sigma)$, we define:

$$R(\tau, \delta, \tau') \equiv \forall \alpha \bullet \alpha \in S_{tuple}(\delta) \Leftrightarrow \tau \bullet \alpha \in S_{tuple}(\tau')$$

The Divide operation takes the form

> **divide** σ **by** v **giving** ρ

As with other operations, the input sources σ and v must denote valid relations that are either defined in the schema or are results of previous operations, and ρ must be a unique identifier to denote the result of the division. The intensions of σ and v must be such that

$$S(v) \subset S(\sigma)$$

The Divide operation can then be characterised by the following:

- $S(\rho) \equiv S(\sigma) - S(v)$

- $T(\rho) \equiv \{ \tau \mid \tau_1 \in T(\sigma) \wedge R(\tau_1, \Delta, \tau) \wedge T(v) \subseteq IM(\tau) \}$

  where
  $S_{tuple}(\Delta) = S(\rho)$,
  $S_{tuple}(\delta) = S(v)$, and
  $IM(\tau) = \{ t' \mid t \in T(\sigma) \wedge R(t, \delta, t') \wedge R(t, \Delta, \tau) \}$

6.3. Set Operations

Relations are basically sets. We should, therefore, be able to apply standard set operations on them. To do this, however, we must observe a basic rule: a set operation on two or more sets is meaningful if the sets comprise values of the same type. This is so that comparison of values from different sets is meaningful. It is quite pointless, for example, to attempt an intersection of a set of integers and a set of names. We can still perform the operation, of course, but we can already tell at the outset that the result will be a null set because any value from one will never be equal to any value from the other.

To ensure this rule is observed for relations, we need to state what it means for two relations to comprise values of the same type. As a relation is a set of tuples, the values we are interested in are the tuples themselves. So when is it meaningful to compare two tuples for equality? Clearly, the *structure* of the tuples must be identical, ie. the tuples must be of equal length and their corresponding elements must be of the same type. Only then can two tuples be equal, ie. when their corresponding element values are equal. The structure of a tuple, put another way, is in fact the *intension* or *schema* of the relation it occurs in. Thus, meaningful set operations on relations require that the source relations have identical intensions/schemas. Such relations are said to be *union-compatible*.

The set operations included in relational algebra are Union, Intersection, and Difference. Keeping in mind that they are applied to whole tuples, these operations behave in exactly the standard way. It goes without saying that their results are also relations with intensions identical to the source relations.

The Union operation takes the form

<source-relation-1> <u>union</u> <source-relation-2> <u>giving</u> <result-relation>

where <source-relation-*i*> are valid relations or results of previous operations and are union-compatible, and <result-relation> is a unique identifier denoting the resulting relation.

Figure 6-3 illustrates this operation.

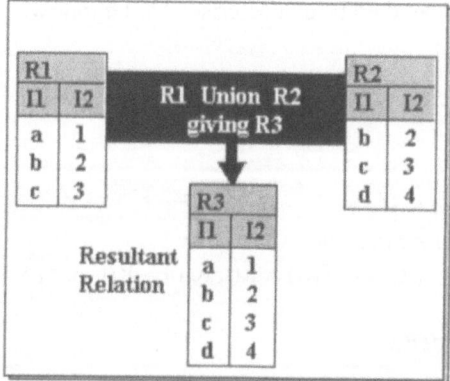

Figure 6-3 Relational union operation

The Intersection operation takes the form

<source-relation-1> <u>intersect</u> <source-relation-2> <u>giving</u> <result-relation>

where <source-relation-*i*> are valid relations or results of previous operations and are union-compatible, and <result-relation> is a unique identifier denoting the resulting relation.

Figure 6-4 illustrate this operation.

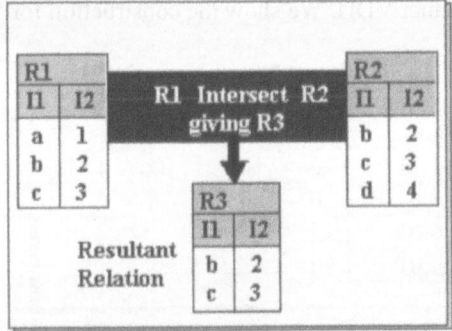

Figure 6-4 Relational intersection operation

The Difference operation takes the form

<source-relation-1> <u>minus</u> <source-relation-2> <u>giving</u> <result-relation>

where <source-relation-*i*> are valid relations or results of previous operations and are union-compatible, and <result-relation> is a unique identifier denoting the resulting relation.

Figure 6-5 illustrate this operation.

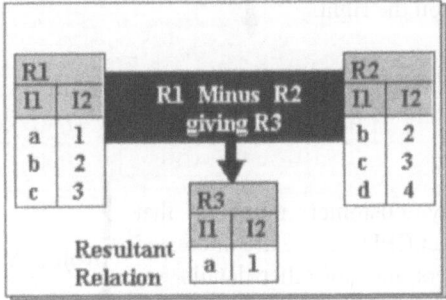

Figure 6-5 Relational difference operation

As an example of the need for set operations, consider the query: "which customers purchased the product CPU but not the product VDU?"

The sequence of operations to answer this question is quite lengthy, but not difficult. Probably the best way to construct a solution is to work backwards and observe that if we had a set of customers who purchased CPU (say W1) and another set of customers who purchased VDU (say W2), then the solution is obvious: we only want customers that appear in W1 but not in W2, or in other words, the operation "W1 minus W2".

The problem now has been reduced to constructing the sets W1 and W2. Their constructions are similar, the difference being that one focuses on the product CPU while the other the product VDU. We show the construction for W1 below.

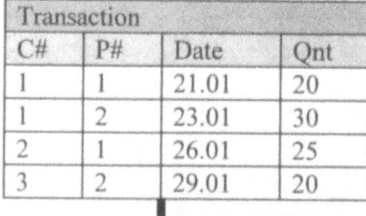

Transaction			
C#	P#	Date	Qnt
1	1	21.01	20
1	2	23.01	30
2	1	26.01	25
3	2	29.01	20

Product		
P#	Pname	Pprice
1	CPU	1000
2	VDU	1200

join Transaction AND Product over P# giving X

X					
C#	P#	Date	Qnt	Pname	Pprice
1	1	21.01	20	CPU	1000
1	2	23.01	30	VDU	1200
2	1	26.01	25	CPU	1000
3	2	29.01	20	VDU	1200

The above Join operation is needed to bring in the product name into the resulting relation. This is then used as the basis of a selection, as shown on the right.

select X where Pname = CPU giving

Y1					
C#	P#	Date	Qnt	Pname	Pprice
1	1	21.01	20	CPU	1000
2	1	26.01	25	CPU	1000

Y1 now has only customer numbers that purchased the product CPU. As we are interested only in the customers and not other details, we perform the projection on the right.

project Y1 over C# giving Z1

Customer			
C#	Cname	Ccity	Cphone
1	Codd	London	2263035
2	Martin	Paris	5555910
3	Deen	London	2234391

Z1
C#
1
2

join Customer AND Z1 over C# giving W1

Finally, details of such customers are obtained by joining Z1 and Customer, giving the desired relation W1.

W1			
C#	Cname	Ccity	Cphone
1	Codd	London	2263035
2	Martin	Paris	5555910

The construction for W2 is practically identical to that above except that the selection operation specifies the condition "Pname = VDU". The reader may like to perform these steps as an exercise and verify that the following relation is obtained:

W2			
C#	Cname	Ccity	Cphone
1	Codd	London	2263035
3	Deen	London	2234391

Now we need only perform the difference operation "W1 minus W2 giving Result" to construct a solution to the query:

Result			
C#	Cname	Ccity	Cphone
2	Martin	Paris	5555910

Formal Definition

If σ denotes a relation, then let

$S(\sigma)$ denote the finite set of attribute names of σ (ie. its intension)

$T(\sigma)$ denote the finite set of tuples of σ (ie. its extension)

The form of set operations is

σ **<set operator>** λ **giving** ρ

where <set operator> is one of 'union', 'intersect' or 'minus'; σ, λ are source relations and ρ the result relation. The source relations must be union-compatible, ie. $S(\sigma) = S(\lambda)$.

The set operations are characterised by the following:

- $S(\rho) = S(\sigma) = S(\lambda)$ for all <set operator>s
- for 'union'
  $T(\rho) \equiv \{\, t \mid t \in T(\sigma) \vee t \in T(\lambda) \,\}$
- for 'intersect'
  $T(\rho) \equiv \{\, t \mid t \in T(\sigma) \wedge t \in T(\lambda) \,\}$
- for 'minus'
  $T(\rho) \equiv \{\, t \mid t \in T(\sigma) \wedge t \notin T(\lambda) \,\}$

6.4. Null values

In populating a database with data objects, it is not uncommon that some of these objects may not be completely known. For example, in capturing new customer information through forms that customers are requested to fill, some fields may have been left blank (some customers may take exception to revealing their age or phone numbers!). In these cases, rather than not have any information at all, we can still record those that we know about. But what *value* do we insert into the unknown fields of data objects? Leaving a field blank is not good enough as it can be interpreted as an empty string which may be a valid value for some domains. We need a value that denotes 'unknown' and that cannot be confused with valid domain values.

It is here that the *Null* value is used. We can think of it as a special value different from any other value from any attribute domain. At the same time, we may think of it as belonging to every attribute domain in the database, ie. it may appear as a value for any attribute and not violate any type constraints. Syntactically, different DBMSs may use different symbols to denote null values. For our purposes, we will use the symbol '?'.

How do null values affect relational operations? All relational operations involve comparing values in tuples, including Projection (which involves comparison of result tuples for duplicates). The key to answering this question is in how we evaluate boolean operations involving null values. Thus, for example, what does "? > 5" evaluate to? The unknown value could be greater than 5. But then again, it may not be. That is, the value of the boolean expression cannot be determined on the basis of available information. So perhaps we should consider the result of the comparison as unknown as well?

Unfortunately, if we did this, the relational operations we've discussed cease to be well-defined! They all rely on comparisons evaluating categorically to one of two values: TRUE or FALSE. For example, if the above comparison ("? > 5") was generated in the process of selection, we would not know whether to include or exclude the associated tuple in the result if we were to admit a third value

(UNKNOWN). If we wanted to do that, we must go back and redefine all these operations based on some form of three-valued logic.

To avoid this problem, most systems that allow null values simply interpret any comparison involving them as FALSE. The rationale is that even though they *could* be true, they are not demonstrably true on the basis of what is known. That is, the result of any relational operation conservatively includes only tuples that demonstrably satisfy conditions of the operation. Adopting this convention, all the operations defined previously still hold without any amendment. Some implications on the outcome of each operation are considered below.

For the Select operation, an unknown value cannot identify a tuple. This is illustrated in Figure 6-6 which shows two Select operations applied to the relation R. Note that between the two operations, the selection criteria ranges over the entire domain of the attribute I2. One would expect therefore, that any tuple in R1 would either be in the result of the first or the second. This is not the case, however, as the second tuple in R1 (<b,?>) is not selected in either operation—the unknown value in it falsifies the selection criteria of both operations!

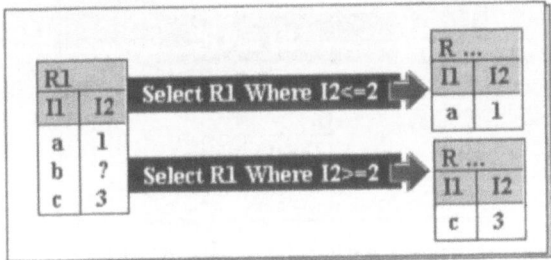

Figure 6-6 Selecting over null values

For Projection, tuples containing null values that are otherwise identical are not considered to be duplicates. This is because the comparison "? = ?", by the above convention, evaluates to FALSE. This leads to the situation as illustrated in Figure 6-7 below. The reader should note from this example that the symbol '?', while it denotes some value much like a mathematical variable, is quite unlike the latter in that it's occurrences do not always denote the same value. Thus "? = ?" is not demonstrably true and therefore considered FALSE.

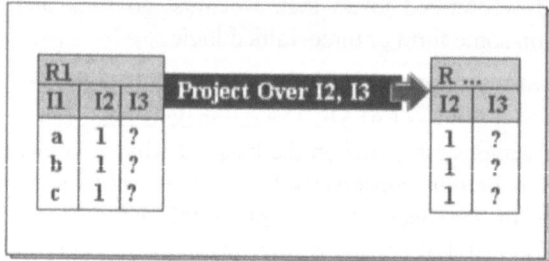

Figure 6-7 Projecting over null values

In a Join operation, tuples having null values under the common attributes are not concatenated. This is illustrated in Figure 6-8 ("?=1", "1=?" and "?=?" are all FALSE).

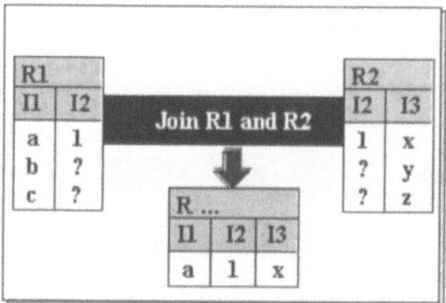

Figure 6-8 Joining over null values

In Division, the occurrence of even one null value in the divisor means that the result will be an empty relation, as any value in the dividend's common attribute(s) will fail when matched with it. This is illustrated in Figure 6-9 below. Note, however, that this is not necessarily the case if only the dividend contains null values under the common attribute(s) - division may still be successful on tuples not containing null values.

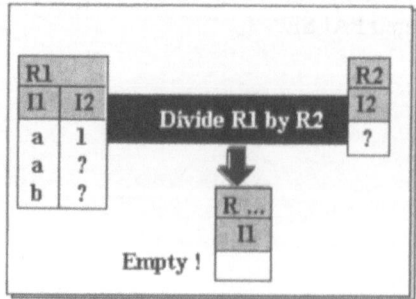

Figure 6-9 Division with null divisors

In set operations, because tuples are treated as a single unit in comparisons, a single rule applies: tuples otherwise identical but containing null values are considered to be different (as was the case for Projection above). Figure 6-10 illustrates this for each set operation. Note that because of the occurrence of null values, the tuples in R2 are not considered duplicates of R1's tuples. Thus their union simply collects tuples from both relations; subtracting R2 from R1 simply results in R1; and their intersection is empty.

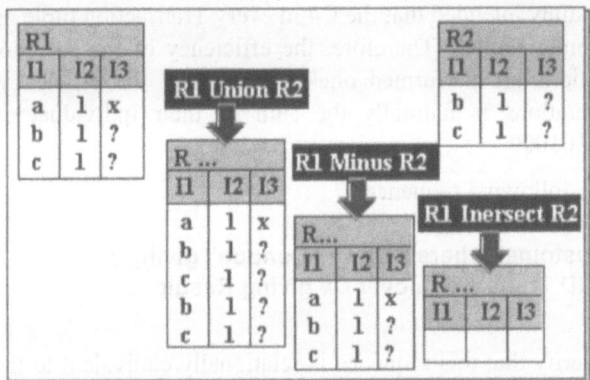

Figure 6-10 Set operations involving null values

6.5. Optimisation

Each relational operation entails a certain amount of work: retrieving a tuple, examining a tuple's attribute values, comparing attribute values, creating new tuples, repeating a process on each tuple in a relation, etc. For a given operation, the amount of work clearly varies with the cardinality of source relation(s). For example, a selection performed on a relation twice the cardinality of another (of the same degree) would involve twice as much work.

We can also compare the relative amount of work needed between different operations based on the number of tuples processed. An operation with two source inputs, for example, need to repeat its logic on every possible tuple-pair formed by taking a tuple from each input relation. Thus if we had two relations of cardinalities M and N respectively, a total of M×N tuple-pairs must be processed, ie. M (or N) times more than, say, a selection operation on each individual relation. Of course, this is not an exact relative measure of work, as there are also differences in the amount of work expended by different operations at the tuple level. By and large, however, we are interested in the *order of magnitude* of work (rather than the exact amount of work) and this is fairly well approximated by the number of tuples processed.

We will call such a measure the *efficiency* of an operation. Thus, the efficiency of selection and projection is the cardinality of its single input relation, while the efficiency of join, divide and set operations is the product of the respective cardinalities of their two input relations.

Why should the efficiency of operations interest us? Consider the following sequence of operations:

> **join Customer AND Transaction over C# giving X;**
> **select X where CCity = "London" giving Result**

Suppose the cardinality of Customer was 100 and that of Transaction was 1000. Then the efficiency of the join operation is 100×1000 = 100000. The cardinality of X is 1000 (as it is certainly intended that the C# in every Transaction tuple matches a C# in one of the Customer tuples). Therefore, the efficiency of the selection is 1000. As these two operations are performed one after another, the efficiency of the entire sequence of operations is naturally the sum of their individual efficiencies, ie. 100000+1000 = 101000.

Now consider the following sequence:

> **select Customer where CCity = "London" giving X;**
> **join X AND Transaction over C# giving Result**

The reader can verify that this sequence is relationally equivalent to the first, ie. they produce identical results. But how does its efficiency compare with that of the first? Let us calculate using the same assumptions about the cardinalities. The efficiency of the selection is 100. To estimate the efficiency of the join, we need to make an assumption on the cardinality of X. Let's say that 10 customers live in London. Then the efficiency of the join is 10×1000 = 10000, and the efficiency of the sequence as a whole is 100+10000 = 10100 - ten times more efficient than the first!

Of course, the reader may think that the assumption about X's cardinality was contrived to give this dramatic performance improvement. The point, however, is that the second sequence can do no worse than the first, ie. if all customers in the Customer relation live in London, then it performs as poorly as the first. More likely, however, we expect a performance improvement.

The above example illustrates a very important point about relational algebra: there can be more than one (sequence of) expression that describe a desired result. The main aim of optimisation, therefore, is to translate a given (sequence of) expression into its most efficient equivalent form. Such optimisation may be done manually by a human user or automatically by the database management system. Automatic optimisation may in fact do better because the automatic optimiser has access to information that is not readily available to a human optimiser, eg. current cardinalities of source relations, current data values, etc. But the overwhelming majority of relational DBMS's available today merely execute operations requested by users as is. Thus, it is important that users know how to perform optimisations manually.

For manual optimisation, it is perhaps less important to derive *the* most efficient form of a query than to follow certain guidelines, heuristics or rules-of-thumb that lead to more efficient expressions. Frequently the latter will lead to acceptable performance and expending more effort to find the optimal expression may not significantly improve that performance if good heuristics are used. There is, in fact, a simple and effective rule to remember when writing queries: delay as long as possible the use of expensive operations! In particular, we should wherever possible put selection ahead of other operations because it reduces the cardinality of relations. Figure 6-11 illustrate the application of this principle. The reader should be able to verify that the two sequences of operations are logically equivalent and that intuitively the selection operations before the joins can significantly improve the efficiency of the query.

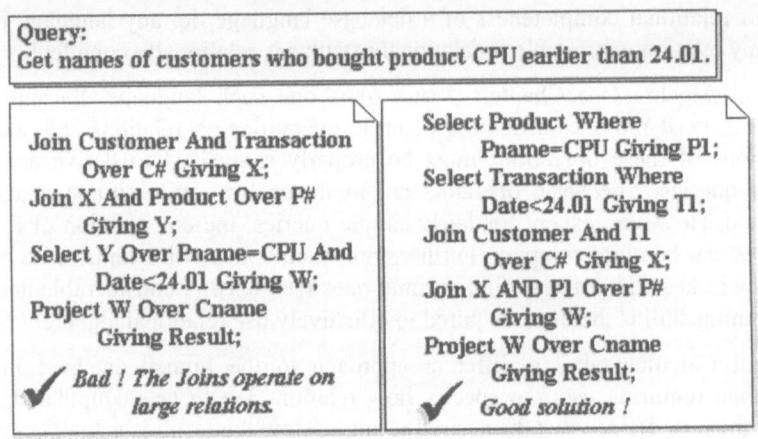

Figure 6-11 Delay expensive operations

7. Relational Calculus I

7.1 Introduction

We established earlier the fundamental role of relational algebra and calculus in relational databases (see 5.1). More specifically, relational calculus is the basis for the notion of relational completeness of a database language, ie. any language that can define any relation expressible in relational calculus is relationally complete.

Relational Algebra (see Chapters 5 and 6) is one such language. Its approach is procedural, ie. it provides a number of basic operations on relations and successive applications of these operations must be properly sequenced to derive answers to database queries. The basic operators are in themselves quite simple and easy to understand. However, except for fairly simple queries, the construction of operation sequences can be quite complex. Furthermore, such constructions must also consider efficiency issues and strive to find optimal ones (see 6.5). A considerable amount of programming skill is therefore required to effectively use relational algebra.

Relational Calculus takes a different approach to the human–database interface. Rather than requiring users to specify how relations are to be manipulated, it only requires them to define *what* the desired result is. How the result is actually computed, ie. the operations used, their sequencing and optimisation, is left to the database management system to work out. As it doesn't deal with procedures (ie. sequencing of operations), this approach is frequently termed *non-procedural* or *declarative*.

Relational Calculus is mainly based on the well-known Propositional Calculus, which is a method of calculating with sentences or declarations. Such sentences or declarations, also termed propositions, are ones for which a truth value (ie. "true" or "false") may be assigned. These can be simple sentences, such as "the ball is red", or they may be more complex involving one or more simple sentences, such as "the ball is red AND the playing field is green". The truth value of complex sentences will of course depend on the truth values of their components. This is in fact what the calculus 'calculates', using rules for combining truth values of component sentences.

In Relational Calculus, the sentences we deal with are simpler and refer specifically to the relations and values in the database of interest. Simple sentences typically take the form of comparisons of values denoted by variables or constants, eg. $X \geq 3$, $X < Y$, etc. More complex sentences are built using logical connectives And ('&') and Or ('|'), eg. $X > 7$ & $X < Y$ | $X \leq 5$. Simple and complex sentences like these are examples of Well-Formed Formulae, which we will define fully later.

Regardless of their exact syntax, a formula is in principle a logical function with one or more free variables. For purposes of illustration, we will write such functions as in the following annotated example:

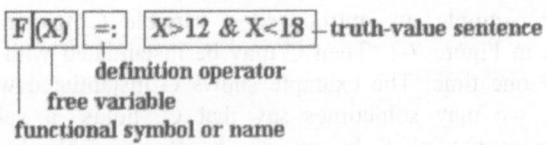

In the above example, there is one free variable, X. The value of the function can be computed for specific instances of X. Thus,

$$F(15) \equiv (15 > 12 \ \& \ 15 < 18) \equiv (\text{true} \ \& \ \text{true}) \equiv \text{true}$$
$$F(10) \equiv (10 > 12 \ \& \ 10 < 18) \equiv (\text{false} \ \& \ \text{true}) \equiv \text{false}$$

Additionally, free variables are deemed to range over a set of permitted values, ie. only such values can instantiate them. We shall see the significance of this later, as applied to relations. But just to illustrate the concept for now, consider the following function over two free variables:

$$F(X,Y) \ =: \ X > Y \ \& \ Y < 12$$

Suppose X ranges over {8, 15} and Y ranges over {7,14}. Then F(8, 14) and F(15, 7) are allowable instantiations of the function, with truth values false and true respectively, whereas F(1000,200) is not a valid instantiation. Such restrictions of values over which free variables range become significant when we interpret a formula as the simple query: "get the set of values of free variables for which the formula evaluates to true". Thus, for the above formula, we need only construct the following table involving only the permitted values:

X	Y	F(X,Y)
8	7	true
8	14	false
15	7	true
15	14	false

The desired set of values can then be read from the rows where F(X,Y) evaluated to true, ie. the set {(8,7), (15,7)}.

Relational Calculus is an application of the above ideas to relations. We will develop these ideas in greater detail in the following sections.

7.2 Tuple Variables

Free variables in logical functions can in principle range over any type of value. A feature that distinguishes Relational Calculus from other similar calculi is that the free variables range over relations. More specifically, any free variable ranges over the extension of a designated relation, ie. the current set of tuples in the relation. Thus, a free variable may be instantiated with a tuple selected from the designated relation.

Suppose, for example, we introduced a variable C to range over the relation Customer, as in Figure 7-1. Then C may be instantiated with any <u>one</u> of the three tuples at any one time. The example shows C instantiated with the second tuple. Equivalently, we may sometimes say that C 'holds' a value instead of being instantitated with that value[1]. In any case, because variables like C range over tuples (or is only permitted to hold a tuple), they are termed *tuple variables*.

Figure 7-1 A tuple variable C ranging over the Customer relation

A tuple has component parts, and unless we have a means of referring to such parts, the logical functions we formulate over relations will have limited expressive power. Given, for example, two variables X and Y that range over two different relations with a common domain, we may want to specify a condition where their current instantiations are such that the values under the common domain are identical. Thus while X (and Y) denote a tuple as a whole, we really wish to compare tuple component values. The syntactic mechanism provided for this purpose takes the form:

<tuple-variable-name>.<attribute-name>

and is interpreted to mean the value associated with <attribute-name> in the current instantiation of <tuple-variable-name>. Thus, assuming the instantiation of C as in Figure 7-1:

    C.C# = 2
    C.Cname = 'Martin'
    ...etc

This denotation of a particular data item within a tuple variable is often referred to as a projection of the tuple variable over a domain (eg. "C.Cname" is a projection of tuple variable C over the domain Cname).

Relational Calculus is a collection of rules of inference of the form:

<target list> : <logical expression>

where <target list> is a list of free variables and/or their projections that are referenced in <logical expression>. This list is thought of as the "target list" because the set of instantiations of the list items that makes <logical expression> true is the desired result. In other words, an inference rule may be thought of as a query, and may be informally understood as a request to find all variable instantiations that

---

[1] This terminology may perhaps be favoured by programmers who are used to programming language variables and to thinking about them as memory locations that can 'hold' one value at a time.

satisfy <logical expression> and, for each such instantiation, to extract the data items mentioned in <target list>.

For example, consider the inference rule in Figure 7-2. It references one free variable, C, which ranges over Customer. The <target list> specifies items we are interested in - only the phone number in this case - but only of those tuples that satisfy the <logical expression>. In other words, the rule may be paraphrased as the query to "get the set of phone numbers of customers who live in London". Note that the use of the variable C *both* in <target list> and in <logical expression> denotes the *same* instantiation, thereby ensuring that "C.Cphone" is extracted from the same tuple that satisfies the comparison "C.Ccity = London". The computed set in this case would be {2263035, 2234391}, corresponding to the phone numbers in the first and last tuples - these being the only tuples satisfying "C.Ccity = London".

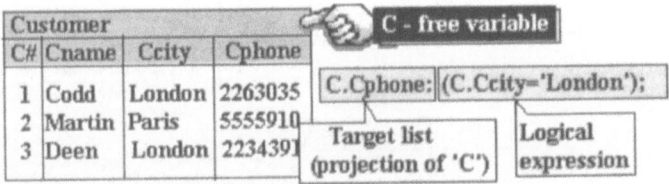

Figure 7-2 An inference rule over the Customer relation

The reader should note the simplicity and declarative character of the inference rule, which merely states the desired result (the <target list>) and the conditions that must be satisfied (the <logical expression>) for a value to be included in the result. Contrast this with relational algebra which would require the following construction:

```
select Customer where Ccity = 'London' giving X;
project X over Cphone giving Result
```

The above example only used a single variable. However, a single variable can only range over a single relation, while often the data items of interest are spread over more than one relation. In such cases, we will need more than one tuple variable.

Figure 7-3 illustrates such a case involving two variables, P and T, ranging over relations Product and Transaction respectively. Note that the inference rule at the top of the figure

- lists items from both variables in the target list (ie. P.Pname, T.C#)

- compares in the logical expression projections of the two different variables over the same domain (T.P# = P.P#)

It further illustrates specific instantiations of each variable and evaluation of the logical expression in the context of these instantiations. In this case, the logical expression is true and therefore the items in the target list are extracted from the variables (shown in the "result" table). It is important to note that a given inference, as in this illustration, is entirely in the context of a specific instantiation of each tuple variable. It is meaningless, for example, to evaluate "T.P# = P.P#" using one instance of P and "P.Price > 1000" using another. The total number of inferences that can be attempted for any given rule is therefore the product of the cardinality of each variable's range.

The inference rule in this example may be paraphrased as the query "find the customer numbers and product names, priced at more than 1000, that they purchased". As an exercise, the reader should attempt to construct this query in relational algebra (hint: it will involve the basic operators Select, Project and Join).

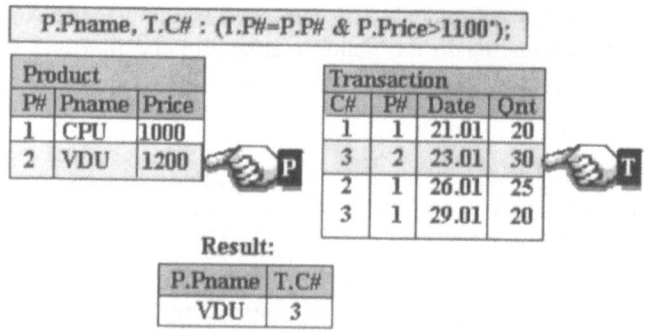

P.Pname, T.C# : (T.P#=P.P# & P.Price>1100');

Product

P#	Pname	Price
1	CPU	1000
2	VDU	1200

Transaction

C#	P#	Date	Qnt
1	1	21.01	20
3	2	23.01	30
2	1	26.01	25
3	1	29.01	20

Result:

P.Pname	T.C#
VDU	3

Figure 7-3 Multiple variable inference

7.3 Quantifiers

Logical expressions may also include variable *quantifiers*, specifically:

1. the *existential* quantifier, denoted by the symbol '$\exists$', and

2. the *universal* quantifier, denoted by the symbol '$\forall$'

These quantifiers quantify variables. An existentially quantified variable, say x, is written "$\exists x$" and is read as "there exists an x such that…". A universally quantified variable is written as "$\forall x$" and is read as "for all x …".

Quantification is applied to a formula and is written preceding it. For example,

$\exists x (x < y \& y < 12)$

would be read as "there exists an x such that x is less than y and y is less than 12". The formula to which the quantification is applied is called the *scope* of quantification. Occurrences of quantified variables in the scope of quantification are said to be bound (existentially or universally). The scope is normally obvious from the written expressions, but if ambiguities might otherwise arise, we will use parenthesis to delimit scope.

Informally, the formula "$\exists x (<\text{expr}>)$" asserts that there exists *at least one* value of x (from among its range of values) such that <expr> is true. This assertion is false only when no value of x can be found to satisfy <expr>. On the other hand, if the assertion is true, there may be more than one such value of x, but *we don't care which*. In other words, the truth of an existentially quantified expression is not a function of the quantified variable(s)[2].

As an example, consider the unquantified expression

$$x < y \ \& \ y < 12$$

and suppose x ranges over $\{4,15\}$ and y over $\{7,14\}$. The truth table for the expression is:

x	y	x<y & y<12
4	7	true
4	14	false
15	7	false
15	14	false

Now consider the same expression but with x existentially quantified:

$$\exists x \ (x < y \ \& \ y < 12)$$

Since we don't care which value of x makes the expression true as long as there is at least one, its truth depends only on the unbound variable y:

y	∃x (x<y & y<12)
7	true
14	false

An existentially quantified expression therefore has a distinctly different meaning from the same expression unquantified. In particular, when <logical expression> of an inference rule is existentially quantified, it becomes a query on the free variables only, since it is a function of only those variables.

Product			
P#	Pname	Price	
1	CPU	1000	
2	VDU	1200	

Transaction			
C#	P#	Date	Qnt
1	1	21.01	20
3	2	23.01	30
2	1	26.01	25
2	2	29.01	20

Figure 7-4 Product and Transaction relations with associated tuple variables

Consider, for example, the Product and Transaction relations in Figure 7-4, with tuple variables P ranging over the former and T over the latter. The rule

$$\text{P.Pname: } \exists T \ (T.P\# = P.P\# \ \text{And} \ T.C\# = 1)$$

---

[2] The truth of a quantified expression does depend, of course, on the range of permitted values of the quantified variables.

is interpreted as the query to find values of the free variable P such that there exists at least one value of the bound variable T satisfying the formula "T.P# = P.P#   And T.C# = 1".

As before, evaluation of the expression is in the context of some instantiations of the variables. All possible values of P must be considered, but for each we need only find one value of T to satisfy expression. Once we have done that, other possible values of T, if any, may be ignored. For example, with P instantiated to the first tuple of Product, we consider in turn tuples of Transaction as values of T. We will find in fact that the first already satisfies the expression and we may therefore ignore the others. With P set to the second tuple, however, we will find no value for T to satisfy the expression. The result for this example therefore is only one value for P, with P.Pname=CPU.

As another example, consider the relations in Figure 7-5 with associated tuple variables as shown. Suppose, we are interested in finding the names of customers who bought the product CPU. That is, our target is the value X.Cname, but only if X is a customer who has bought the product CPU. In other words, there must exist a Y such that "X.C# = Y.C#". This would establish that X bought a product, denoted by Y.P# (the product number). Furthermore, this product must be a CPU, ie. there must exist a Z such that "Y.P# = Z.P#" and "Z.Pname = CPU". Thus, the rule corresponding to our query is

$$X.Cname: \exists Y \, \exists Z \, (\, X.C\# = Y.C\# \, \& \, Y.P\# = Z.C\# \, \& \, Z.Pname = CPU \,)$$

The reader can verify that the answer satisfying this query is {Codd, Martin}.

Customer				X
C#	Cname	Ccity	Cphone	
1	Codd	London	2263035	
2	Martin	Paris	5555910	
3	Deen	London	2234391	

Transaction				Y
C#	P#	Date	Qnt	
1	1	21.01	20	
3	2	23.01	30	
2	1	26.01	25	
2	2	29.01	20	

Product			Z
P#	Pname	Price	
1	CPU	1000	
2	VDU	1200	

Figure 7-5 Product, Customer and Transaction relations with associated tuple variables

Using again the relations in Figure 7-5, let's look at a more complex query: get the names of customers who bought the product CPU and VDU. At first glance, this seems a simple extension of the above query:

$$X.Cname: \exists Y \, \exists Z \, (\, X.C\# = Y.C\# \, \& \, Y.P\# = Z.C\# \, \&$$
$$Z.Pname = CPU \, \& \, Z.Pname = VDU \,)$$

But the reader who remembers a similar example in section 6.1 would have noted a problem. Specifically, the subexpression "Z.Pname = CPU & Z.Pname = VDU" can never be true for a given value of Z - a field of a given tuple can only hold one value, so only one or the other can be true but not both! Of course what we mean to specify is that the customer purchased at least one product which is a CPU, and *another* which is a VDU. Since a tuple variable can hold only one value at a time, this clearly cannot be done using only one tuple variable.

The solution, therefore, is to *introduce additional distinct variables to range over the same relation* when more than one tuple is to be considered at a time (note that relational calculus places no restriction on the number of distinct variables that can range over a relation). For this particular example, we need only introduce one additional variable each for the relations Transaction and Product respectively, as shown in Figure 7-6. This will allow us to consider two separate purchases at one time. The correct formulation, therefore, is:

$$X.Cname: \exists T1\ \exists T2\ \exists P1\ \exists P2\ (\ X.C\# = T1.C\#\ \&\ X.C\# = T2.C\#\ \&$$
$$T1.P\# = P1.C\#\ \&\ P1.Pname = CPU\ \&$$
$$T2.P\# = P2.C\#\ \&\ P2.Pname = VDU\ )$$

Figure 7-6 additionally shows particular values of these variables that satisfy our query.

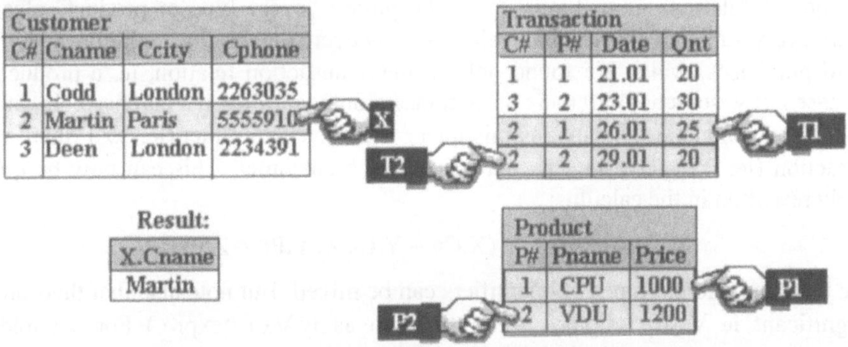

Figure 7-6 Multiple variables ranging over a relation

Let's turn now to the universal quantifier. Informally, the formula "$\forall x$ (<expr>)" asserts that *for every* value of x (from among its range of values) <expr> is true. Like the existential quantifier, the truth of an existentially quantified expression is not a function of the quantified variable(s).

Consider, for example, the unquantified expression
$$x < y \mid y < 12$$
and suppose x ranges over {4,15} and y over {7,14}.

The truth table for the expression is:

x	y	x<y | y<12
4	7	true
4	14	true
15	7	true
15	14	false

Now consider the same expression but with x universally quantified:

$$\forall x \ (x < y \mid y < 12)$$

In a sense, like the existentially quantified variable, we don't care what the values of x are, as long as every one of them makes the expression true for any given y. Thus its truth table is:

y	$\forall x \ (x<y \mid y<12)$
7	true
14	false

The universal quantifier will be needed for queries like the following:

"get the names of customers who bought every type of product"

Assume the relations as in Figure 7-5. The phrase "every type of product" clearly means every tuple of the Product relation. However, the Product relation does not record purchases, which are found only in the Transaction relation, ie. a product is purchased (by someone) if there is a transaction recording its purchase. In other words, a customer (ie. X) satisfies this query if for every product (ie. $\forall Z$) there is a transaction (ie. $\exists Y$) recording its purchase by the customer. This can now be quite simply rewritten in the calculus:

$$X.Cname: \forall Z \ \exists Y \ (X.C\# = Y.C\# \ \& \ Y.P\# = Z.P\#)$$

Note that the different types of quantifiers can be mixed. But note also that their order is significant, ie. $\forall x \ \exists y \ (<expr>)$ is not the same as $\exists y \ \forall x \ (<expr>)$. For example,

$$\forall x \ \exists y \ (y \text{ is the mother of } x)$$

asserts that everyone has a mother. Whereas,

$$\exists y \ \forall x \ (y \text{ is the mother of } x)$$

asserts that there is a single individual (y) who is the mother of everyone!

7.4 Well-Formed Formulae

Let us now be more precise about the valid forms of logical expressions involving tuple variables. Such valid forms are called well-formed formulae (wff) and are defined as follows:

1. $A \, \theta \, M$ is a wff
     if A is a projection of a tuple variable,
        M is a constant or a projection of a tuple variable, and
        θ is one of the comparison operators: $=, \neq, <, >, \leq, \geq$

2. **F1 & F2** and **F1 | F2** are wffs if **F1** and **F2** are wffs

3. **(F)** is a wff if **F** is a wff

4. $\exists x \, (F(x))$ and $\forall x \, (F(x))$ are wffs if $F(x)$ is a wff with a free occurrence of the variable x.

The operator precedence for the '**&**' and '**|**', operators follow the standard precedence rules, ie. '**&**' binds stronger than '**|**'. Thus,

$$\text{'F1 \& F2 | F3'} \equiv \text{'(F1 \& F2) | F3'}$$

Explicit use of parenthesis, as in rule (3) above, is required to override this default precedence. Thus if the intention is for the '|' operator to bind stronger in the above expression, it has to be written as

$$\text{F1 \& (F2 | F3)}$$

We can now be more specific about the form of a query in relational calculus:

$$(\text{<target list>}){:}(\text{<wff>})$$

As final examples for this chapter, consider the following queries:

> Query 1: "Get the names, cities and phone numbers of customers who bought the product CPU before the 25th of January"

Assume the tuple variables C, T and P ranging over relations Customer, Transaction and Product respectively. The appropriate query is as follows:

(C.Cname, C.City, C.Phone) :
$\qquad$ $\exists$T $\exists$P (C.C# = T.C# & T.Date < 25.01 & T.P# = P.P# & P.Pname = CPU)

> Query 2: "Get the names of products bought by customers living in London or by the customer named Smith"

Assume tuple variables as in Query 1 above. The appropriate query is as follows:

(P.Pname) :
$\exists$T $\exists$C (T.P# = P.P# & T.C# = C.C# & (C.City = London | C.Cname = Smith))

Note that the use of parenthesis around the 'or' expression above is necessary.

8. Relational Calculus II

Relational Calculus, as defined in the previous chapter, provides the theoretical foundations for the design of practical Data Sub-Languages (DSL). In this chapter, we will look at an example of one - in fact, the first practical DSL based on relational calculus - the Alpha.

Further to this, we will also look at an alternative calculus - still a relational calculus (ie. relations are still the objects of the calculus) but based on *Domain Variables* rather than *Tuple Variables*. Because of this, the relational calculus covered earlier is more accurately termed *Relational Calculus with Tuple Variables*. The reader will recall that Tuple Variables range over tuples of relations and were central in the formulation of inference rules and in the definition of well-formed formulae. *Domain Variables*, on the other hand, range over domain values rather than tuples and consequently require a different construction of well-formed formulae. We will discuss this alternative in the second part of this chapter.

8.1 The Data Sub-Language Alpha

DSL Alpha is directly based on relational calculus with tuple variables. It provides, however, additional constructions that increase the query formulation power of the language. Such constructions are in fact found in most practical DSL in use today.

8.1.1 Alpha Command

DSL Alpha is a set of *Alpha commands*, each taking the form:

Get <workspace> (<target list>) : <WFF>

<workspace> is an identifier or label that names a temporary working relation to hold the result of the command (similar to the named working relation in the 'giving' clause of relational algebra - see section 5.3). The attributes of this relation are specified by <target list> which is a list of tuple variable projections as in the previous chapter. <WFF> is of course a well-formed formulae of relational calculus that must be satisfied before the values in <target list> are extracted as a result tuple.

As an example, suppose the variable P ranges over the Product relation as shown in Figure 8-1. Then the following construction is a valid Alpha command:

Get W(P.Pname) : P.Price ≤ 1000

Product		
P#	Pname	Price
1	CPU	1000
2	VDU	1200

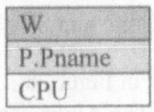

W
P.Pname
CPU

Figure 8-1 Example relations

The reader can see that except for the keyword 'Get' and the naming of the result relation ('W' in this example), the basic form is identical to the one used in the previous chapter, which would simply be written

$$(P.Pname) : P.Price \le 1000$$

The semantics of the Alpha command is also exactly the same, except that the result is a named relation, as shown in the illustration.

8.1.2 Range Statement

In our exposition of relational calculus, tuple variables used in queries were introduced informally. We did this in the above example too (viz. "suppose the variable P ..."). This will not do, of course, if we wish the language to be interpreted by a computer. Thus, tuple variables must be introduced and associated with the relations over which they range using formal constructions. In DSL Alpha, this is achieved by the *range declaration statement*, which takes the basic form:

Range <relation name> <variable name>

where <relation name> must name an existing relation and <variable name> introduces a unique variable identifer. The variable <variable name> is taken to range over <relation name> upon encountering such a declaration. The above example can now be written more completely and formally as:

> Range Product P;
> Get W(P.Pname) : P.Price ≤ 1000

DSL Alpha statements and commands, as the above construction shows, are separated by semi-colons (';').

DSL Alpha also differs from relational calculus in the way it quantifies variables. First, for a practical language, mathematical symbols like '∀' and '∃' need to be replaced by symbols easier to key in. DSL Alpha uses the symbols '**ALL**' and '**SOME**' to stand for '∀' and '∃' respectively. Second, rather than using the quantifiers in the <WFF> expression, they are introduced in the range declarations. Thus, the full syntax of range declarations is:

Range <relation name> <variable name> [SOME | ALL]

Note that the use of quantifiers in the declaration is optional. If omitted, the variable is taken to be a free variable whenever it occurs in an Apha command.

Let us look at a number of examples.

> Query 1: "Get the names and phone numbers of customers who live in London"

Assume the Customer relation as in Figure 8-2. This query will only need a single free variable to range over customer. The Alpha construction required is:

Range Customer X;
Get WA(X.Cname, X.Cphone): X.Ccity = London

Figure 8-2 also highlights the tuples in Customer satisfying the WFF of the command and the associated result relation WA.

Figure 8-2 Query 1

> Query2: "Get the names of products bought by Customer #2"

For this query, we will need to access the Transaction relation, with records of which customer bought which product, and the Product relation, which holds the names of products. Assume these relations are as given in Figure 8-3. The object of our query is the Pname attribute of Product, thus the tuple variable for Product must necessarily be a free variable:

Range Product A;

The condition of the query requires us to look in the Transaction relation for a record of purchase by Customer #2 - as long as we can find one such record, the associated product is one that we are interested in. This is a clear case of existential quantification, and the variable introduced to range over Transaction is therefore given by:

Range Transaction B SOME;

The Alpha command for the query can now be written:

Get W (A.Pname): A.P# = B.P# And B.C# = 2

The associated tuples satisfying the WFF above are highlighted in the figure (the result relation is not shown).

Product		
P#	Pname	Price
1	CPU	1000
2	VDU	1200

Transaction			
C#	P#	Date	Qnt
1	1	21.01	20
3	2	23.01	30
2	1	26.01	25
2	2	29.01	20

Figure 8-3 Query 2

Query 3: "Get the names and phone numbers of customers in London who bought the product VDU"

This is a more complex example that will involve three relations, as shown in Figure 8-4. The target data items are in the Customer relation (names and phone numbers). So the tuple variable assigned to it must be free:

    Range Customer X;

Part of the condition specified is that the customer must live in London (ie. X.Ccity = London), but the rest of the condition (" ... who bought the product VDU") can only be ascertained from the Transaction relation (record of purchase by some customer) and Product relation (name of product). In both these cases, we are just interested in finding one tuple from each, ie. that there exists a tuple from each relation that satisfies the query condition. Thus, the variables introduced for them are given by:

    Range Transaction Y SOME;
    Range Product Z SOME;

The Alpha command can now be written as:

    Get W(X.Cname, X.Cphone):
    X.Ccity = London And X.C# = Y.C# And Y.P# = Z.P# And Z.Pname = VDU

Figure 8-4 highlights one instantiation of each variable that satisfies the above WFF.

Product		
P#	Pname	Price
1	CPU	
2	VDU	

Transaction			
C#	P#	Date	Q
1	1	21.01	20
1	2	23.01	30
2	1	26.01	25
2	2	29.01	20

Customer			
C#	Cname	Ccity	Cphone
1	Codd	London	2263035
2	Martin	Paris	5555910
3	Deen	London	2234391

Figure 8-4 Query 3

Query 4: "Get the names of customers who bought all types of the company's products"

As with the previous example, this one also requires access to three relations as shown in Figure 8-5. A customer will satisfy this query if for every product there is a transaction recording that he/she purchased it. This time, therefore, we have a case for universal quantification - "...all types of the company's products" - which will require that the variable ranging over Product be universally quantified. The variable for Transaction, onthe other hand, is existentially quantified ("...there is a transaction..."). The full Alpha construction therefore is:

> Range Customer C;
> Range Product P ALL;
> Range Transaction T SOME;
> Get W (C.Cname): P.P# = T.P# And T.C# = C.C#

Figure 8-5 highlights tuples from the various relations that satisfy this construction.

Note that the order of quantified variable declarations is important. The order above is equivalent to "∀P ∃T". If variable T was declared before P, it would be equivalent to "∃T ∀P" which would mean something quite different! (see section 7.3)

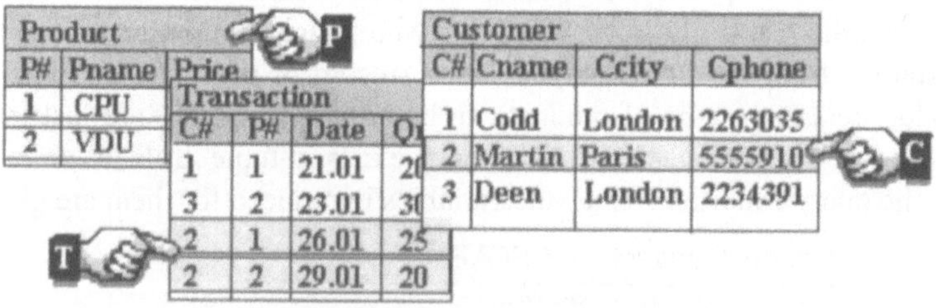

Figure 8-5 Query 4

Query 5: "Get the name of the most expensive product"

This query involves only one relation: the Product relation (assume the Product relation as in the above examples). Now, the "most expensive product" is that for which every product has a price less than or equal to it. Or, in relational calculus, X is such a product provided that "∀Y X.Price ≥ Y.Price". Thus two variables are required, both ranging over Product but one of them is universally quantified:

> Range Product X;
> Range Product Y ALL;
> Get W(X.Pname): X.Price ≥ Y.Price

It is perhaps interesting to note in passing that the choice by DSL Alpha designers to quantify variables at the point of declaration rather than at the point of use makes

Alpha commands a little harder to read - it is not clear which variables are quantified just by looking at the Alpha command. One must search for the variable declaration to see how, if at all, it is quantified.

8.1.3 Additional Facilities

DSL Alpha provides additional facilities that operate on the results of its commands. While these are outside the realm of relational calculus, they are useful and practical functions that enhances the utility of the language. These facilities fall loosely under two headings: *qualifiers*, and *library functions*.

The qualifiers affect the order of presentation of tuples in the result relation, based on the ordering of values of a specified attribute in either an ascending or descending order, ie. they may be thought of as sort functions over a designated attribute. Note that in relational theory the order of tuples in a relation is irrelevant since a relation is a *set* of values. So the qualifiers affects only the presentation of a relation.

Syntactically, the qualifier is appended to the WFF and takes the following form:

{ UP | DOWN } <attribute name>

As an example, consider the requirement for the names of products bought by Customer #2 in descending order of their prices. The Alpha construction for this would be:

    Range Product X;
    Range Transaction Y SOME;
    Get UWA(X.Pname, X.Price): (X.P# = Y.P# And Y.C# = 2) DOWN X.Price

Figure 8-6 shows the relations highlighting tuples satisfying the WFF. It also shows the result relation UWA which can be seen to be ordered in descending order of price.

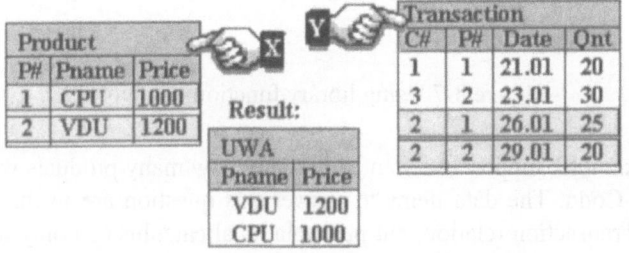

Figure 8-6 Result of qualified command

The library functions, on the other hand, derives (computes) new values from the data items extracted from the database. Another way to put this is that the result relation of the basic Alpha command is further transformed by library functions to yield the final result. Why would we want to do this? Consider for example that we have a simple set of integers, say {1,2,3}. There are a variety of values we may wish to derive from it, such as

- the number of items, or cardinality, of the set (library function COUNT, ie. COUNT{1,2,3}=3)
- the sum of the values in the set (library function TOTAL, ie. TOTAL {1,2,3}=6)
- the minimum, or maximum, value in the set (library function MIN and MAX, ie. MIN {1,2,3} = 1, or MAX {1,2,3} = 3)
- the average of values in the set (library function AVERAGE, ie. AVERAGE {1,2,3} = 2)

Extending this idea to relations, and in particular the Alpha command, library functions are applied to attributes in the target list, taking the form:

\<library function\>(\<attribute name\>)

As an example, consider the need to find the number of customers who bought the product VDU. This is quite a practical requirement to help management track how well some products are doing on the market. Pure relational calculus, however, has no facility to do this. But using the library function COUNT in DSL Alpha, we can write the following:

```
Range Transaction T;
Range Product P SOME;
Get AAA( COUNT(T.C#) ): T.P# = P.P# And P.Pname = VDU
```

Figure 8-7 highlights the tuples satisfying the WFF and shows the result relation.

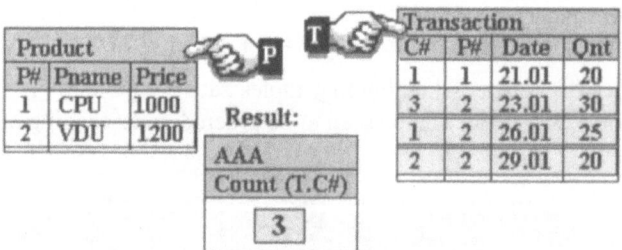

Figure 8-7 Using library function (COUNT)

As another example, suppose we wanted to know how many products were bought by the customer Codd. The data items to answer this question are in the quantity field (Qnt) of the Transaction relation, but pure relational calculus can only retrieve the set of quantity values associated with purchases by Codd. What we need is the sum of these values.

The library function TOTAL of DSL Alpha allows us to do this:

```
Range Transaction T; Range Customer C SOME;
Get BBB( TOTAL( T.Qnt ) ): T.C# = C.C# And C.Cname = Codd
```

Figure 8-8 summarises the execution of this Alpha command.

Customer			
C#	Cname	Ccity	Cphone
1	Codd	London	22630
2	Martin	Paris	5555910
3	Deen	London	2234391

Transaction			
C#	P#	Date	Qnt
1	1	21.01	20
1	2	23.01	30
2	1	26.01	25
2	2	29.01	20

Result:

BBB
Total (T.Qnt)
50

Figure 8-8 Using library function (TOTAL)

As a final remark, we note that we have only sampled a few library functions. It is not our aim to cover DSL Alpha comprehensively, but only to illustrate real DSLs based on the relational calculus, and to look at added features or facilities needed to turn them into practical languages.

8.2 Relational Calculus with Domain Variables

8.2.1 Domain Variables

As noted in the introduction, there is an alternative to using tuple variables as the basis for a relational calculus, and that is to use domain variables. Recall that a domain (see section 2.2) in the relational model refers to the current set of values of a given kind under an attribute name and is defined over all relations in the database, ie. an attribute name denotes the same domain in whatever relation it occurs. A domain variable ranges over a designated domain, ie. it can be instantiated to, or hold, any value from that domain.

For example, consider the domain Cname found in the Customer relation. This domain has three distinct values as shown in Figure 8-9. If we now introduced a variable, 'Cn', and designate it to range over Cname, then Cn can be instantiated to any of these values (the illustration shows it holding the value 'Martin').

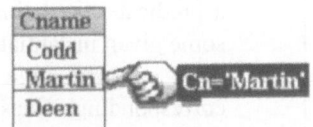

Cname
Codd
Martin
Deen

Cn='Martin'

Figure 8-9 A domain variable

As with tuple variables:

- a domain variable can hold only one value at any time
- domain variables can be introduced for any domain in the database
- more than one domain variable may be used to range over the same domain

Note also that the value of a domain variable is an atomic value, ie. it does not comprise component values as was the case with tuple variables. Thus there is no need for any syntactic mechanism like the 'dot notation' to denote component atomic values of tuple variables. It also means that in constructing simple comparison expressions, domain variables appear directly without any embellishments, eg. A > 1000, B = London, C ≤ 2000, D ≠ Paris, etc. (assuming of course that the variables A, B, C and D have been designated to range over appropriate domains).

In a relational calculus with domain variables we can write predicates of the form:

<relation name>(x₁, ... , xₙ)

where
- <relation name> is the name of a relation currently defined in the database schema, and
- each xᵢ is a domain variable ranging over a domain from the intension of <relation name>

Thus, suppose we have the situation as in Figure 8-10. It is then syntactically valid to write:

Customer(A, B)

as 'Customer' is a valid relation name, and the variables 'A' and 'B' range over domains that are in the intension of the Customer relation.

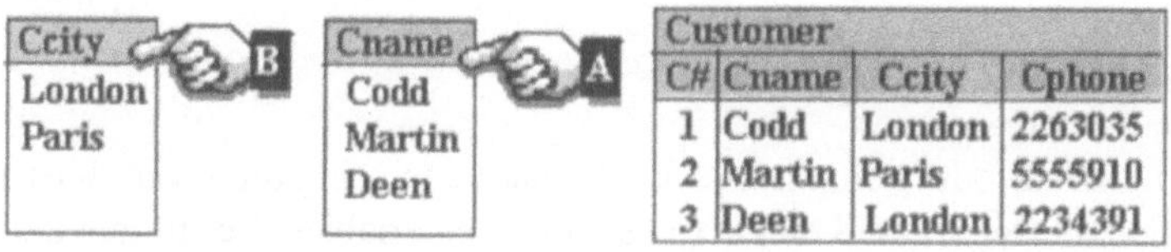

Figure 8-10 Variables ranging over domains of a relation

The meaning of such a predication can be stated as follows:

> a predicate "<relation name>(x₁, ... , xₙ)" is true for some given instantiation of each variable xᵢ if and only if there exists a tuple in <relation name> that contains corresponding values of the variables x₁, ... , xₙ

Thus, for example, Customer(A,B) is true when A=Codd and B=London, since the first tuple of Customer has the corresponding values. In contrast, Customer(A,B) is false when A=Codd and B=Paris, as no tuple in Customer have these values.

In fact, the values that make Customer(A,B) true are:

Cname	Ccity
Codd	London
Martin	Paris
Deen	London

that is, in relational algebra terms, a projection of <relation name> over the domains that variables $x_1, \ldots, x_n$ range over.

A query in relational calculus with domain variables take the form:

(<target list>) : (<logical expression>)

where

- <target list> is a comma-separated list of domain variable names, and

- <logical expression> is a truth-valued expression involving predicates and comparisons over domain variables and constants (the rules for constructing well-formed <logical expressions> will be detailed later)

The result of such a query is a set of instantiations of variables in <target list> that make <logical expression> true.

For example, consider the database state in Figure 8-11 and the query

$$(x,y) : (\text{Product}(x,y) \ \& \ y > 1000)$$

which can be paraphrased as "get product names and their prices for those products costing more than 1000".

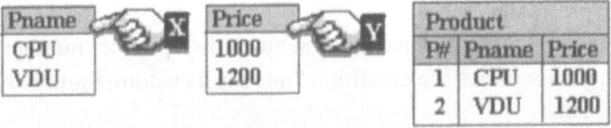

Pname		Price		Product		
CPU	X	1000	Y	P#	Pname	Price
VDU		1200		1	CPU	1000
				2	VDU	1200

Figure 8-11 Database state for the query "(x,y): (Product(x,y) & y > 1000)"

The only pair of (x,y) instantiation satisfying logical expression in this case is (VDU,1200), ie. the result of the query is

x	y
VDU	1200

Domain variables, like tuple variables, may also be quantified with either the universal or existential quantifier. Expressions involving quantified domain variables are interpreted in the same way as for quantified tuple variables (see 7.3).

Consider the query: "get the names of products bought by customer #1". The required data items are in two relations: Product and Transaction, as follows.

Product		
P#	Pname	Price
1	CPU	1000
2	VDU	1200

Transaction			
C#	P#	Date	Qnt
1	1	21.01	20
1	2	23.01	30
2	1	26.01	25
2	2	29.01	20

We can paraphrase the query to introduce variables and make it easier to formulate the correct formal query:

> x is such a product name if there is a product number y for x and there is a customer number z that purchases y and z is equal to 1

The phrase "x is such a product name" makes it clear that it is a variable for the 'Pname' domain, and as this is our target data value, x must be a free variable. The phrase "there is a product number y for x" clarifies two points: (1) that y is a variable for the P# domain, and (2) that it's role is existential. Similarly, the phrase "there is a customer number z that purchases y" states that (1) z is a variable for the domain C#, and (2) it's role is existential. This can now be quite easily rewritten as the formal query (assuming the variables x,y and z range over Pname, P# and C# respectively):

$$(x) : \exists y \ \exists z \ (\text{Product}(x,y) \ \& \ \text{Transaction}(y,z) \ \& \ z = 1)$$

where the subexpressions
- Product(x,y)   captures the condition "there is a product number y for x"
- Transaction(y,z) captures the condition "there is a customer number z that purchases y", and
- z = 1 clearly requires that the customer number is 1

The reader should be able to work out the solution to the query as an exercise.

As a final example, consider the query: "get the names of customers who bought all types of the company's products". The reader can perform an analysis of this query as was done above to confirm that the relevant database state is as shown in Figure 8-12 and that the correct formal query is:

$$(x) : \forall y \ \exists z \ (\text{Customer}(x,z) \ \& \ \text{Transaction}(y,z))$$

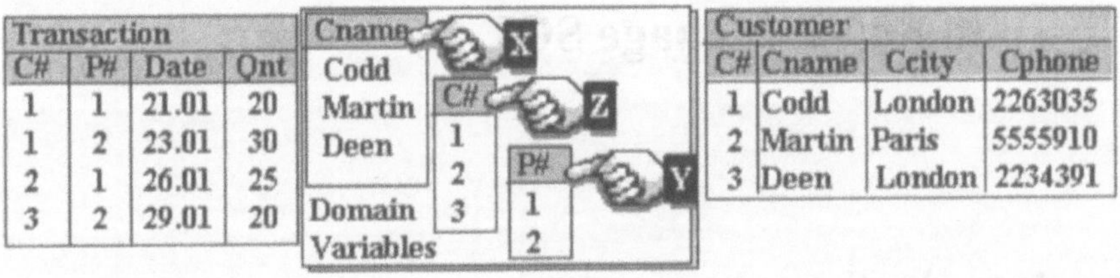

Figure 8-12 Database state for "(x) : ∀y ∃z (Customer(x,z) & Transaction(y,z))"

This example illustrates a universally quantified domain variable y ranging over P#. For this query, this means that the "Transaction(y,z)"part of the logical expression must evaluate to true for every possible instantiation of y given a particular instantiation of z. Thus, when x = Codd and z = 1, both Transaction(1,1) and Transaction(2,1) must evaluate to true. They do in this case and Codd will therefore be part of the result set. But, when x = Martin and z = 2, Transaction(1,2) is true but Transaction(2,2) is not! So Martin is not part of the result set. Continuing in this fashion for every possible instantiation of x will eventually yield the full result.

8.2.2 Well-Formed Formula

We have not formally defined above what constitutes valid <logical expression>s. We do so here, but for the sake of a uniform terminology, we will use the phrase well-formed formula (WFF) instead of <logical expression> just as we did for relational calculus with tuple variables. Thus a formal query in relational calculus with domain variables take the form:

$$(\text{<target list>}) : (\text{WFF})$$

where <target list> is a comma-separated list of *free* variable names, and a WFF is defined by the following rules:

1. *P(A,...)* is a WFF if *P* is a relation name and *A,...* is a list of free variables

2. *A θ M* is a WFF if *A* is a variable, *M* is a constant or a variable, and
$$\theta \in \{=, \neq, <, >, \leq, \geq\}$$

3. *F1 & F2* and *F1 | F2* are WFFs if *F1* and *F2* are WFFs

4. *(F)* is a WFF if *F* is a WFF

5. *∃x (F(x))* and *∀x (F(x))* if *F(x)* is a WFF with the variable *x* occurring free in it

As usual, the operator precedence for the '&' and '|', operators follow the standard precedence rules, ie. '&' binds stronger than '|'. Thus,

'F1 & F2 | F3' ≡ '(F1 & F2)| F3'

Explicit use of parenthesis, as in rule (4) above, is required to override this default precedence. Thus if the intention is for the '|' operator to bind stronger in the above expression, it has to be written as

F1 & (F2 | F3)

9. Data Sub-Language SQL

9.1 Introduction

In this chapter, we shall learn more about the essentials of the relational model's standard language that will allow us to manipulate the data stored in the databases. This language is powerful yet flexible, thus making it popular. It is in fact one of the factors that has led to the dominance of the relational model in the database market today.

Following Codd's papers on the relational model and relational algebra and calculus languages, research communities were prompted to work on the realisation of these concepts. Several implemented versions of the relational languages were developed, amongst the most noted were SQL (Structured Query Language), QBE (Query-By-Example) and QUEL (Query Language). Here, we shall look into SQL with greater detail as it the most widely used relational language today. One often hears of remarks that say, "It's not relational if it doesn't use SQL". It is currently being standardised now as a standard language for the Relational Data Model.

SQL had its origins back in 1974 from IBM's System R research project as Structured English Query Language (or SEQueL) for use on the IBM VS/2 mainframes. It was developed by Chamberlain et al. The name was subsequently changed to Structured Query Language or SQL. It is pronounced "sequel" by some and S-Q-L by others. IBM's products such as SQL/DS and the popular DB2 emerged from this. SQL is based on the Relational Calculus with tuple variables. In 1986, the American National Standards Institute (ANSI) adopted SQL standards, contributing to its widespread adoption. Whilst many commercial SQL products exist with various "dialects", the basic command set and structure remain fairly standard.

Although SQL is called a query language, it is capable of more than just getting data off relations in the databases. It can also handle data updates and even data definitions - add new data, change existing data, delete or create new structures. Thus SQL is capable of:

1. *Data Query*
The contents of the database are accessed via a set of commands whereby useful information is returned to the end user

2. *Data Maintenance*
The data within the relations can be created, corrected, deleted and modified

3. *Data Definition*
The structure of the database and its relations can be defined and created

The end user is given an interface, as we have seen in Chapter 3, to interact with the database via menus, query operations, report generators, etc. Behind this lies the SQL engine that performs the more difficult tasks of creating relation structures, maintaining the systems catalogues and data dictionary, etc.

SQL belongs to the category of the so-called Fourth-Generation Language (4GL) because of its power, conciseness and low-level of procedurality. As a non-procedural language it allows the user to specify *what* must be done without detailing *how* it must be done. The user's SQL request specification is then translated by the RDBMS into the technical details needed to get the required data. As a result, the relational database is said to require less programming than any other database or file system environment. This makes SQL relatively easy to learn.

9.2   Operations

9.2.1   Mapping: The SQL Select Statement

The basic operation in SQL is called *mapping*, which transforms values from a database to user requirements. This operation is syntactically represented by the following block:

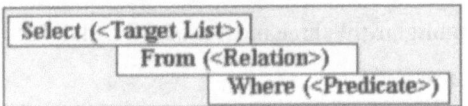

Figure 9-1. SQL Select

This uncomplicated structure can used to construct queries ranging from very simple inquiries to more complex ones by essentially defining the conditions of the predicate. It thus provides immense flexibility.

The SQL Select command combines the Relational Algebra operators Select, Project, Join and the Cartesian Product. Because a single declarative-style command can be used to retrieve virtually any stored data, it is also regarded by many to be an implementation of the Relational Calculus. If we need to extract information from only one relation of the database, we may encounter similarities and a few differences between the Relational Calculus-based DSL Alpha and SQL. In this case we may substitute key words of DSL Alpha for matching key words of SQL as follows:

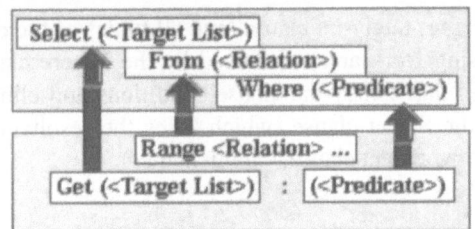

Figure 9-2. Similarities of DSL Alpha and SQL Select

Let us refer back to the earlier example with the Customer relation.

Suppose we wish to "Get the names and phone numbers of customers living in London". With DSL Alpha, we would specify this query as:

> Range Customer X;
> Get (X.Cname, X.Cphone): X.Ccity=London;

whereas in SQL its equivalent would be:

> Select Cname, Phone
>   From Customer
>   Where Ccity = 'London'

In either case, the result would be the retrieval of the following two tuples:

This simple query highlights the three most used SQL clauses:

1. The SELECT clause
This effectively gets the *columns* that we are interested in getting from the relation. We may be interested in a single column, thus we may for example write "Select Cphone" if we only wish to list just the telephone numbers. We may also however be interested in listing the customer's name, city and telephone number; in which case, we write "Select Cname, Ccity, Cphone".

2. The FROM clause
We need to identify the *relations* that our query refers to and this is done via the From clause. The columns that we have chosen from the Select clause must be found in the relation names of the From clause as in "From Customer".

3. The WHERE clause
This holds the *conditions* that allows us to restrict the tuples of the relation(s). In the example "Where Ccity=London" asserts that we wish to select only the tuples which contain the city name that is equal to the value 'London'.

The system first processes the From clause (and all tuples of the chosen relation(s) are placed in the processing work area), followed by the Where clause (which chooses, one by one, the tuples that satisfy the clause conditions and eliminating those which do not), and finally the Select clause (which takes the resultant tuples and displays only the values under the Select clause column names).

9.2.2 Output Restriction

Most queries do not need every tuple in the relation but rather only a subset of the tuples. As described previously in section 5.3, the following mathematical operators can be used in the predicate to restrict the output:

Symbol	Meaning
=	Equal to
<	Less than
>	Greater than
<=	Less than or equal to
>=	Greater than or equal to
<>	Not equal to

Additionally, the logical operators AND, OR and NOT may be used to place further restrictions. These logical operators, along with parentheses, may be combined to produce quite complex conditional expressions.

Suppose we need to retrieve the tuples from the Transaction relation such that the following conditions apply:

1. The transaction date is before 26 Jan and the quantity is at least 25

2. Or, the customer number is 2

The SQL statement that could get the desired result would be:

```
Select C#, Date, Qnt From Transaction
            Where (Date < '26.01' And Qnt >= 25) Or C# = 2
```

9.2.3 Recursive Mapping: Sub-queries

The main idea of SQL is the recursive usage of the mapping operation instead of using the existential and universal quantifiers. So far in our examples, we always know the values that we want to put in our predicate. For example,

```
Where Ccity = 'London'
Where Date < '26.01' And Qnt > 25
```

Suppose we now wish to "Get the personal numbers of customers who bought the product CPU". We could start off by writing the SQL statement:

```
Select C#
    From Transaction
        Where P#= ?
```

We cannot of course write "Where P#=CPU" because CPU is a part name not its number. However as we may recall, part number P# is stored in the Transaction relation, but the part name is in fact in another relation, the Product relation.

Thus one needs to first of all get the part name from Product via another SQL statement:

```
Select P#
     From Product
          Where Pname = 'CPU'
```

Having obtained the equivalent P#, the value is then used to complete the earlier query. The way this is to be expressed is by writing the whole mapping operator in the right hand side of comparison expressions of another mapping operator. This effectively means the use of an inner block (sub-query) within the outer block (main query) as depicted in the figure below.

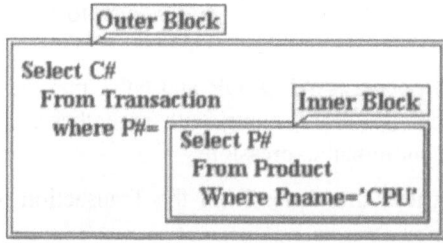

Figure 9-3. Query nesting

The query in the outer block thus executes by using the value set generated earlier by the sub-query of the inner block.

It is important to note that because the sub-query replaces the value in the predicate of the main query, the value retrieved from the sub-query must be of *the same domain* as the value in the main predicate.

9.2.4 Multiple Nesting

It is also possible that may be two or more inner blocks within an outer SQL block. For instance, we next wish to: "Get a date when customer Codd bought the product CPU". The SQL statement we would start out with would probably look like this:

```
Select Date
     From Transaction
          Where P#=?
          And C#=?
```

As in the earlier query, the part number P# can be obtained via the part name Pname in the relation Product. The customer name, Codd, however has to have its equivalent customer number which has to be obtained from C# of the relation Customer.

Thus to complete the above query, one would have to work two sub-queries first as follows:

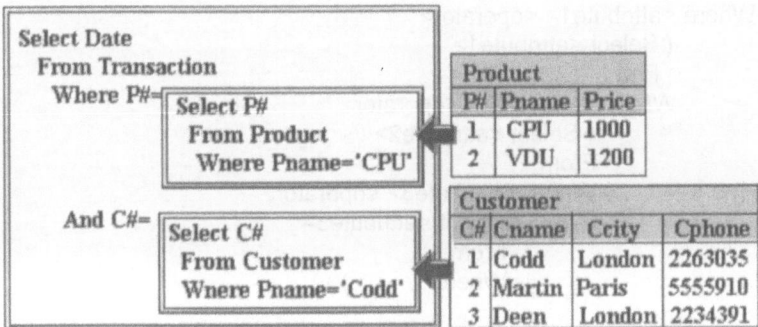

Figure 9-4. Interpretation of sub-queries

Note that the original SQL notation utilises brackets or parentheses to determine inner SQL blocks as:

```
Select Date
From Transaction
Where P# =
        ( Select P#
          From Product
          Where Pname = CPU)
And C# =
        ( Select C#
          From Customer
          Where Cname = Codd)
```

Similarly, an inner block many contain further inner SQL blocks. For instance, if we wish to "Get the names of customers who bought more than 20 pieces of the product CPU" we need to specify:

```
Select Cname
From Customer
Where C# =
        ( Select C#
        From Transaction
        Where P# =
                ( Select P#
                  From Product
                  Where Pname = CPU )
        And Qnt > 20 )
```

Thus we may visualise the nesting of sub-queries as:

```
Select ...
From ....
Where <attribute1> <operator>
        ( Select <attribute1>
          From ...
        Where <attribute2> <operator>
              ( Select <attribute2>
              From ...
              Where <attribute3> <operator>
                    ( Select <attribute3>
                    From ...
                    Where ...    ) ) )
```

The number of inner blocks or levels of nesting may, however, be limited by the storage available in the workspace of the DBMS in use.

9.2.5 Multiple Data Items

Standard comparison operators ($=, >, <, >=, <=, <>$) operate on two data items, as in $x = y$ or $p >= 4$. They cannot be applied to multiple data items. However, a particular SQL block normally returns a set of values (i.e. not a single value which can be used in a comparison).

For instance: "Get the product numbers of items which were bought by customers from London".

```
Select P#
From Transaction
Where C# =
        ( Select C#
        From Customer
        Where Ccity = 'London' )
```

Given the sample database of the earlier examples, the result of the inner SQL block would yield two values for C#, which are 1 and 3, (or more precisely, the set { 1, 3 }). The outer SQL block, in testing C# = { 1, 3 } would effectively test if { 1,2 } = { 1, 3} or not. Thus the above SQL statement is not correct!

To overcome the error caused by the testing of multiple values returned by the sub-query, SQL allows the use of comparison expressions in the form:

$$\text{<attribute name>} \left\{ \begin{array}{c} \text{In} \\ \text{Not In} \end{array} \right\} \text{<set of values>}$$

This logical expression is true if the current value of an attribute is included (or not included, respectively in the set of values.

For instance,

Smith **In** { Codd, Smith, Deen }   is True,

and

Smith **Not In** { Codd, Smith, Deen }   is False.

Thus in re-writing the earlier erroneous statement, we now replace the equal operator (=) with the set membership operator 'In' as follows:

```
Select P#
From Transaction
Where C# In
       ( Select C#
       From Customer
       Where Ccity = 'London' )
```

This time it would yield the outer SQL block would effectively test C# in { 1, 3}. The outer SQL block would now only retrieve the P#s that are only in the set { 1, 3 }, i.e. testing { 1, 2 } In { 1, 3 }. This would result in returning P# 1 only, which is the expected right answer.

Illustrating with another example, consider the query to "Find the names of customers who bought the product CPU". Its corresponding SQL statement would thus be:

```
Select Cname From Customer
Where C# In

       ( Select C#
        From Transaction
        Where P# In

              ( Select P# From Product
               Where Pname = 'CPU' ) )
```

Executing this step-by-step:

(1) From the inner-most block,

```
Select P# From Product
Where Pname = CPU
```

would first yield P# 1 from Product, i.e. { 1 }.

(2) The next block, would thus be

```
Select C# From Transaction
Where P# In { 1 }
```

and this would yield C# s 1 and 2 (as they bought P# 1), i.e. { 1, 2 }

(3) And finally, the outer-most block would execute

```
Select Cname From Customer
Where C# In { 1, 2 }
```

would result in the names of customers 1 and 2, which are Codd and Martin respectively.

We next go on to a slightly more complex example. Suppose we now wish to "Get a name of such customers who bought the product CPU but did not buy the product VDU".

In SQL, the statement would be:

```
Select Cname From Customer
Where C# In
        ( Select C# From Transaction Where P# In
                ( Select P#  From Product  Where Pname = 'CPU' )
And C# Not In
        ( Select C# From Transaction Where P# In
                ( Select P#  From Product Where Pname = 'VDU' ) )
```

Why don't you try to figure out, step-by-step, the sequence of results from the inner-most blocks up to the final result of execution of the outer-most block?

Note that the comparison operators

$$\text{<attribute name>} \left\{ \begin{array}{l} \textbf{In} \\ \textbf{Not In} \end{array} \right\} \quad \text{<set of values>}$$

are used instead of existential qualifiers ($\exists$). It is an implementation of multiple logical OR conditions which is more efficiently handled.

Similarly, comparison expressions
    <attribute name> = **ALL** <set of values>
are used instead of universal qualifiers ($\forall$).

This logical expression is valid (i.e. produces the logical value "True") if the collection of attribute name values in the database includes the given set of values.

For instance, "Get personal numbers of those customers who bought all kinds of company's products", would have the following SQL statement for it:

```
Select C# From Transaction
Where P# =
        ALL ( Select P#
                From Product )
```

The inner block would yield the set { 1, 2 } of P# values. Executing the outer block would effectively test if the 3 customers in the Transaction relation, i.e. C# 1, 2 and 3 would have P# in { 1, 2 }.

This test is as follows:

C#	Transaction (C#, P#=1)	Transaction (C#, P#=2)	All P#
1	True	True	**True !**
2	True	False	False
3	False	True	False

The only customer that has P# equal to all P# as found in Product would be C# 1.

9.3   Further Retrieval Facilities

9.3.1 Joining Relations

In the examples that have been used so far, our retrievals have been of values taken from one relation, as in "Select C# From Transaction". However, often we have to retrieve information from two or more relations simultaneously. In other words, a number of relations names may be used in the From clause of SQL. For example, if we wish to access the relations Customer and Transaction, we may write the SQL statement as follows:

```
Select ...
From Customer, Transaction
Where...
```

The target list in the Select clause may contain the attributes form various relations, as in

```
Select Cname, Date, Qnt
From Customer, Transaction
Where...
```

where, if you recall, Cname is an attribute of Customer and Date and Qnt are attributes of Transaction.

Similarly, comparison expressions in the Where clause may include attribute names from various relations,

```
Select Cname, Date, Qnt
From Customer, Transaction
Where (Customer.C# = Transaction.C#)  And  P# = 1
```

Note that a so-called qualification technique which is used to refer to attributes of the same name belonging to different relations. Customer.C# refers to the C# of the Customer relation whereas Transaction.C# refers to the C# of the Transaction relation.

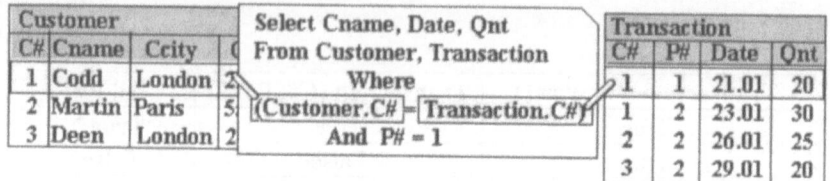

Figure 9-5. Qualifying attributes

Thus the query "Get customer names, dates and number of pieces for transactions of the product number 1" will result in:

Cname	Date	Qnt
Codd	21.01	20

It must be noted that the two (or more) relations that must be combined on at least one common *linking attribute* (as in the Relational Algebra's JOIN operator). As in the above example, the link is established on C# as in the clause

Where Customer.C# = Transaction.C#

9.3.2 Alias

In order to avoid a possible ambiguity in a query definition SQL also allows to use an *alias* for the relation name in the From clause. The alias is an alternate name that is used to identify the source relation and the attribute names may include an alias as a prefix:

<alias>.<attribute name>

Suppose we use T and C as the aliases for the Transaction and Customer relations respectively. We may use these to label the attributes as in:

Select ... From Customer C, Transaction T
Where C.C# = T.C# And ...

An alias is especially useful when we wish to join a relation to itself because of grouping as in the query to "Find the names and phone numbers of customers living in the same city as the customer Codd":

Select C2.Cname, C2.Cphone
From Customer C1, Customer C2
Where C2.Ccity = C1.Ccity
And C1.Cname = 'Codd'

The resulting interpretation of the SQL statement is depicted in Figure 9-6 below:

Customer = C1					Select C2.Cname, C2.Cphone	Customer = C2			

Select C2.Cname, C2.Cphone
From Customer C1, Customer C2
Where
  (C1.Ccity = C2.Ccity)
  And C1.Cname = 'Codd'

Customer = C1				Customer = C2			
C#	Cname	Ccity		C#	Cname	Ccity	Cphone
1	Codd	London		1	Codd	London	2263035
2	Martin	Paris		2	Martin	Paris	5555910
3	Deen	London		3	Deen	London	2234391

Result:

C2.Cname	C2.Cphone
Codd	2263035
Deen	2234391

Figure 9-6. Using an alias

9.4   Library Functions and Arithmetic Expressions

The SQL Select clause (target list) may contain also so-called SQL library functions that will perform various arithmetic summaries such as to find the smallest value or to sum up the values in a specified column. The attribute name for such library functions must be derived from the relations specified in the From clause as follows:

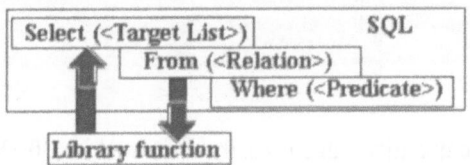

Figure 9-7. Using a library function with SQL Select

The common SQL functions available are:

Function name	Task
COUNT	To count the number of tuples containing a specified attribute value
SUM	To sum up the values of an attribute
AVG	To find the arithmetic mean (average value) of an attribute
MAX	To find the maximum value of an attribute
MIN	To find the minimum value of an attribute

Examples

(1) Get the average quantity of VDUs per transaction

```
Select AVG (Qnt) From Transaction
Where P# =
       ( Select P# From Product
         Where Pname = 'VDU' )
```

Working first with the inner Select clause, we get a P# of 2 from the Product relation as the part number for the product named VDU. Thus the query is now reduced to

```
Select AVG(Qnt)  From Transaction
  Where P# = 2
```

Accessing the Transaction relation now would yield the following two tuples

Transaction			
C#	P#	Date	Qnt
1	1	21.01	20
1	2	23.01	30
2	1	26.01	25
2	2	29.01	20

where the average quantity value is easily computed as (30+20)/2 which is 25.

(2) Get the total quantity of VDUs transacted would similarly be expressed as

```
Select SUM (Qnt) From Transaction
Where P# =
       ( Select P# From Product
         Where Pname = 'VDU' )
```

where the total value is easily computed as (30 + 20) giving 50.

An asterisk (*) in the Select clause is interpreted as "all attributes names of the relations specified in the From clause".

```
Select * From Transaction
```

is equivalent to

```
Select C#, P#, Date, Qnt From Transaction
```

Thus a query to "Get all available information on customers who bought the product VDU" can be written as:

```
Select * From Customer
Where C# In
     ( Select C# From Transaction
       Where P# In
          ( Select  P# From Product
            Where Pname = 'VDU' ) )
```

The interpretation of this query would be worked out as shown in the following sequence of accesses, starting from the access of the product relation to the Transaction and finally to the Customer relation:

Product			Transaction				Customer			
P#	Pname	Price	C#	P#	Date	Qnt	C#	Cname	Ccity	Cphone
1	CPU	1000	1	1	21.01	20	√1	Codd	London	2263035
√2	VDU	1200	1	√2	23.01	30	√2	Martin	Paris	5555910
			2	1	26.01	25	3	Deen	London	2234391
			2	√2	29.01	20				

Figure 9-8. Working through 3 nested Selects

The outcome would be the following relation:

C#	Cname	Ccity	Cphone
1	Codd	London	2263035
2	Martin	Paris	5555910

(2) Get a total number of such customers who bought the product VDU, would be written as:

```
Select COUNT (*) From Customer
Where C# In
       ( Select C#  From Transaction
       Where P# In
              ( Select  P# From Product
                Where Pname = 'VDU' ) )
```

and this would yield a value of 2 for Count (*).

Arithmetic expressions are also permitted in SQL, and the possible operations include:

- addition +
- subtraction -
- multiplication *
- division /

Expressions may be written in the Select clause as:

```
Select C#, P#, Qnt*Price From Transaction, Product
Where Transaction.P# = Product.P#
```

which is used to "Get a total price for each transaction" resulting in:

Product				Transaction				Result:		
P#	Pname	Price		C#	P#	Date	Qnt	C#	P#	Qnt*Price
1	CPU	1000		1	1	21.01	20	1	1	20000
2	VDU	1200		1	2	23.01	30	1	2	36000
				2	1	26.01	25	2	1	25000
				2	2	29.01	20	2	2	24000

Arithmetic expressions, likewise, can also be used as parameters of SQL library functions. For example, "Get a total price of all VDUs sold to customers" may be written as the following SQL statement:

```
Select SUM (Qnt*Price) From Transaction, Product
Where Transaction.P# = Product.P#
And Product.Pname = 'VDU'
```

Work this out. You should get an answer of 60000.

The attribute names for both library functions and arithmetic expressions must be derived from the relations specified in the From clause. Thus, it should be noted that the following query definition is NOT correct.

```
Select SUM (Qnt*Price) From Transaction
Where Transaction.P# = Product.P#
And Product.Pname = 'VDU'
```

Additionally, SQL also permits the use of library functions not only in the Select clause but also in the Where clause as a part of comparison expressions.

The query to "Get all available information on such customers who bought the most expensive product" would be:

```
Select *  From Customer
Where C# In
         ( Select C# From Transaction
          Where P# In
                 ( Select P# From Product
                   Where Price = MAX (Price) ) )
```

9.5   Additional Facilities

9.5.1 Ordering

The result of a mapping operation may be sorted in ascending or descending order of the selected attribute value.

The form of the Order clause is

Order By <attribute name> Up | Down

Consider the following example:

"Get a list of all transactions of the product CPU sorted in descending order of the attribute Qnt"

```
Select * From Transaction
Where P# In
        ( Select P# From Product
          Where Pname = 'CPU' )
Order By Qnt Down
```

The result would be

C#	P#	Date	Qnt
2	1	26.01	25
1	1	21.01	20

If instead, the last clause had been "Order By Qnt Up", the result would be listed in ascending order:

C#	P#	Date	Qnt
1	1	21.01	20
2	1	26.01	25

The Order By clause is only a logical sorting process, the actual contents of the original relations are not affected.

Multi-level ordered sequence may also be performed as in:

```
Select * From Transaction
    Order By C# Up,
             Qnt Down
```

9.5.2 Handling Duplicates

The result of an SQL mapping operation is however not perceived as a relation, i.e. it may include duplicate tuples. Consider for example:

```
Select C# From Transaction
Where P# In
        ( Select P# From Product
          Where Price >= 1000 )
```

The result is actually

Imagine if we have thousands of transactions and yet a handful of customers. The result would yield hundreds (even thousands) of duplicates. Fortunately, duplicate tuples can be removed by using the Unique option in the Select clause of the operation as follows:

```
Select C# Unique From Transaction
Where P# In
        ( Select P# From Product
          Where Price >= 1000 )
```

and this will yield a much reduced result with only the distinct (unique) customer numbers:

9.5.3 Grouping of Data

Usually, the result of a library function is calculated for the whole relation. For example, consider wanting to find the total number of transactions,

```
Select Count (*)        From Transaction
```

Transaction			
C#	P#	Date	Qnt
1	1	21.01	20
1	2	23.01	30
2	1	26.01	25
2	2	29.01	20

Given this relation, the result of Count (*) is 4

However, sometimes we need to calculate a library function, not for the entire relation, but only for a subset of it. Such subsets of tuples are called *groups*. For instance, in the relation Transaction, a collection of tuples with the same value of attribute C# is a "group". In this case, C# is called "Group By" attribute.

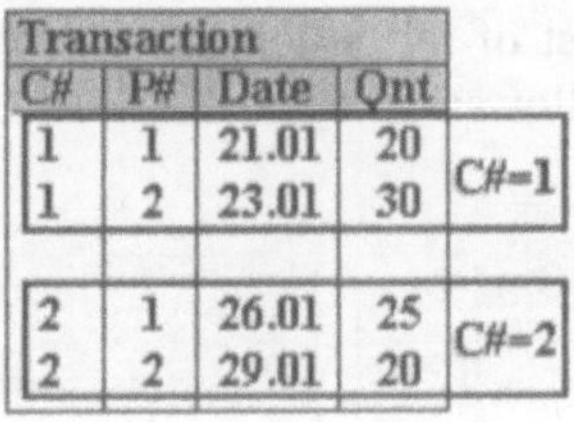

Transaction				
C#	P#	Date	Qnt	
1	1	21.01	20	C#=1
1	2	23.01	30	
2	1	26.01	25	C#=2
2	2	29.01	20	

Figure 9-9. Grouping by customer numbers

The form of the Group By clause is

Group By <attribute name>

Consider the following example:

"Get the list of all customer numbers and the quantity of products bought by each of them".

Note that the relation will have many transactions for any one customer. The transactions for each customer will have to be grouped and the quantities totaled. This is then to be done for each different customer. Thus the SQL statement would be:

Select C#, Sum(Qnt) From Transaction Group By C#

Thus all transactions with the same C#s are grouped together and the quantities summed to yield the summarised result:

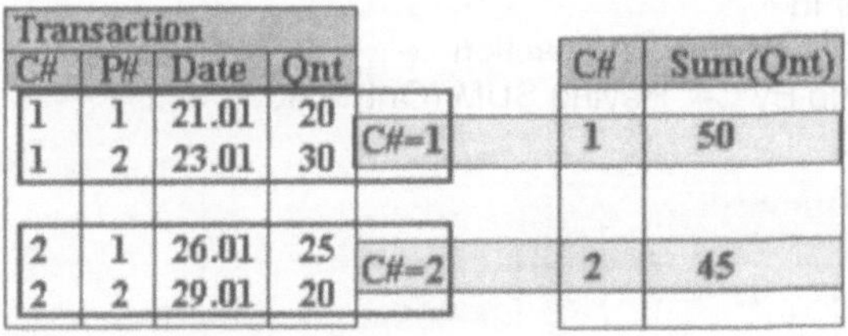

Transaction						C#	Sum(Qnt)
C#	P#	Date	Qnt			1	50
1	1	21.01	20	C#=1			
1	2	23.01	30				
2	1	26.01	25	C#=2		2	45
2	2	29.01	20				

Why would the following statement be impossible to execute?

Select * From Transaction Group By P#

Normally, the Where clause would contain conditions for the selection of tuples as in:

> Select Cname, Sum (Qnt) From Customer, Transaction
> Where Customer.C# = Transaction.C#
> Group By C#

This statement will "Get a list of all customer names and the quantity of products bought by each of them" as follows:

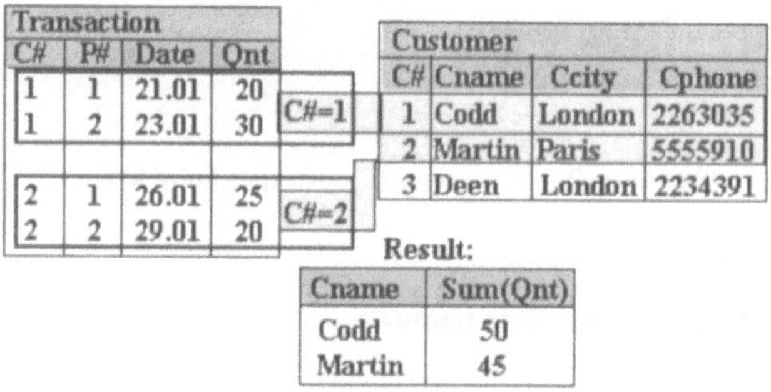

Transaction			
C#	P#	Date	Qnt
1	1	21.01	20
1	2	23.01	30
2	1	26.01	25
2	2	29.01	20

C#=1

C#=2

Customer			
C#	Cname	Ccity	Cphone
1	Codd	London	2263035
2	Martin	Paris	5555910
3	Deen	London	2234391

Result:

Cname	Sum(Qnt)
Codd	50
Martin	45

Figure 9-10. Restriction followed by grouping

9.5.4 Further Filtering: Having

We can further filter out unwanted groups generated by the Group By clause by using a "Having" clause which will include in the final result only those groups that satisfy the stated condition. Thus the additional "Having" clause provides a possibility to define conditions for selection of groups.

For example, if we wish to just "Get such customers who bought more than 45 units of products", the SQL statement would be:

> Select * From Customer
>   Where C# In
>   (Select C# From Transaction
>   Group By C# Having SUM (Qnt) > 45)

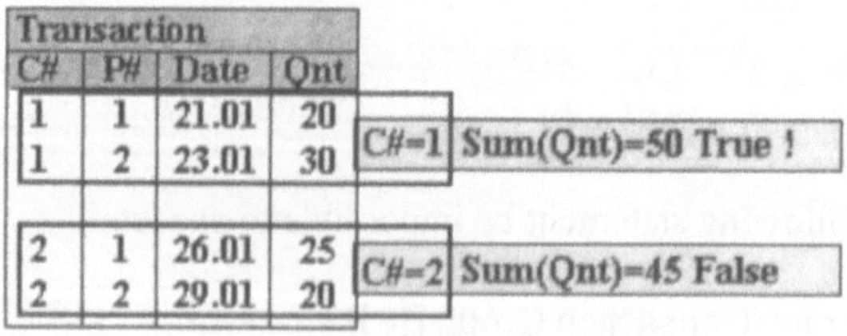

Transaction			
C#	P#	Date	Qnt
1	1	21.01	20
1	2	23.01	30
2	1	26.01	25
2	2	29.01	20

C#=1 Sum(Qnt)=50 True !

C#=2 Sum(Qnt)=45 False

Figure 9-11. Grouping followed by restriction

In this case, those grouped customers with 45 units or less will not be in the final result. The result will thus only be:

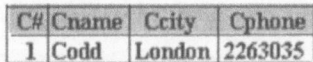

C#	Cname	Ccity	Cphone
1	Codd	London	2263035

It is important to note that in the further filtering of values, the Where clause is used to exclude values *before* the Group By clause is applied, whereas the having clause is used to exclude values *after* they have been grouped.

10. Query-By-Example (QBE)

10.1 Introduction

Data Query Languages were developed in the early seventies when the man-machine interface was, by today's standards, limited and rudimentary. In particular, interaction with the computer was through the processing of batched jobs, where jobs (computation requests such as "run this program on that data", "evaluate this database query", etc) were prepared off-line on some computer readable media (eg. punch cards), gathered into a 'batch' and then submitted for processing. No interaction takes place between the user and computer while the jobs were processed. End results were instead typically printed for the user to inspect (again off-line) and to determine the next course of action. The batch cycle continued until the user had obtained the desired results.

This was pretty much the way database queries were handled (see Figure 10-1). As data coding devices were exclusively textual in nature and as processing is non-interactive, queries must be defined textually and each query must be self-contained (ie. has all the components required to complete the evaluation). The design of early languages were influenced by, and in fact had to comply with, these constraints to be usable. Thus, for example, the SQL query:

> Select P# from Transaction
> where C# IN (Select C# from Customer
>   where Ccity = London   )

could be easily encoded as a job for batched submission. Needless to say, the turnaround time in such circumstances were high, taking hours or even days before a user sees the results of submitted queries. Many hours are typically spent off-line for a job that would take seconds to evaluate, and it is even worse if you made an error in your submission!

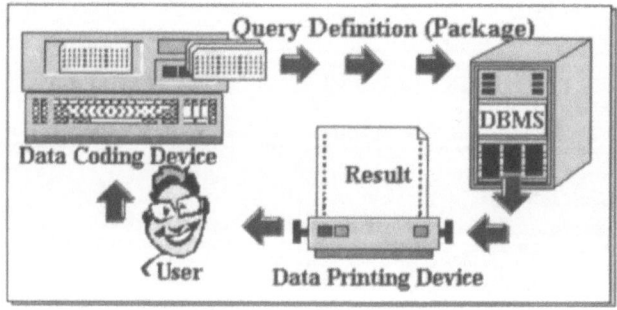

Figure 10-1 Early batch processing of queries

Over the past 20 years, however, man-machine interfaces or human-computer interaction (HCI) has progressed in leaps and bounds. Today, graphical user interfaces (GUI) are taken for granted and the batched mode of processing is largely a past relic replaced by highly interactive computing. Nevertheless, many database query languages today still retain the old 'batch' characteristics and do not exploit features of interactive interfaces. This is perhaps not surprising as, first, a large body of techniques for processing textual languages had grown over the years (eg. compiling and optimisation) and, second, they were well suited for embedding in more general purpose programming languages. The latter especially provides great flexibility and power in database manipulation. Also, as the paradigm shifted to interactive computing, its application to database queries was not immediately obvious. But end-user computing is, in any case, increasing and many tasks that previously required the skills of expert programmers are now being performed by end-users through visual, interactive interfaces.

Query-By-Example (QBE) is the first interactive database query language to exploit such modes of HCI. In QBE, a query is a construction on an interactive terminal involving two-dimensional 'drawings' of one or more relations, visualised in tabular form, which are filled in selected columns with 'examples' of data items to be retrieved (thus the phrase query-*by-example*). The system answers the query by fetching data items based on the given example and drawing the result on the same screen (see Figure 10-2).

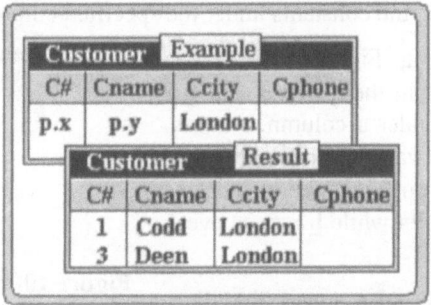

Figure 10-2 A QBE query and its results

Typically, the 'drawing' of relations are aided by interactive commands made available through pull-down menus (see Figure 10-3). The menu selection is constrained to relations available in the schema and thus eliminates errors in specifying relation structures or attribute names as can occur in text-based languages like SQL. The interface provided is in effect a structured editor for a graphical language.

For the remainder of this chapter, we will focus exclusively on the principal features of QBE. In contrast to SQL, QBE is based on relational calculus with domain variables (see 8.2). To close this introduction, we should mention that QBE was developed by M.M. Zloof at the IBM Yorktown Heights Laboratory.

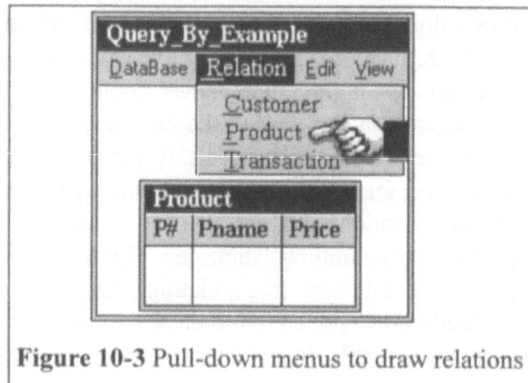

Figure 10-3 Pull-down menus to draw relations

10.2 Variables and Constants

In filling out a selected table with an example, the simplest item that can be entered under a column is a free variable or a constant. A free variable in QBE must be an *underlined* name (identifier) while a constant can be a number, string or other constructions denoting a single data value. A query containing such combinations of free variables and constants is a request for a set of values instantiating the specified variables while matching the constants under the specified columns.

As an example, look at Figure 10-4. Two variables are introduced in the query: **a** and **b**. By placing a variable under a column, we are in effect assigning that variable to range over the domain of that column. Thus, the variable **a** ranges over the domain P# while **b** ranges over Pname.

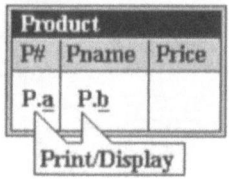

Figure 10-4 Free variables in query

The reader would have also noted that the variables are prefixed by "**P**.". In QBE, this is required if the instantiation found for the specified variable is to be displayed, ie. the prefix "**P**." may be thought of as a command to print. We will say more about prefix commands like this later. Suffice it for now to say that if neither variable in Figure 10-4 was preceded by "**P**." then the result table would display nothing!

The query in Figure 10-4 is in fact equivalent to the following construction of relational calculus with domain variables:

a → P#; b → Pname;
(a, b): (Product (a, b))

Assuming the usual Product relation extension as in previous chapters, the result of the query is shown in Figure 10-5.

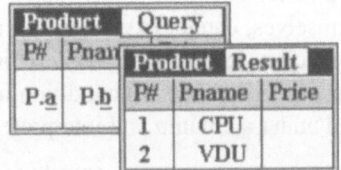

Figure 10-5 Result of query in Figure 10-4

Let us consider another simple example and walk through the basic interactions necessary to formulate the query and get the desired results. Suppose we wanted the names and cities of all customers. The basic interactions are summarised in Figure 10-6.

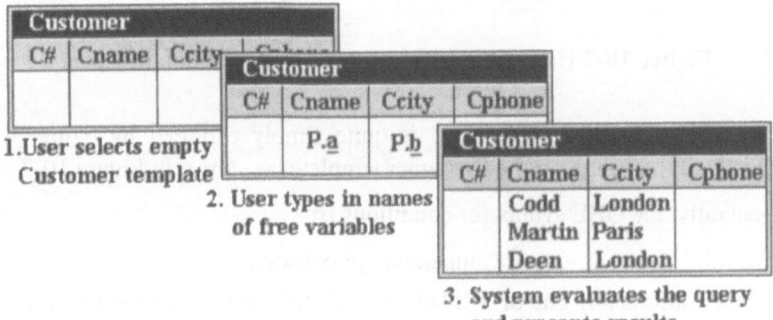

Figure 10-6 Basic sequence of interactions

1. The user first uses a pull-down menu as in Figure 10-3 to select the appropriate relation(s) containing the desired items. For this query, the Customer relation would seem the most appropriate and selecting it would result in an empty template being displayed.

2. Inspecting the template, the user can ascertain that the desired data items are indeed in the selected template (viz. The Cname and Ccity columns). Next, the user invents variable identifiers (**a** and **b**) and types each under the appropriate column. This is all that is required for this query.

3. Finally, the example is evaluated by the system and the results displayed on the screen.

This is the basic interaction even for more complex queries - select relation templates, fill in example items, then let the system evaluate and display the results. Of course, with more complex queries, more than one relation may be used and constructing the example will usually involve more than just free variables, as we shall see in due course.

Free variables unconditionally match data values in their respective domains and thus, by themselves, cannot express conditional queries, such as "get the names and phone numbers of customers who *live in London*" (the italicised phrase is the condition). The simplest specification of a condition in QBE is a *constant*, which is a single data value entered under a column and interpreted as the condition:

<attribute name> = <constant>

Customer	Query		
C#	Cname	Ccity	Cphone
	P.a	London	P.b

Customer			
C#	Cname	Ccity	Cphone
1	Codd	London	2263035
2	Martin	Paris	5555910
3	Deen	London	2234391

Customer	Result		
C#	Cname	Ccity	Cphone
	Codd		2263035
	Deen		2244391

Figure 10-7 Use of a constant to specify a condition in a query

Thus, the condition '*live in London*' is quite simply captured by typing 'London' under the 'Ccity' attribute in the Customer template, as shown in Figure 10-7.

More generally, the QBE syntax for conditions is:

[<comparator>] <constant>

where comparator is any one of '=', '≠', '<', '≤', '>', and '≥', and is interpreted as the condition

<attribute name> <comparator> <constant>

If <comparator> is omitted, it defaults to '=' (as in the above example). As an example of the use of other comparators, the query "get the names of products costing more than 1000" would be as shown in Figure 10-8.

Product	Query	
P#	Pname	Price
	P.a	>1100

Product		
P#	Pname	Price
1	CPU	1000
2	VDU	1200

Product	Result	
P#	Pname	Price
	VDU	

Figure 10-8 Comparators in conditions

A query can also spread over several rows. This is the QBE equivalent form for expressing complex conjunctions and disjunctions of conditions. To correctly interpret multiple row queries, bear in mind the following:

- the ordering of rows is immaterial
- a variable identifier denotes the same instantiation wherever it occurs

The second point above is particularly important when a variable occurs in more than one row. But let's consider first the simpler case where distinct rows do not share any variable. In this case, the rows are unrelated and can be evaluated independently of one another and the final result is simply the union of the results of each row. The collective condition of such a query is thus a *disjunction* of the conditions specified in each row.

For example, consider the query: "Get the names of customers who either live in London or Paris and whose personal number is greater than 1". The QBE query for this is shown inFigure 10-9. Looking at row 1, note that two conditions are specified. These must be satisfied by values from a single tuple, ie. the condition may be restated as

$$C\# > 1 \text{ AND Ccity=London}$$

Similarly, the condition specified in row 2 is

$$C\# > 1 \text{ AND Ccity=Paris}$$

As the two rows do not share variables, the collective condition is a disjunction

$$(C\# > 1 \text{ AND Ccity=London}) \text{ OR } (C\# > 1 \text{ AND Ccity=Paris})$$

which may be simplified to

$$C\# > 1 \text{ AND } (Ccity=\text{London OR Ccity=Paris})$$

Customer			
C#	Cname	Ccity	Cphone
1	Codd	London	2263035
2	Martin	Paris	5555910
3	Deen	London	2234391

Customer			
C#	Cname	Ccity	Cphone
>1	P.x1	London	
>1	P.x2	Paris	

Ccity='London' Or Ccity='Paris'

Figure 10-9 Multiple disjunctive rows

In contrast, if a variable occurs in more than one row, then the conditions specified for each row must be true for the *same* value of that variable. Consider, for example, the query in Figure 10-10 where the variable $\underline{x}$ occurs in both rows.

This means that a value of $\underline{x}$ must be found such that both row 1 and row 2 are simultaneously satisfied. In other words, the condition for this query is equivalent to

$$Ccity = \text{London AND } C\# > 1 \text{ AND } C\# < 4$$

(Given the above Customer relation, only the value "Deen" satisfies both rows in this case.)

Customer			
C#	Cname	Ccity	Cphone
>1	P.$\underline{x}$	London	
<4	$\underline{x}$	London	

C#>1 And C#<4

Figure 10-10 Multiple conjunctive rows

There is another possibly simpler way of describing the meaning and evaluation of multiple row queries. Specifically, we treat each row as a *sub-query*, evaluate each separately, then merge the results (a set of tuples for each sub-query) into a single table. The merging of two sets of tuples is simply a union, if their corresponding sub-queries do not share variables. Otherwise, their intersection *over attributes that share variables* is computed instead.

Thus, for the query in Figure 10-9, the first sub-query (row 1) results in the set {Deen}, while that of the second sub-query (row 2) is {Martin}. As the sub-queries do not share variables, the final result is simply the union of these results: {Deen, Martin}.

In contrast, for the query in Figure 10-10, the first sub-query (row 1) results in {Deen}, while the second (row 2) results in {Codd, Deen}. But as the sub-queries share the variable x under attribute Cname, the merged result is the intersection of the two, ie. {Deen}.

Before proceeding with the next section, we should just mention here some syntactical constraints and options of QBE. First, the prefix "P." can be used on any example item, not just free variables. This underlines its earlier interpretation, ie. it is a command to "print" or "display" the value of the item it prefixes (variable or comparison). Thus, if the query in Figure 10-9 had been:

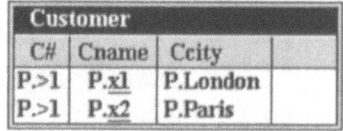

then the displayed result would be:

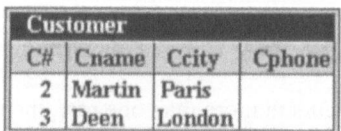

Note that, in general, prefixing a comparison prints the value that satisfies it. Of course, in the case of a constant (implicitly a "=" comparison), the constant itself will be printed.

QBE also allows the user to simplify a query to only essential components. This is largely optional and the user may choose (perhaps for greater clarity) to include redundant constructs. Basically, there are two rules that can be applied:

1. If a particular variable is used only once, then it may be omitted. This saves the user the trouble of otherwise having to invent names. Application of this rule is illustrated in Figure 10-11, where it is applied to the first table (variables $x1$ and $x2$) to result in the second. Note that unless this rule is kept in mind when reading

simplified queries, the appearance of the prefix "**P.**" by itself may not only look odd but confusing too. The prefixes in the second table must be correctly read as prefixing implicit but distinct variables.

2. Duplicate prefixes and constants occurring over multiple rows may be "factorised" into just one row. This is illustrated also in Figure 10-11 where it is applied to the second table to result in the third. Again, unless this rule is kept in mind, queries such as that in the third table may seem meaningless.

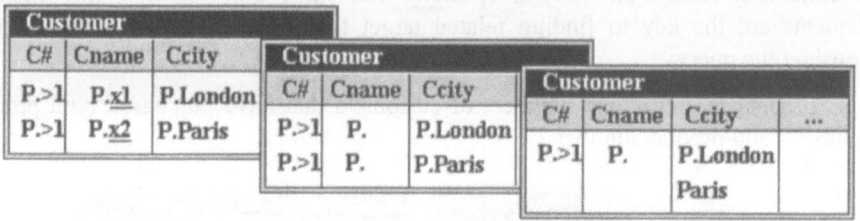

Figure 10-11 Simplifying queries

While the above rules are optional, the following is a syntactic constraint that must be observed: if a free variable occurs in more than one row, then the prefix "P." may be used on at most one of its occurrences.

The query below illustrates a valid construction - note that $\underline{x}$ occurs in two rows but only one of them has the P prefix.

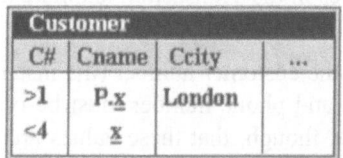

10.3 Example Elements

Each row of a query table may be seen as an example of tuples from the associated relation - specifically, tuples that match the row. A tuple *matches* a row if each attribute value in the tuple matches the corresponding query item in the row. We have seen above exactly when a value matches a query item. In summary:

1. Any value matches a blank query item or a variable

2. A value matches a comparison item if it satisfies the specified comparison

Using these rules, it is relatively easy to ascertain tuples exemplified by a query row. This is illustrated in Figure 10-12. This is why variables in QBE are called *example elements*.

Customer			
C#	Cname	Ccity	Cphone
1	Codd	London	2263035
2	Martin	Paris	5555910
3	Deen	London	2234391

Customer			
C#	Cname	Ccity	Cphone
	P.x1	London	P.y1
	P.x2	Paris	P.y2

Figure 10-12 A query row is an example of matching tuples

In extracting facts from several relations that share attribute domains, example elements are the key to finding related target tuples from the different relations. Consider the query:

"Get the names and phone numbers of customers that have purchased both product number 1 and product number 2".

Transaction			
C#	P#	Date	Qnt
$\underline{x}$	1		
$\underline{x}$	2		

Customer			
C#	Cname	Ccity	Cphone
$\underline{x}$	P.$\underline{a}$		P.$\underline{b}$

Figure 10-13 Example elements over several relations

The Transaction relation has part of the information we are after. Specifically, we look for records of purchase of each item by the same customer, ie. a tuple where the product number is 1, another where the product number is 2, but both with the same customer number. The entries in the Transaction template in Figure 10-13 capture this requirement.

However, this tells us only the customer number (the instantiation of **X**). Information about the customer's name and phone number must be obtained from the Customer relation. We need to ensure, though, that these values are obtained from a customer tuple that represents the same customer found in the Transaction relation. In QBE, this is simply achieved by specifying the *same* example element **X** in the customer number column of the Customer relation (as shown in the Customer template of Figure 10-13).

The query in Figure 10-13 may be evaluated, assuming the following extensions of Transaction and Customer, as follows.

Transaction			
C#	P#	Date	Qnt
1	1	21.01	20
1	2	23.01	30
2	1	26.01	25
3	2	29.01	20

Customer			
C#	Cname	Ccity	Cphone
1	Codd	London	2263035
2	Martin	Paris	5555910
3	Deen	London	2234391

1. The subquery in the first row of the Transaction template is matched by the first and third tuples of the Transaction relation, ie. $X = \{1,2\}$

2. The subquery in the second row of the Transaction template is matched by the second and fourth tuples of the Transaction relation, ie. $X = \{1,3\}$

3. The result of evaluating the Transaction template is therefore $\{1,2\} \cap \{1,3\} = \{1\}$.

4. The subquery in the Customer template matches all the tuples in the Customer relation, ie. the entire relation is the result.

5. The final result is the intersection, over C#, of the results in (3) and (4), ie. $\{<Codd, 2263035>\}$

Figure 10-14 shows another example of a multi-table query and illustrates also the relative ease in "reading" or paraphrasing QBE constructs. First, the Customer subquery makes it clear, from the use of "P." prefix, that the desired result is a set of customer names and their phone numbers (the elements **a** and **b** respectively). The element **x** links Customer to Transaction, ie. a customer included in the result must have purchased something, denoted yet by another element **y**. Furthermore, **y** must be such that it is the product CPU.

Customer					Transaction			Product		
C#	Cname	Ccity	Cphone		C#	P#	Date	P#	Pname	Price
x	P.a		P.b		x	y		y	CPU	

Figure 10-14 Another example of a multi-table query with example elements

In other words, the query can be paraphrased as:

"Get the names and phone numbers of those customers who bought the product CPU".

The preceding two examples should be enough for the reader to realise that (unadorned) example elements spread across tables are in fact existentially quantified. For example, there may be more than one Transaction tuple that can match the customer number found in Customer, but we don't care which! The examples also show that, more generally, a QBE query can spread over a number of rows of a single relation *and* across other relations. A few further examples will serve to highlight QBE's power and features.

In Figure 10-15, we see a complex-looking QBE query. A closer examination will reveal, however, that within each relation template the rows do not share elements, although the elements are shared across relations. In fact, there are two disjoint sets of rows - one taken from the first row of each relation and the other from the second row of each relation. The first set is actually equivalent to the QBE query in Figure 10-14.

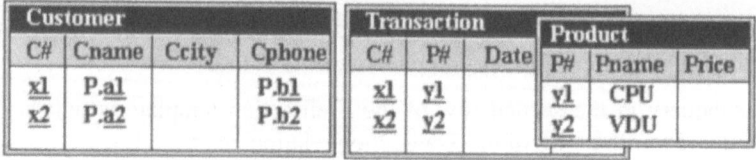

Figure 10-15 Disjunctive multi-table query

The second differs only in the specified product (replace 'CPU' by 'VDU' in the above paraphrased query). By analogy with earlier constructions involving unrelated multiple rows, this type of construction therefore denotes a disjunctive query. In other words, combining the two sets of rows yield the query:

"Get the names and phone numbers of those customers who bought the product CPU or the product VDU"

Earlier, we've seen examples of elements used in multiple rows of the same relation. However, given now an understanding of multi-table queries, such constructions can equivalently be seen as a multi-table query involving the same table! This is shown in Figure 10-16 below.

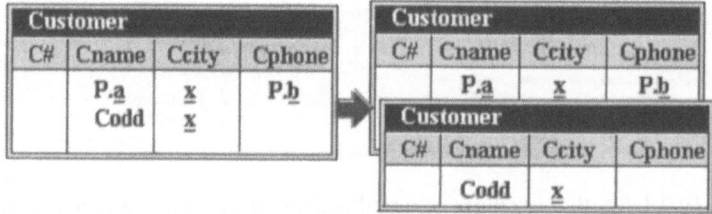

Figure 10-16 Multi-row (with shared elements) and equivalent multi-table form

Example elements may also be negated. Negated elements are written with the prefix '!', eg. **!X** (read "not X"). The negated form can only be used if there is at least one occurrence of the unnegated element elsewhere in the query. It is then interpreted as matching any corresponding domain value that the unnegated form did not match.

Consider, for example, the illustration in Figure 10-17. There are two parts to the illustration, labelled (a) and (b), each with a query table and an extension of the corresponding relation. For purposes of this example, the two query tables constitute a multi-table query, ie. the example element **X** is the same one in both. Note, however, that **X** is negated in (b).

Given the extension of Transaction as shown, the domain values matching the example element **X** in (a) is {1,2}. Turning now to the subquery in (b), the specification of '**!X**' in it means that the only tuples that can match it are tuples such that the C# value is *not* in {1,2}. Given the extension of Customer as shown, this means that only the third tuple matches the example, ie. the answer returned for elements **A** and **B** are 'Deen' and '2234391' respectively.

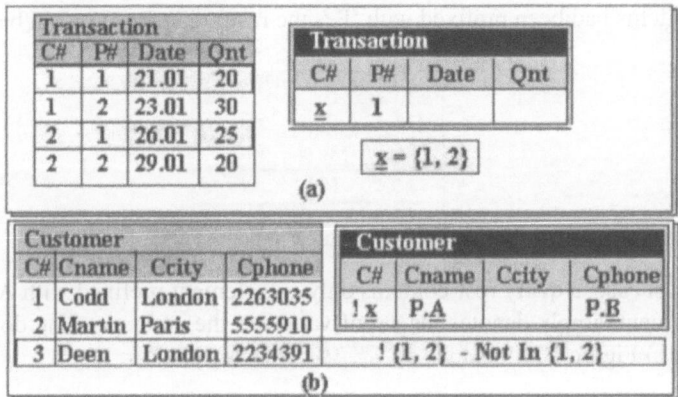

Figure 10-17 Negated element

10.4 The Prefix ALL

The prefix ALL can be applied to example elements. The occurrence of such an element in an arbitrary query row of an arbitrary relation denotes a set of values such that each, together with a particular instantiation of other items in the row, matches a tuple of the relation. As an example, consider the following relation and query:

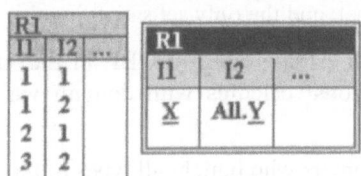

Figure 10-18 Example relation and query with ALL

In this case, there is only one other item in the query row: another element $\underline{X}$. The set of values denoted by 'All.$\underline{Y}$' therefore needs to be determined for each value that $\underline{X}$ takes. Thus,

- when $\underline{X} = 1$, there are two possible values for $\underline{Y}$, ie. 1 and 2. Thus, 'All.$\underline{Y}$' is the set {1,2}

- when $\underline{X} = 2$, there is only one value for $\underline{Y}$, ie. the set {1}

- when $\underline{X} = 3$, there is also only one value for $\underline{Y}$, ie. the set {2}

If the query items had been prefixed with 'P.', the result displayed would be:

R1		
I1	I2	...
1	{1,2}	
2	{1}	
3	{2}	

In the simplest case, a query row contains only one element prefixed with ALL. In this case, the element simply denotes the set of values in the corresponding domain. This is illustrated in Figure 10-19 below.

R2		
I2	I3	...
1	a	
2	b	

R2	Query	
I2	I3	...
ALL.X		

R2	Result	
I2	I3	...
{1, 2}		

Figure 10-19 Simple use of ALL

The use of ALL is more interesting when it involves multitable queries. For example, combining the query in Figure 10-18 and Figure 10-19 into a single query, we effectively restrict **X** to just the value 1. This is because **ALL.Y** occurs in both tables and must denote the same set, and the only set satisfying this is {1,2}.

It should be clear now that ALL is used in QBE in the same way that a universal quantifier is used in relational calculus with domain variables. To highlight this, consider the query:

"Get the names of customers who bought all types of the company's product"

Three relations are required to resolve this query: Customer, Transaction and Product. The QBE query is shown in Figure 10-20 which is also annotated with explanations.

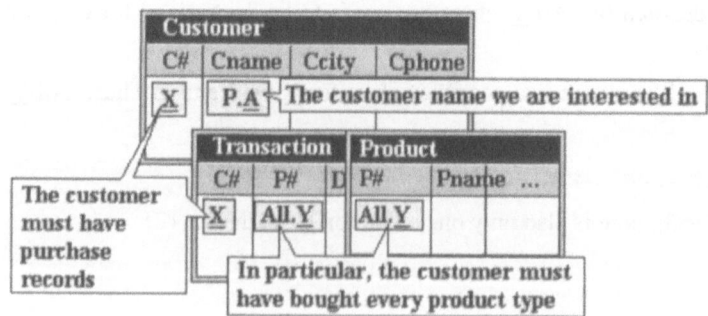

Figure 10-20 The query "Get the names of customers who bought all types of the company's product"

One final word about ALL: it does not remove duplicate values, in contrast to an unprefixed element which will return only unique matching values. This is illustrated in Figure 10-21 below. We shall see in the next section how this property is used (if fact, is necessary) in order to answer certain classes of practical queries.

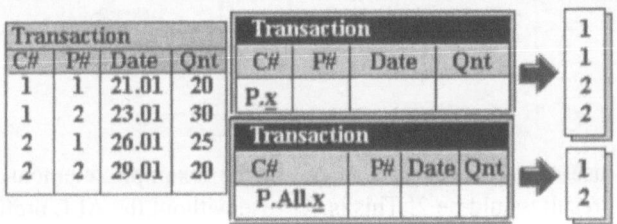

Figure 10-21 ALL does not remove duplicates!

10.5 Library Functions

As with SQL, QBE also provides arithmetic operations and a number of built-in functions which are necessary to manipulate the values in ways not otherwise within the scope of relational calculus, eg. to count the number of occurrences of returned values or to sum them up. As you may expect by now, these operations are provided in the form of prefixes. For example, suppose we wish to know how many transactions were related to the purchase of a particular product, say product number 1.

We can extract, for example, all customer numbers in transactions involving product number 1:

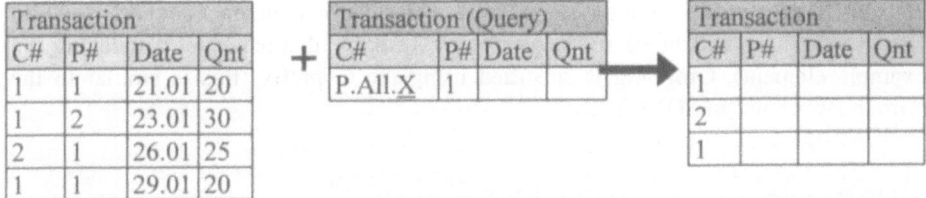

But what we are really interested in is counting the number of such values. QBE allows us to do this with the prefix CNT (equivalent to the function COUNT in SQL), which counts the number of values matching the element it prefixes.

Thus the same query above, different only in the addition of the CNT prefix, achieves the desired result:

Transaction				+	Transaction (Query)				→	Transaction			
C#	P#	Date	Qnt		C#	P#	Date	Qnt		C#	P#	Date	Qnt
1	1	21.01	20		P.CNT.All.X	1				3			
1	2	23.01	30										
2	1	26.01	25										
1	1	29.01	20										

Note that the use of ALL is *necessary*. If the example element was simply "**P.CNT.X**", the result would be 2! This is because without the ALL prefix, the values matching the element **X** are returned with duplicate values removed (as illustrated earlier in Figure 10-21).

Another frequently used function is SUM, which sums up the values matching the example element it prefixes. Suppose, we wish to know the total number of product number 1 that has been sold. Instead of counting the number of customers that purchased it, we sum instead the quantities recorded in the relevant transactions. Thus:

Transaction				+	Transaction (Query)				→	Transaction			
C#	P#	Date	Qnt		C#	P#	Date	Qnt		C#	P#	Date	Qnt
1	1	21.01	20			1		P.SUM.All.X					65
1	2	23.01	30										
2	1	26.01	25										
1	1	29.01	20										

QBE also allows us to group tuples in a relation based on a specified example element. That is, tuples with the same value of the example element are collected into one group (there will be as many groups as there are distinct values matching the example element). Grouping is specified using the G prefix (this is similar to the 'Group By' clause in SQL). Thus:

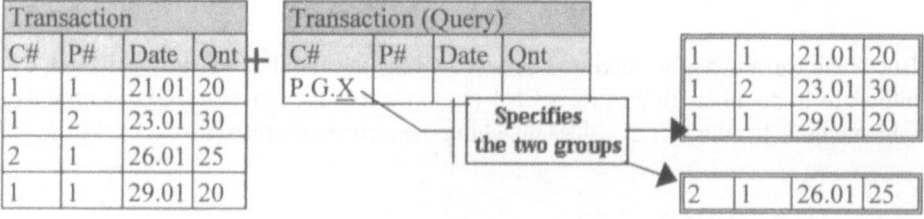

Aritmetic functions may be applied to groups. Thus, if we wanted to know the total number of items purchased by each customer, we can modify the above query as follows:

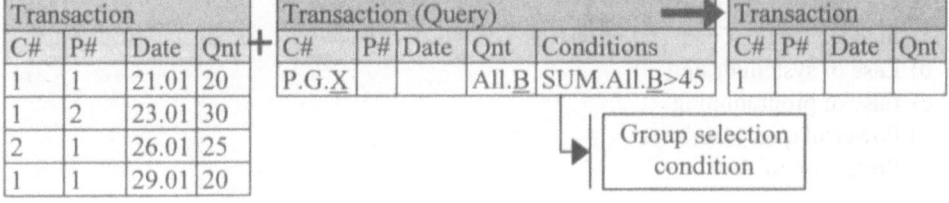

Transaction			
C#	P#	Date	Qnt
1	1	21.01	20
1	2	23.01	30
2	1	26.01	25
1	1	29.01	20

Transaction (Query)			
C#	P#	Date	Qnt
P.G.X			P.SUM.All.B

Transaction			
C#	P#	Date	Qnt
1			70
2			25

Groups may additionally be selected based on conditions that are specified in an additional column (this corresponds to the 'Having clause' of SQL). This additional conditions column may be created by means of a special menu item in the QBE interface.

Thus, if we are only interested in finding customers who have purchased more than 45 items, our query would be as follows:

Transaction			
C#	P#	Date	Qnt
1	1	21.01	20
1	2	23.01	30
2	1	26.01	25
1	1	29.01	20

Transaction (Query)				
C#	P#	Date	Qnt	Conditions
P.G.X			All.B	SUM.All.B>45

Group selection condition

Transaction			
C#	P#	Date	Qnt
1			

In summary, grouping and arithmetic functions can be used in combination to obtain useful *derived* values from the database.

11. Architecture of Database Systems

11.1 Introduction

Software systems generally have an *architecture*, ie. possessing of a structure (form) and organisation (function). The former describes identifiable components and how they relate to one another structurally; the latter describes how the functions of the various structural components interact to provide the overall functionality of the system as a whole. Since a database system is basically a software system (albeit complex), it too possesses an architecture. A typical architecture must define a particular configuration of and interaction between data, software modules, meta-data, interfaces and languages (see Figure 11-1).

The architecture of a database system determines its capability, reliability, effectiveness and efficiency in meeting user requirements. But besides the visible functions seen through some data manipulation language, a good database architecture should provide:

a) Independence of data and programs
b) Ease of system design
c) Ease of programming
d) Powerful query facilities
e) Protection of data

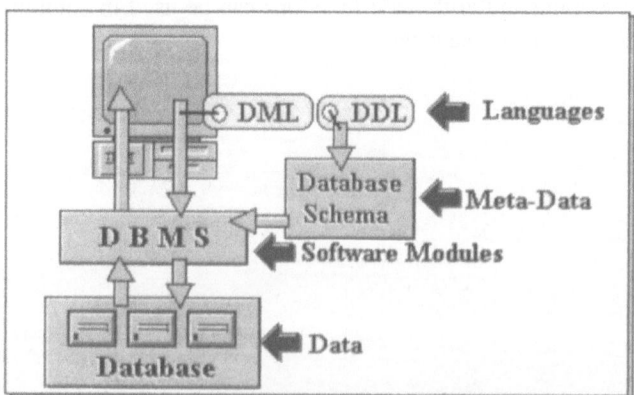

Figure 11-1 General database system architecture

The features listed above become especially important in large organisations where corporate data are held centrally. In such situations, no single user department has responsibility over, nor can they be expected to know about, all of the organisation's data. This becomes the job of a *Database Administrator* (DBA) who has a daunting range of responsibilities that include creating, expanding, protecting and maintaining the integrity of all data while adressing the interests of different present and future user communities. To create a database, a DBA has to analyse and assess the data requirements of all users and from these determine its logical structure (database schema). This, on the one hand, will need to be efficiently mapped onto a physical structure that optimises retrieval performance and the use of storage. On the other, it would also have to be mapped to multiple user views suited to the respective user applications. For large databases, DBA functions will in fact require the full time services of a team of many people. A good database architecture should have features that can significantly facilitate these activities.

11.2 Data Abstraction

To meet the requirements above, a more sophisticated architecture is in fact used, providing a number of levels of data abstraction or data definition. The database schema, also known as *Conceptual Schema*, mentioned above represents an information model at the *logical level* of data definition. At this level, we abstract out details like computer storage structures, their restrictions, or their operational efficiencies. The view of a database as a collection of relations or tables, each with fixed attributes and primary keys ranging over given domains, is an example of a logical level of data definition.

The details of efficiently organising and storing objects of the conceptual schema in computers with particular hardware configurations are dealt with at the *internal (storage) level* of data definition. This level is also referred to as the *Internal Schema*. It maps the contents of the conceptual schema onto structures representing tuples, associated key organisations and indexes, etc, taking into account application characteristics and restrictions of a given computer system. That is, the DBA describes at this level how objects of the conceptual schema are actually organised in a computer. Figure 11-2 illustrates these two levels of data definition.

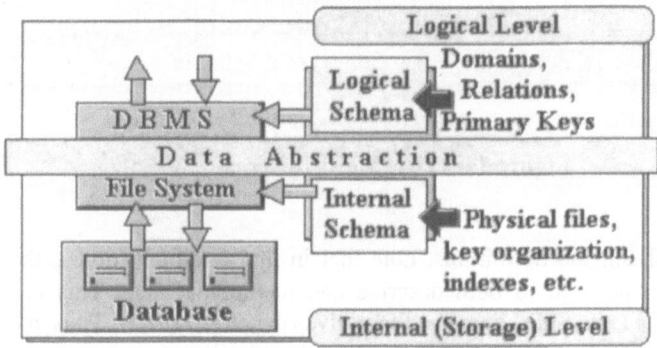

Figure 11-2 The logical and internal levels of data abstraction

At a higher level of abstraction, objects from the conceptual schema are mapped onto *views* seen by end-users of the database. Such views are also referred to as *External Schemas*. An external schema presents only those aspects of the conceptual schema that are relevant to the particular application at hand, abstracting out all other detaiils. Thus, depending on the requirements of the application, the view may be organised differently from that in the conceptual schema, eg. some tables may be merged, attributes may be suppressed, etc. There may thus be many views created - one for each type of application. In contrast, there is only one conceptual and one internal schema. All views are derived from the same conceptual schema. This is illustrated in Figure 11-3 which shows two different user views derived from the same conceptual schema.

Thus, modern database systems support three levels of data abstraction: External Schemas (User Views), Conceptual Schema, and Internal (Storage) Schema.

The DDL we discussed in earlier chapters is basically a tool only for conceptual schema definition. The DBA will therefore usually need special languages to handle the external and internal schema definitions. The internal schema definition, however, varies widely over different implementation platforms, ie. there are few common principles for such definition. We will therefore say little more about them in this book.

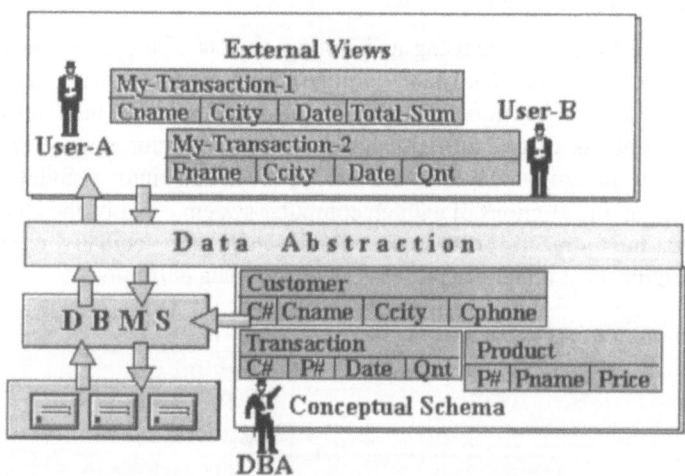

Figure 11-3 User views (external schema)

As to external schema definitions, note that in the relational model, the Data Sub-Languages can be used to both describe and manipulate data. This is because the expressions of a Data Sub-Language themselves denote relations. Thus, a collection of new (derived) relations can be defined as an external schema.

For example, suppose the following relations are defined:

    Customer(C#, Cname, Ccity, Cphone)
    Product(P#, Pname, Price)
    Transaction(C#, P#, Date, Qnt)

We can then define an external view with a construct like the following:

    Define View My_Transaction_1 As
        Select Cname, Ccity, Date, Total_Sum=Price*Qnt
        From Customer, Transaction, Product
        Where Customer.C# = Transaction.C#
            & Transaction.P# = Product.P#

which defines the relation (view):

    My_Transaction_1(Cname, Ccity, Date, Total_Sum)

This definition effectively maps the conceptual database structure into a form more convenient for a particular user or application. The extension of this derived table is itself derived from the extensions of the source relations. This is illustrated in Figure 11-4 below.

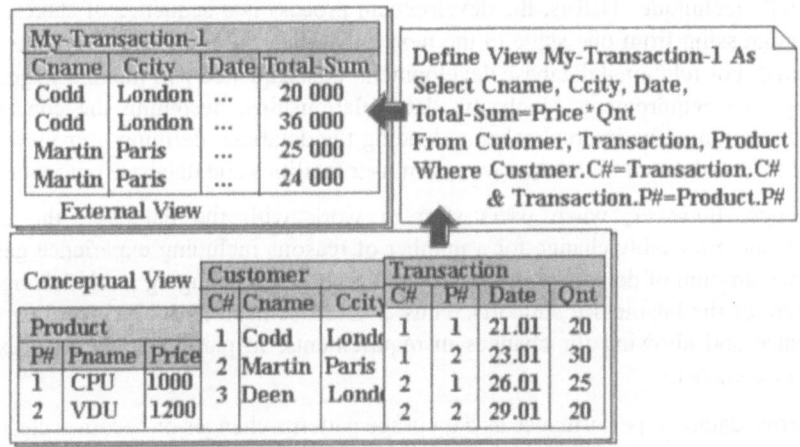

Figure 11-4 External view definition

This is a very important property of the relational data model: *a unified approach to data definition and data manipulation.*

11.3 Data Administration

Functions of a DBA include:

- Creation of the database

To create a database, a DBA has to analyse and assess the requirements of the users and from these determine its logical structure. In other words, the DBA has to design a conceptual schema and a first variant of an internal schema. When the internal schema is ready, the DBA must load the database with actual data.

- Acting as intermediary between users and the database

A DBA is responsible for all user facilities determined by external schemas, ie. the DBA is responsible for defining all external schemas or user views.

- Ensuring data privacy, integrity and security

In analysing user requirements, a DBA must determine who should have access to which data and subsequently arrange for appropriate privacy locks (passwords) for identified individuals and/or groups. The DBA must also determine integrity constraints and arrange for appropriate data validation to ensure that such constraints are never violated. Last, but not least, the DBA must make arrangements for data to be regularly backed up and stored in a safe place as a measure against unrecoverable data losses for one reason or another.

At first glance, it may seem that a database can be developed using the conventional "waterfall" technique. That is, the development process is a sequence of stages, with work progressing from one stage to the next only when the preceding stage has been completed. For relational database development, this sequence will include stages like eliciting user requirements, analysing data relationships, designing the conceptual schema, designing the internal schema, loading the database, defining user views and interfaces, etc, through to the deployment of user facilities and database operations.

In practice, however, when users start to work with the database, the initial requirements inevitably change for a number of reasons including experience gained, a growing amount of data to be processed, and, in this fast changing world, changes in the nature of the business it supports. Thus, a database need to evolve, learning from experience and allowing for changes in requirements. In particular, we may expect periodic changes to:

- improve database performance as data usage patterns changes or becomes clearer

- add new applications to meet new processing requirements

- modify the conceptual schema as understanding of the enterprise's perception of data improves

Changing a database, once the conceptual and internal schemas have been defined and data actually loaded, can be a major undertaking even for seemingly small conceptual changes. This is because the data structures at the storage layer will need to be reorganised, perhaps involving complete regeneration of the database. A good DBMS should therefore provide facilities to modify a database with a minimum of inconvenience. The desired facilities can perhaps be broadly described to cover:

- performance monitoring
- database reorganisation
- database restructuring

By performance monitoring we mean the collection of usage statistics and their analysis. Statistics necessary for performance optimisation generally fall under two headings: static and dynamic statistics. The static statistics refer to the general state of the database and can be collected by special monitoring programs when the database is inactive. Examples of such data include the number of tuples per relation, the population of domains, the distribution of relations over available storage space, etc. The dynamic statistics refer to run-time characteristics and can be collected only when the database is running. Examples include frequency of access to and updating of each relation and domain, use of each type of data manipulation operator and associated response times, frequency of disk access for different usage types, etc.

It is the DBA's responsibility to analyse such data, interpret them and where necessary take steps to reorganise the storage schema to optimise performance. Reorganising the storage schema also entails the subsequent physical reorganisation of the data themselves. This is what we mean by database reorganisation.

The restructuring of the conceptual schema implies changing its contents, such as:

- adding/removing data items (ie. columns of a relation)
- adding/removing entire relations
- splitting/recombining relations
- changing a relation's primary keys
- ...etc

For example, assuming the relations as on page 3, suppose we now wish to record also for each purchase transaction the sales representative responsible for the sale. We will need therefore to add a column into the Transaction relation, say with column name R# :

Transaction(C#, P#, R# Date, Qnt)

new attribute added

The intention, of course, is to record a unique value under this column to denote a particular sales representative. Details of such sales representatives will then be given in a new relation:

Representative(R#, Rname, Rcity, Rphone)

A retructured conceptual schema will normally be followed by a database reorganisation in the sense explained above.

11.4 Data Independence

Data independence refers to the independence of one user view (external schema) with respect to others. A high degree of independence is desirable as it will allow a DBA to change one view, to meet new requirements and/or to optimise performance, without affecting other views. Relational databases with appropriate relational sub-languages have a high degree of data independence.

For example, suppose that the view

My_Transaction_1(Cname, Ccity, Date, Total_Sum)

as defined on page 4 no longer meet the user's needs. Let's say that Ccity and Date are no longer important, and that it is more important to know the product name and quantity purchased. This change is easily accommodated by changing the select-clause in the definition thus:

Define View My_Transaction_1 As Select Cname, Pname, Qnt, Total_Sum=Price*Qnt From Customer, Transaction, Product Where Customer.C# = Transaction.C# & Transaction.P# = Product.P#	This replaces the original specification of Ccity and Date items

If each view is defined separately over the conceptual schema, then as long as the conceptual schema does not change, a view may be redefined without affecting other views. Thus the above change will have no effect on other views, unless they were built upon My_Transaction_1.

Data independence is also used to refer to the independence of user views relative to the conceptual schema. For example, the reader can verify that the change in the conceptual schema in the last section (adding the attribute R# to Transaction and adding the new relation Representative), does not affect My_Transaction_1 - neither the original nor the changed view!. In general, if the relations and attributes referred to in a view definition are not removed in a restructuring, the view will not be affected. Thus we can accommodate new (additive) requirements without affecting existing applications.

Lastly, data independence may also refer to the extent to which we may change the storage schema without affecting the conceptual or external schemas. We will not elaborate on this as we have pointed out earlier that the storage level is too diverse for meaningful treatment here.

11.5 Data Protection

There are generally three types of data protection that any serious DBMS must provide. These were briefly described in Chapter 1 and we summarise them here:

1. Authorisational Security
This refers to protection against unauthorised access and includes measures such as user identification and password control, privacy keys, etc.

2. Operational Security
This refers to maintaining the integrity of data, ie. protecting the database from the introduction of data that would violate identified integrity constraints.

3. Physical Security

This refers to procedures to protect the physical data against accidental loss or damage of storage equipment, theft, natural disaster, etc. It will typically involve making periodic backup copies of the database, transaction journalling, error recovery techniques, etc.

In the context of the relational data model, we can use relational calculus as a notation to define integrity constraints, ie. we define them as formulae of relational calculus. In this case, however, all variables must be bound variables as we are specifying properties over their ranges rather than looking for particular instantiations satisfying some predicate. For example, suppose that for the Product relation, the Price attribute should only have a value greater than 100 and less than 99999. This can be expressed (in DSL Alpha style) as:

> **Range Product X ALL;**
> **(X.Price > 100 & X.Price < 99999)**

This is interpreted as an assertion that must always be true. Any data manipulation that would make it false would be disallowed (typically generating messages informing the user of the violation). Thus, not only does the relational data model unify data definition and manipulation, but its *control* as well.

In the area of physical security, database backups should of course be done periodically. For this purpose, it is perhaps best to view a database as a large set of physical pages, where each page is a block of fixed size serving as the basic unit of interaction between the DBMS and storage devices. A database backup is thus essentially a copy of the entire set of pages onto another storage medium that is kept in a secure and safe place. Aside from the obvious need for backups against damage of storage devices, theft, natural disasters and the like, backups are necessary to recover a consistent database in the event of a database 'crash'. Such crashes can occur in the course of a sequence of database transactions, particularly transactions that modify the database content.

Suppose, for example, that the last backup was done at time t_0, and subsequent to that, a number of update transactions were applied one after another. Suppose further that the first n transactions were successfully completed, but during the $(n+1)^{th}$ transaction a system failure occurred (eg. disk malfunction, operating system crash, power failure, etc) leaving some pages in a corrupted state. In general, it is not possible to just reapply the failed transaction - the failure could have corrupted the updates performed by previous transactions as well, or worse, it could have damaged the integrity of the storage model as to make some pages of the database unreadable! We have no recourse at this point but to go back to the last known consistent state of the database at time t_0, ie. the entire contents of the last backup is reinstated as the current database. Of course, in doing so, all the transactions applied after t_0 are lost.

At this point it may seem reasonable that, to guard against losing too much work, backups should perhaps be done after each transaction - then at most only the work of one transaction is lost in case of failure. However, many database applications today are transaction intensive typically involving many online users generating many transactions frequently (eg. online airline reservation system). Many databases, on the other hand, are very large and an entire backup could take hours to complete. While backup is being performed the database must be inactive. Thus, it should be clear that this proposition is impractical.

As it is clearly desirable that transactions since the last backup are also somehow saved in the event of crashes, an additional mechanism is needed. Essentially, such mechanisms are based on *journalling* successful transactions applied to a database. This simply means that a copy of each transaction (or affected pages) is recorded in a sequential file as they are applied to the database.

The simplest type of journalling is the *Forward System Journal*. In this, whenever a page is modified, a copy of the modified page is also simultaneously recorded into the forward journal.

To illustrate this mechanism, let the set of pages in a database be $P = \{p_1, p_2, \ldots p_n\}$. If the application of an update transaction T on the database changes P_T, where $P_T \subseteq P$, then $\mathbf{T}(P_T)$ will be recorded in the forward journal. We use the notation $\mathbf{T}(P_T)$ to denote the set of pages P_T *after* the transaction T has changed each page in P_T. Likewise, we write $\mathbf{T}(p_i)$ to denote a page p_i after it has been changed by transaction T. Furthermore, if T was applied successfully (ie. no crash during its processing), a separator mark, say ';', would be written to the journal. Thus, after a number of successful transactions, the journal would look as follows

$$< \mathbf{T}(P_{T1}) ; \mathbf{T}(P_{T2}) ; \ldots \mathbf{T}(P_{Tk}) ; >$$

As a more concrete example, suppose transaction T1 changed $\{p_1, p_2, p_3\}$, T2 changed $\{p_2, p_3, p_4\}$, and T3 changed $\{p_3, p_4, p_5\}$, *in that order* and all successfully carried out. Then the journal would contain:

$$< \mathbf{T1}(\{p_1, p_2, p_3\}) ; \mathbf{T2}(\{T1(p_2), T1(p_3), p_4\}) ; \mathbf{T3}(\{T2(T1(p_3)), T2(p_4), p_5\}) ; >$$

Now suppose a crash occurred just after T3 has been applied. The recovery procedure consists of two steps:

a) replace the database with the latest backup

b) read the system journal in the forward direction (hence the term 'forward' journal) and, for each set of journal pages that precedes the separator ';', use it to replace the corresponding pages in the database. Effectively, this duplicates the effect of applying transactions in the order they were applied prior to the crash.

The technique is applicable even if the crash occurred during the last transaction. In this case, the journal for the last transaction would be incomplete and, in particular, the separator ';' would *not* be written out. Say that transaction T3 was interrupted after modifying pages p_3 and p_4 but before it could complete modifying p_5. Then the journal would look as follows:

$$< \mathbf{T1}(\{p_1, p_2, p_3\}) ; \quad \mathbf{T2}(\{T1(p_2), T1(p_3), p_4\}) \boxed{\mathbf{T3}(\{T2(T1(p_3)), T2(p_4), \ldots\}}) >$$

Incomplete entry

In this case, recovery is exactly as described above except that the last incomplete block of changes will be ignored (no separator ';'). Of course, the work of the last transaction is lost, but this is unavoidable. It is possible, however, to augment the scheme further by saving the transaction itself until its effects are completely written to the journal. Then T3 above can be reapplied, as a third step in the recovery procedure.

While the forward journal can recover (almost) fully from a crash, its disadvantage is that it is still a relatively slow process - hundreds or even thousands of transactions may have been applied since the last full backup, and the corresponding journals of each of these transactions must be copied back in sequence to restore the state of the database. In some applications, very fast recovery is needed.

In these cases, the *Backward System Journal* will be the more appropriate journalling and recovery technique. With this technique, whenever a transaction changes a page, the page contents *before* the update is saved. As before, if the transaction succesfully completes, a separator is written. Thus the backward journal for the same example as above would be:

$<\{ p_1, p_2, p_3 \} ; \{ T1(p_2), T1(p_3), p_4 \} ; \{ T2(T1(p_3)), T2(p_4), ... \} >$

Since each block of journal pages represents the state immediately before a transaction is applied, recovery consists of only one step: read the journal in the backward direction until the first separator and replace the pages in the database with the corresponding pages read from the journal. Thus, the backward journal is like an 'undo' file - the last block cancels the last transaction, the second last cancels the second last transaction, etc.

Features such as those discussed above can significantly facilitate the management of corporate data resources. Such features, together with the overall architecture and the Data Model examined in previous chapters, determine the quality of a DBMS and are thus often used as part of the principal criteria used in critical evaluation of competing DBMSs.

11.6 Further Reading

Those of you wanting a more detailed introduction to the relational data model, are strongly recommended to read [Date 1995]. The book is written in a tutorial style with many of the issues, such as the database languages, presented through a progressive series of examples. Another book by the same author [Date 1993] is a readable account of the SQL standard. The book contains many examples and a reader can learn enough to be able to write simple SQL programs or to understand an existing program.

The books [Kroenke 1995], [Benyon 1997] and [Ullmann & Widom1997] are written in a similar tutorial style and describe the Relational Data Model in greater detail providing useful recommendations on actual database design.

Database theory is well presented in [Elmaseri and Navathe 1994] and [Ullmann 1988].

The book [Smith & Barnes 1987] bridges the gap between physical data structures and logical database models. Assuming knowledge of elementary data structures, it describes file processing techniques and introduces fundamentals of database systems as you become aware of design and implementation issues.

The book [Silverston, Inmon, and Graziano 1997] can be useful for those who are interested in the actual application of database systems. It provides a common set of database structures for specific functions common to most businesses, such as sales, marketing, order processing, budgeting, and accounting. The book presents and discusses in greater details different design and implementation techniques. Readers can apply one of such data structures to their own company to meet specific data needs.

References:

[Benyon 1997] Benyon D. *Information and Data-Modelling* (2nd. Edition), Mc Graw Hill (1997).

[Date 1995] Date, C.J. *Introduction to Database Systems* (6th Edition), Addison-Wesley Publ. company (1995).

[Date 1993] Date, C.J. *A Guide to the SQL Standard.* (3rd Edition), Addison-Wesley Publ. company (1993).

[Elmaseri and Navathe 1994] Elmaseri, K. and Navathe, D. *Fundamentals of Database Systems* (2nd. Edition), Benjamin / Cumming (1994).

[Kroenke 1995] Kroenke D.M. *Database Processing.* (5th. Edition), Prentice Hall (1995).

[Silverston, Inmon, and Graziano 1997] Silverston L., Inmon W. H. and Graziano K. *The Data Model Resource Book: A Library of Logical Data Models and Data Warehouse Designs,* John Willey & Sons (1997).

[Smith & Barnes 1987] Smith, P.D. and Barnes, M.G. *Files and Databases: An Introduction,* Addison-Wesley Publ. company (1987).

[Ullmann 1988] Ullmann, J.D. *Principles Of Database and Knowledge-Base Systems, Volume I: Classical Database Systems,* Computer Science Press (1988).

[Ullmann & Widom1997] Ullmann, J.D. and Widom, S. *A First Course in Database Systems,* Prentice Hall (1997).

Part II
Object-Oriented Databases

12. Abstract Data Objects

12.1 Introduction

Object-oriented systems are currently receiving much attention and making great impacts in many areas of computer science. They have their roots in programming, as an alternative approach to procedure-driven programming, and is reflected in the development of such programming languages as Simula, Smalltalk and C++. It has since been adopted and extended, particularly to cover the broader range of software engineering activities including modelling, specifications and design phases of software construction. Even the field of artificial intelligence, especially knowledge engineering, have (somewhat independently and in parallel with development in programming) found the object-oriented approach to be particularly effective.

Somewhat a later development is the application of the object-oriented paradigm to databases and database management systems. This interest was perhaps fueled by requirements in new areas of database applications - in particular, hypermedia systems. Such applications call for data modelling capabilities not supported by traditional models of databases or current implementations of database management systems (such as relational or network data models and DBMSs based on them).

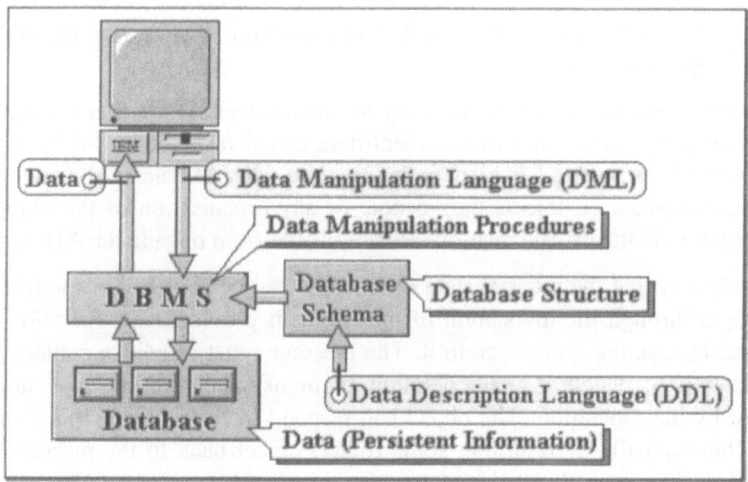

Figure 12-1 Database architecture

Conceptually, database systems are based on the idea of separating a database *structure* from its *contents*. This was explained in section 1.3 (see also Figure 1-5 there). To briefly recapitulate, the database structure is also called a *schema* (or *meta-*

structure - because it describes the structure of data objects). A schema describes all possible states of a database, in the sense that no state of the database can contain a data object that is not the result of instantiating an entity schema, and likewise no state can contain an association (link) between two data objects unless such an association was defined in the schema. Moreover, data manipulation procedures can be separated from the data as well. Thus the architecture of database systems is portrayed as shown in Figure 12-1.

The axioms of conventional data modelling are:

1. Attributes, data objects and relationships belong to predefined types;
2. The schema or metastructure of a database must be specified in advance;
3. Data manipulation facilities are based on a propositional calculus (allowing comparisons of attribute values)

12.2 Abstract Data Objects

The principal idea behind object-oriented approaches is that of *encapsulating data* in *abstract data objects*, or ADO for short (the use of this term is practically synonymous with that of abstract data types, or ADT, which is also commonly used in the literature; where no confusion can arise, however, and when it results in better reading, we will simply use 'object' or 'data object' to mean an ADO). An ADO has the following properties:

1. It has a unique identity.

2. It has a private memory and a number of operations that can be applied to the current state of that memory.

3. The values held in the private memory are themselves ADOs that are referenced *from within* by means of variable identifiers called *instance variables*. Note the emphasis "*from within*", which underlines the idea of encapsulation, ie. such instance variables or objects they denote or any organisation of the objects into any structure in the private memory are not visible from outside the ADO.

4. The only way that the internal state of an ADO can be accessed or modified from outside is through the invocation of operations it provides. An operation can be invoked by *sending a message* to it. The message must of course contain enough information to decide which operation to invoke and provide also any input needed by that operation. The object can respond to the message in a number of ways, but typically by returning some (other) object back to the message sender and/or causing some observable change (eg. in a graphical user interface).

Operations of an ADO are also referred to as *methods*. Not all methods have to be visible, however - some methods may be needed only internally and, like the structure and contents of private memory, are hidden from outside view. Those methods that are visible externally are called *public methods* and constitute the *public interfaces* of the object. Users or clients of the object need only be aware of its unique identity and its public interfaces to be able to use it.

These properties of an ADO may be pictorially depicted as in the figure below:

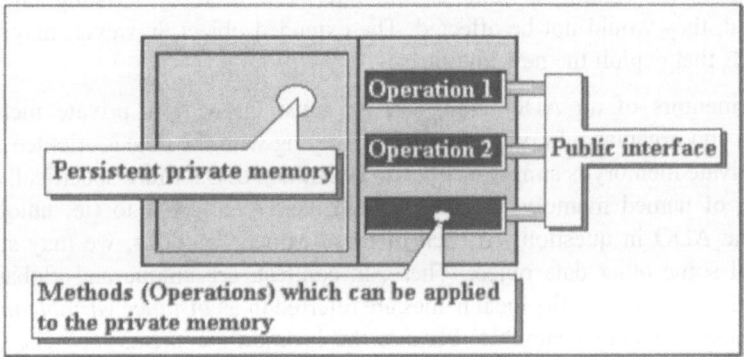

Figure 12-2 Depiction of an abstract data object

For example, the ADO with identity "Person Nick" may be depicted as in Figure 12-3. This object represents a particular person and its private memory will contain values pertaining to that person. These values are accessed and manipulated only through the public interfaces. Thus, the message "Get-Salary" will invoke the corresponding method which will retrieve and return the person's salary. The "Set-Salary" message on the other hand will invoke the corresponding method to modify that value in private memory representing the person's salary.

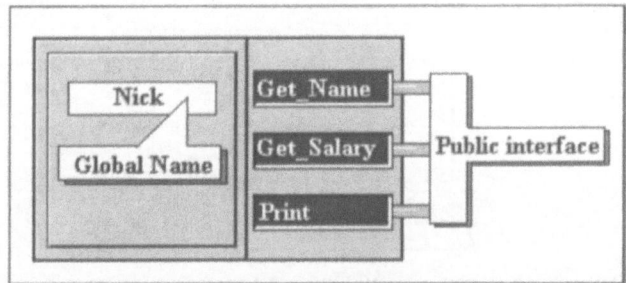

Figure 12-3 Data object example

Note that as a user or client of this object, we have no knowledge of, nor do we need to know or care about, its private memory structure. The salary, for instance, may be a value stored explicitly in the object's memory, or computed dynamically using other values (such as daily rates and number of days worked), or retrieved from some other object. What matters to the client is only the public interface.

Much of the power of the object-oriented approach lies here in data encapsulation. It means that the implementor of some ADO is free to choose any implementation structure he/she deems appropriate, or change it later, say, for greater efficiency. As long as the agreed public interfaces remain the same, clients will be assured of the same (perhaps improved) service. Changes may also add new functionality, ie. new public interfaces. Again, as long as the interfaces used by existing clients are maintained, they would not be affected. The extended object, however, may take on new clients that exploit the new interfaces.

As implementors of an ADO, however, we must know how private memory is structured and organised. In principle, and in keeping with the object-oriented view of values, private memory is simply a collection of other ADOs. More specifically, it is a collection of named memory locations. These names are *local* to (ie. unique only within) the ADO in question. At each of these named locations, we may store the identity of some other data object. These, in contrast, are unique and global to the database. For this reason, the local names are referred to as *instance variable names* or simply *variable names* ('variable' because the location's contents may change, and 'instance', as we shall see later, is synonymous with ADO). Arbitrarily complex associations between objects may therefore be constructed through their memories.

Consider, for example, the collection of objects in Figure 12-4.

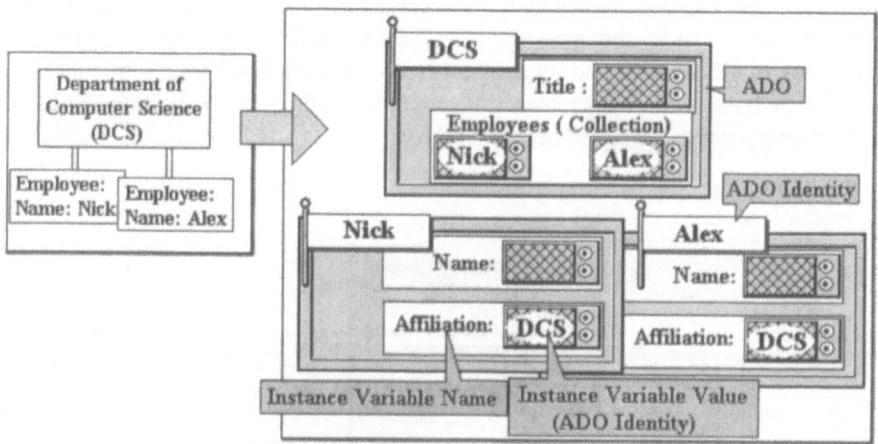

Figure 12-4 Object collection with their private memories

The schematic on the left depicts the situation we wish to represent in object-oriented terms, viz. there is a department of computer science with a collection of employees (two are shown). Each employee has a number of attributes (the 'Name' attribute is shown).

The schematic on the right depicts one possible representation, which comprises three data objects. Each object has a unique identity ('DCS', 'Alex' and 'Nick' respectively) and a private memory which contains a collection of instance variable names and their values (eg. in the ADO 'Alex', the variable 'Affiliation' has value 'DCS'). The public methods of these objects are unimportant for now and are omitted.

Note that the value of a variable is in effect a reference to an ADO, using the object identity rather than a copy of the object. This "reference semantics" of object containment means that a particular object can be referenced from within many other objects, ie. a form of re-use of data objects. Thus, each of the objects 'Nick' and 'Alex' refers to the object 'DCS' as its affiliation. The object 'DCS' in turn has both references to 'Nick' and 'Alex' in its private memory. Together, these associations capture the relationship (expressed in the left schematic) between a department and its employees.

Of course, variable names may be arbitrarily chosen. The names, in themselves, do not constrain the values they may contain and the same data object may be re-used in different variable names of different objects. So another ADO, say 'University', may have a variable named 'Departments' whose contents are a collection of references to department objects. The data object 'DCS' can then also be a value in this collection.

12.3 Methods

An ADO's methods are code that operate on its private memory in response to an incoming message. As we have seen above, private memory is a collection of other objects. Thus, a method basically achieves what it needs to do by sending messages in turn to appropriate objects in the private memory. This is illustrated below.

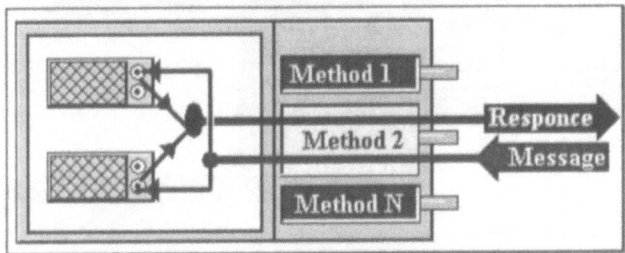

1. Method 2 is activated by an incoming message
2. It in turn invokes appropriate objects in private memory by sending each a message it puts together (possibly using values in the incoming message)
3. Invoked objects eventually return responses
4. Method 2 collects responses and compose a response that is directed back to the sender

Figure 12-5 Method behaviour

For example, suppose the 'DCS' object responds to a message 'GET_NAME', responding with a text string denoting the name of the department. This is shown in Figure 12-6.

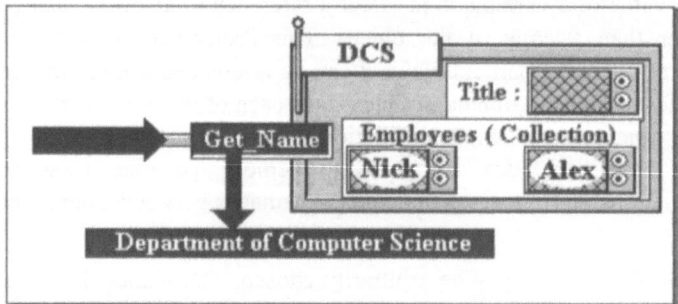

Figure 12-6 The example object 'DCS' responding to a message

Suppose further that the object 'Nick' has a method called 'WORKS_FOR', intended to return the name of the department that Nick works for. Of course, this information is contained in the object 'DCS' in Nick's private memory. So the method 'WORKS_FOR'' may be implemented by simply sending the message 'GET_NAME' to 'DCS', waiting for the response and then relaying this back to the sender. This is illustrated in the following figure.

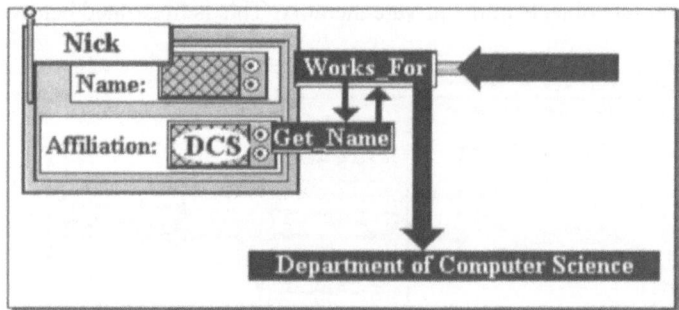

Figure 12-7 Delegating (part of) the work to other objects

If methods achieve their work by sending messages to other objects, and these objects in turn send more messages to yet other objects, and so on, when will any result be generated in response? The answer is that there are *system-defined objects* whose internal structure or method definitions are not our concern. What is important about these system objects is that they provide a number of public interfaces that guarantee a response if invoked with appropriate messages. The simplest type of system objects behave like variables in conventional programming languages, ie. they have only one variable in their memory and provide public interfaces such as 'GET_VALUE' and 'SET_VALUE' that respectively reads and sets the variable. The 'Name' variable in Figure 12-7 could presumably hold such objects.

In applying the object-oriented paradigm to databases, the ADOs are the principal units of data populating the database. ADOs may be created and once created will persist until they are explicitly deleted. They exist independently of particular user sessions, and different sessions may access or modify them.

The following illustration shows a database of three objects on the left. Assuming that the object 'DCS' was sent a 'DELETE' message, that object will cease to exist. The outcome is to remove 'DCS' from the database. Note that in this case, the consistency of the database is also maintained by removing any use of 'DCS' in the private memories of other data objects.

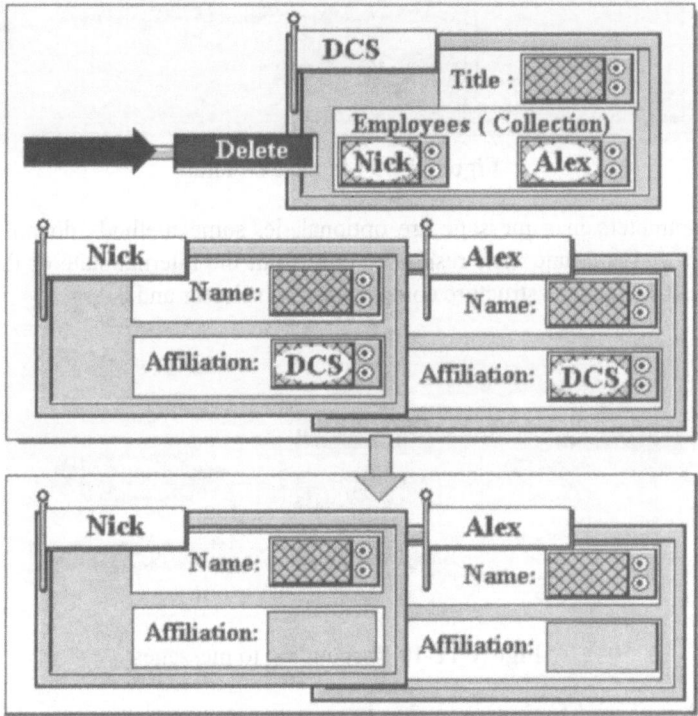

Figure 12-8 Effect of data object deletion

12.4 Messages

We have talked about messages above rather loosely. Public methods of objects must clearly be formal, however, and will only recognise messages that are appropriately structured and carrying the right sorts of data. Sending a message to an object is not unlike calling a function or procedure in conventional programming languages. So we may expect that the message must specify

1. the method name that should respond to the message, also called the 'selector' component of the message,

2. the object to which the message is directed, also called the 'target' or 'receiver' of the message, and

3. the actual parameters (of the right sorts) for the method's code to operate on. Parameters are themselves ADOs.

This message structure is illustrated in the figure below.

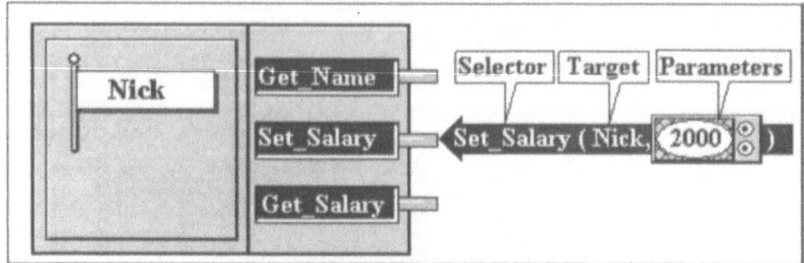

Figure 12-9 Message structure

Actual parameters in a message are optional, ie. some methods do not need input parameters and compute their responses only from the internal state of the object. In these cases the message structure comprise only a selector and a target.

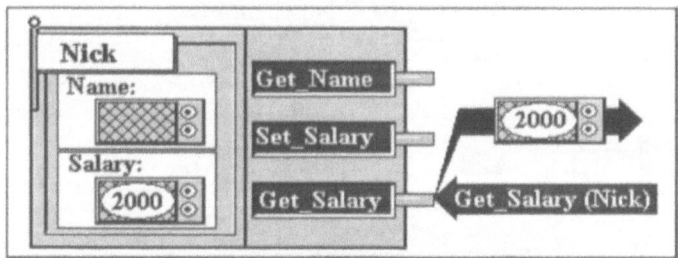

Figure 12-10 Responding to messages

A method may send back some value in response to a message, or it may not. This will depend on the problem domain and how we choose to design our methods. In the case of the "**Set Salary**" method above, no return value is necessary - only the effect of setting the '**Salary**' value is important. A method that does respond with a value actually returns a data object. This is illustrated in the Figure 12-10. The message "**Get Salary(Nick)**" retrieves the object in the '**Salary**' variable and passes it back in a return message to the sender.

It is important to notice that since the response to a message (when there is one) is itself a data object, it can be the target of another message. In such cases, we may treat messages in much the same way as we do functional expressions, ie. a message may be viewed as a function denoting a data object and can therefore be used where a data object is a valid expression. For example, assuming that "**Print**" is a public method of the data object "**2000**" in the above example, then the following is a valid message:

Print(Get-Salary(Nick))

That is, the message "Get-Salary(Nick)" evaluates to the value returned, which is the data object "2000", which then becomes the receiver of the message with selector "Print".

12.5 Summary

We have introduced :

1. ADOs as principal components of an object-oriented database. Each ADO has an identity, its own private memory and responds to a number of messages. A message is always directed to a particular ADO and is in effect a request to carry out one of its operations.

2. The public interface of an ADO is the set of operations or methods that may be invoked through sending appropriately structured messages to it.

3. A method is some code that prescribes the processing to be undertaken when it is invoked by an incoming message. This processing will typically involve sending further messages to data objects in private memory.

4. A system object is a pre-defined ADO. Its internal memory structure or methods definitions are hidden and unimportant to us. They are otherwise like any user-defined ADO and may be used by application-specific objects.

Unlike relational databases, the data structures of objects in an object-oriented database are encapsulated (hidden) and cannot be manipulated directly by generalised procedures. This is because generalised procedures are only possible if the data structure is known and uniform over all objects, eg. the relation or table in the relational model is a known and uniform structure, allowing generalised procedures such as query operations to manipulate tabular structures independently of actual contents. Instead, each ADO presents a public set of methods that operate over its private data structures. This allows great flexibility in the design and definition of objects while at the same time allows object capabilities to be shared and re-used amongst persistent objects.

ADOs are values, in much the same sense that '5' is an integer value or that a particular set is a relational value. They constitute the *contents* of an object-oriented database. A separation of structure and content may be achieved by describing *classes* of ADOs, in much the same way that a relational schema describes a set of tuples. A particular ADO will then be an *instance* of some class description, which will define the memory structure and methods common to all ADOs in the class. This will be the subject of the next chapter.

13. Data Classes

13.1 Introduction

From the discussions of the previous chapter, the basic architecture of an object-oriented database may be illustrated as in Figure 13-1 below. The persistent data of tables in the relational model is replaced by a collection of persistent ADOs, and the generalised data manipulation procedures are replaced by the public interfaces of objects.

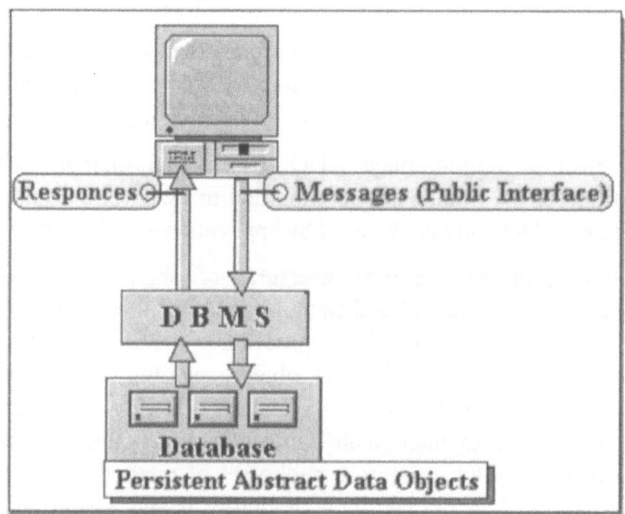

Figure 13-1 Object-Oriented database architecture

The ADO concept of encapsulating data and operations over them, however, poses a problem in the database creation. The creation of an ADO, by its nature, requires private memory to be defined and methods associated with it. But typical databases will have thousands of objects, and having to define each object individually is clearly impractical.

13.2 Data Classes

To avoid such problems, object-oriented systems introduce the concept of *Data Classes*. A data class is a description of a number of similar ADOs. In other words, each ADO belongs to a particular data class, or equivalently, is said to be an *instance* of that data class. The ADOs of a class are 'similar' in the following sense: they have in common the same public interfaces and private memory structure (see Figure 13-2).

They are not the 'same', however, because each may have different memory contents and thus behave differently in response to the same message. A data class description is therefore a metastructure description, separating structure from content, in much the same way that a relational schema was a metastructure in the relational data model.

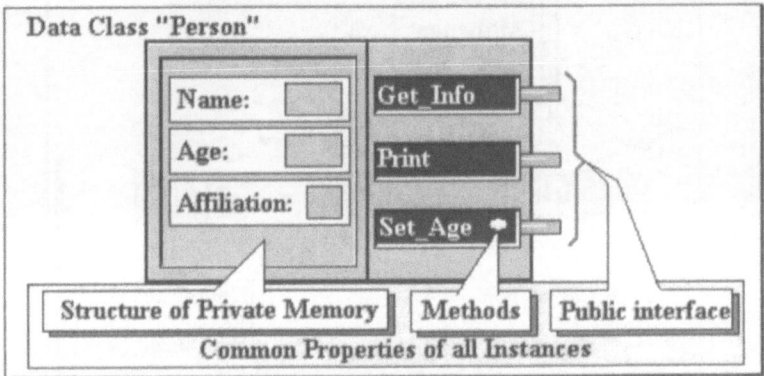

Figure 13-2 A data class

Content is introduced by creating instances of data classes. For this purpose, every data class has an implicit method called 'NEW'. In response to a message with selector 'NEW', a data class will return a unique object that has the private memory structure and methods as described by the data class (excluding, of course, the method 'NEW' itself). Subsequently, messages may be sent to such objects invoking any of their public methods to manipulate internal data (eg. insert, remove, change, etc). A data class may thus be viewed as a template, or a 'cookie cutter', or even as a 'factory' for producing ADOs (ie. the instances).

Figure 13-3 shows this role of a data class. In response to each 'NEW' message a unique instance is created. Also illustrated is the sending of the 'Print' message to the instance 'Nick' and to the instance 'Alex'. Both instances can respond to this message, since each was created in the image of the same data class description which has the corresponding method definition. The results they return, however, may be different since each instance's private memory is independent of one another.

Besides user-defined data classes, an object-oriented system typically includes a number of system classes. In fact, user-defined classes must in the end build upon system classes. We may assume that a system class, like any data class, defines a private memory structure and public methods. The private memory structure is of course hidden and inaccessible to user-defined classes and objects. What is important, though, is that instances of system classes, or system objects, may be used (through their public interfaces) by other objects.

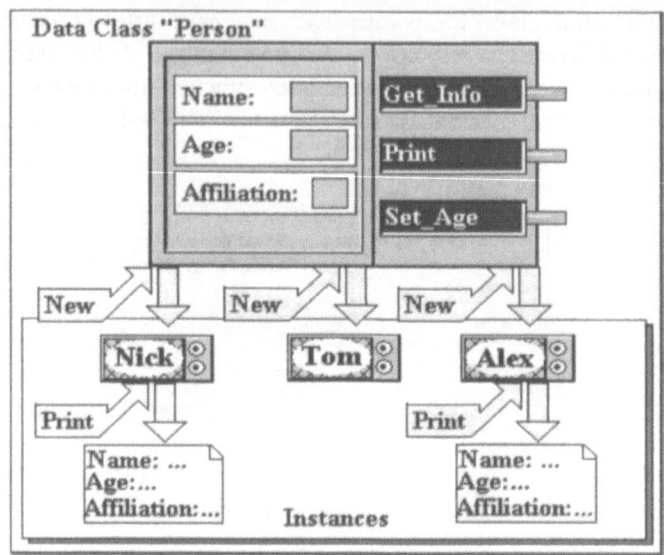

Figure 13-3 A data class and its instances

As an example, a typical system class might be the class called 'Numeric'. Instances of this class are intended to denote particular numeric values. Its public methods may include operations like 'Plus' (+), 'Minus' (-), 'Assign' and 'Get'. This class can then be used, for example, to create instances such as '25' and '31' (which we assume will carry in their respective private memories representations of the values 25 and 31). We can then form the message:

Plus(25, 31)

which is a message directed to the instance '25', selecting the method 'Plus' and providing the object '31' as a parameter. The method 'Plus', as the name suggests, will return an object that holds the sum of the values 25 and 31 (let's call this object '56'). Note that it doesn't matter, in fact, if the message was directed to the instance '31' and providing '25' as the parameter - the result will be the same, ie. 'Plus', in this case is associative like the standard arithmetic operator '+'.

Such system objects may of course be re-used by user-defined ADOs or other system objects. So, for example, we may have another numeric object called 'Age', and messages such as the following can be constructed:

Assign(Age, Plus(25, 31))

In an object-oriented database system, there are also system classes to structure data. Such classes are generically referred to as Data Structures. They will have other objects in their private memories (*members* of the structure) and typically provide public interfaces to insert new members, remove existing members and also to broadcast messages to all current members.

Let's say, for example, that there is a data structure class called 'Collection', with methods 'Insert', 'Remove' and 'Broadcast'. We may then create an instance of this class, say 'Col-1', and populate its private memory with other objects by sending it messages of the form

Insert(Col-1, Obj)

where 'Obj' is some object identity. We can also remove existing objects in 'Col-1' using messages like

Remove(Col-1, Obj)

provided 'Obj' is a member of 'Col-1'. And since every member of 'Col-1' is an ADO itself, we may of course direct messages to individual members, or using the 'Broadcast' method provided, direct a message to all members simultaneously, eg.

Broadcast(Col-1, Plus(1))

This particular message assumes that every member is a numeric object. The 'Broadcast' method will, for each member m in the collection, issue the message "Plus(m, 1)". This facility is useful when some operation is to be applied to every object in the collection (it can be seen as a special case of repetition constructs in conventional programming languages, such as for loops). Of course, the message to broadcast can be any message to which members can respond.

The method 'NEW', in addition to creating a new instance of a data class, may also initialise the private memory of the instance. The initial values, if any, are themselves ADOs and are included in the message to the data class. Thus, a fuller form of the 'NEW' message structure is:

NEW(<data class>, <var>: <value>, ..., <var>: <value>)

where <var> is an instance variable name defined in <data class>, and <value> is an object identifier.

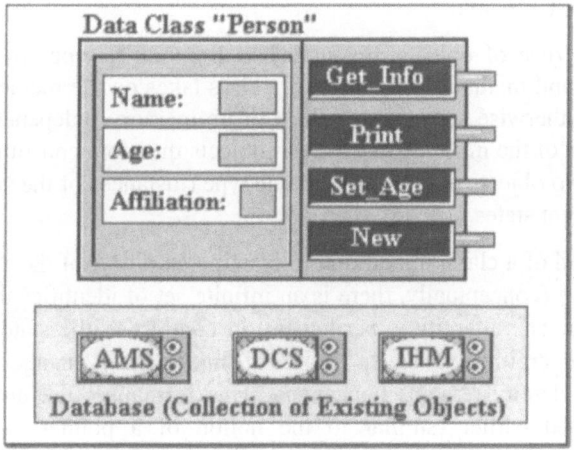

Figure 13-4 Example data class

There are basically two ways objects may be specified in the 'NEW' message. Suppose, for example, there is a data class called 'Person', and that there is already a database of existing objects with identities as shown in Figure 13-4.

Then an object identity may be specified in the <value> part of the message, for example:

NEW(Person, Affiliation: DCS)

This will result in the creation of an instance with the variable 'Affiliation' set to the object named 'DCS' .

A second method of specifying initial object values comes from noting that the 'NEW' message itself returns an object. Thus, the <value> parts of a message can be 'NEW' messages!

For example:

```
NEW(   Person,
        Name: NEW( String, "Nick" ),
        Age:  NEW( Numeric, "40" ),
        Affiliation: DCS
    )
```

We assume that 'String' and 'Numeric' are data classes that are already defined. This message will thus initialise the 'Name' variable with a new 'String' object and the 'Age' variable with a 'Numeric' object. (Note that the syntax used here is informal. It is not our intention to describe any particular object-oriented system or its specific language constructions. We are more concerned with describing concepts and features of object-oriented systems in general. We frequently turn therefore to fairly intuitive graphical notations).

The two ways of specifying objects can of course be combined in one message, as illustrated by the last example.

A class defines a *type* of objects, distinguished from other types by its particular memory structure and methods. An object of a class takes on the memory structure it describes, but is otherwise free to set values in its memory independently of other objects. The values of the instance variables of objects therefore constitute the *state* of the object. Thus two objects may be of the same type (instances of the same class) but may possess different states.

The 'NEW' method of a class, in addition to creating an object of the class, assigns a unique identity to it (conceptually, there is an infinite set of identities that the system can choose from!). This identity is *permanent*, in contrast to the state of the object which can change arbitrarily. Thus, Nick's affiliation may change in the above example, but his identity remains unchanged. This formalises the notion of object reference mentioned earlier (similar to the notion of a pointer in conventional languages). Without identity, it would not be possible to refer to objects independently of their state, and object re-use would be impossible, ie. it would not be possible to have the *same* object as the value of an instance variable in more than one object.

The distinction between identity and state, however, does not apply to objects of so-called Base Classes. These are system classes of values that are atomic, such as integers, floating-point numbers, characters, etc. Such base objects do not have memory and thus cannot have a state that can vary independently of its identity. *Its identity is its value*! Thus an integer '8' object denotes both the object's identity and its value. The state of a user-defined object will eventually be constructed from such base objects.

13.3 Definition of Private Memory

To define a data class, we must define

- A unique name for the class,

- A structure for the private memory of the class, and

- A collection of methods shared by all instances of the class

Private memory structure is defined as a *binding* of instance variable names to existing data classes. The idea of a 'binding' here is not unlike the idea of *typing* in (typed) programming languages. For example, variables in such languages are declared using constructs such as

<variable name> : <type>

eg.   x: integer;
       y: real;   ...etc

The meaning of such a declaration is that the named variable is constrained to hold only values from the specified type. Likewise, a binding is an association of an instance variable name and a data class, using declaration constructs such as

<instance variable name> : <data class name>

As a class is basically a type, the meaning of such a binding is that the instance variable is constrained to hold only instances from the specified data class. Such a binding is thus also referred to as a Variable - Domain binding.

Suppose that 'String', 'Numeric' and 'Collection' are system classes. Then the following is a definition of a class and its private memory structure (again, the syntax is notional):

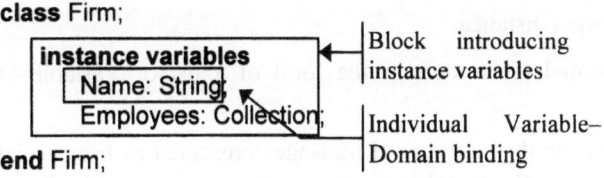

The class 'Firm' in turn can be the domain of instance variables in some other class, for example:

class Person;

    instance variables

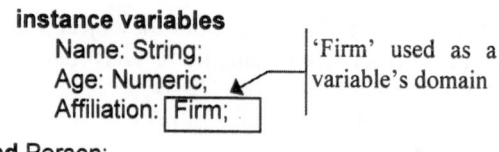

        Name: String;   'Firm' used as a
        Age: Numeric;   variable's domain
        Affiliation: Firm;

end Person;

Bindings therefore define *associations between data classes* which can be graphically depicted in Object-Oriented Data Structure Diagrams. The classes and relationships introduced by the above definitions is shown in Figure 13-5

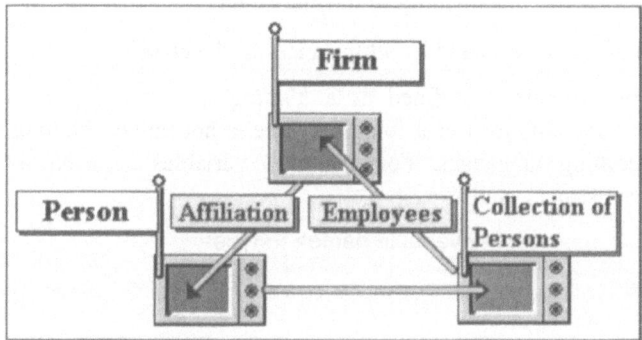

Figure 13-5 Object-Oriented data structure diagram

13.4 Definition of Methods

A method is defined by specifying

- a Message Template, and

- a Method Body

A Message Template defines the structure of messages to which the method will respond. It must include

a) a name to match the selector of an incoming message;

b) a specification of a target instance

c) a specification of formal parameters in the form of a list of Variable–Domain bindings.

The above of course mirrors the structure of messages presented earlier. Variables in the formal parameters part of the template are names that can be used in the message body (they are different from and should not be confused with the instance variables of the class). The domain parts of the bindings must be names of existing classes. Such a formal parameter list will match the parameters of an incoming message if each parameter value is from the corresponding domain in the formal parameter list. The corresponding formal variable will then be bound to that value during execution of the message body.

Suppose for the class 'Firm' above, we wish to define a method to respond to a message to add a new employee. The following then is a possible template:

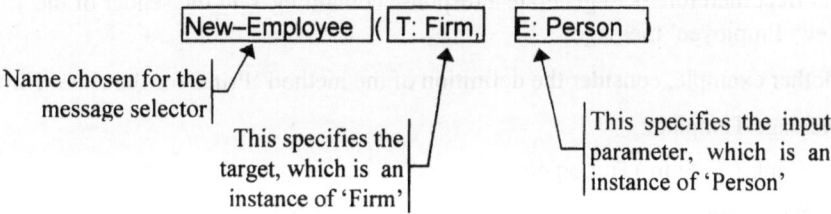

Name chosen for the message selector

This specifies the target, which is an instance of 'Firm'

This specifies the input parameter, which is an instance of 'Person'

With this template, a message such as

New–Employee (X, Y)

will be recognised and accepted by the instance X, if X is an instance of 'Firm' and if Y is an instance of 'Person'. In such a case, the formal variables T and E will be bound to X and Y respectively in the execution of the message body. Any other message structure will be rejected.

If the method also returns a value in response, the template will also specify this by writing a Variable - Domain binding after the formal parameters. For example:

New–Employee (T: Firm, E: Person) R: Logical

The binding "R: Logical" specifies the response the method will generate. We assume 'Logical' is a base system class with **true** and **false** as its only possible instances. Thus the response R will be either **true** or **false**.

The body of a method is specified as a number of message expressions involving the formal variables in the template and instance variables of the class. If a result is specified in the template, some expression must also cause the result variable to be bound to a value. Thus, for the above example, the following might be the method body:

Set (R , Insert (T.Employees, E))

This method body may be interpreted as follows:

- First, issue the message "Insert (T.Employees, E)". The target of this message is the instance found in the instance variable 'Employees' of T, which at this time is bound to the very instance that is responding to the original message. The parameter of the message is the formal variable E which at this time is bound to the instance of 'Person' in the original message.

- Assume that the response to the 'Insert' message is a logical value. That is, the method body expression is reduced to the following when the 'Insert' message responds with a value, say V:

    Set (R, V)

This is also a message that is sent to the variable R to set its value to V. The net effect therefore is to generate a response containing V to the sender of the 'New–Employee' message.

As another example, consider the definition of the method 'Print' for the class 'Firm':

Message Template:

    Print (T: Firm) R: Logical

Method Body:

    Print (T.Name);
    Broadcast (T.Employees, Print);
    Set (R, **true**)

This example underlines the object-oriented style of processing, which is based on message passing. The intention of this method is to print the name of the 'Firm' instance and all its employees. But as the latter are ADOs themselves, the processing at this level cannot directly print to printer their encapsulated information, since such information is hidden. The options at this point therefore are to collect from the objects the relevant information for printing, or to pass the responsibility of printing to the objects themselves. In both cases, messages must be sent to the objects, and the objects must of course have corresponding methods to either return requested information or to perform the printing themselves. The example above assumes that instances of 'String' and 'Person' can handle printing and thus the 'Print' message is passed to them.

13.5 Summary

A data class is a description of ADOs all having the same private memory structure and public interfaces (methods). Each ADO in an object-oriented system belongs to a particular data class and is created as an instance of that class.

A data class is defined by specifying its private memory structure and its methods. The definition of its private memory is essentially a set of bindings of instance variables to existing data classes. Methods are typically defined by messages that are sent to other objects in the system. The definition of a data class is called a *Class Definition Expression*.

We distinguish between system data classes on the one hand, and user-defined data classes on the other. The former are a part of a given object-oriented (database management) system. The latter are the results of class definition expressions, drawing on system classes and other user-defined classes, that collectively describes the behaviour (data structures and operations) of a particular database system.

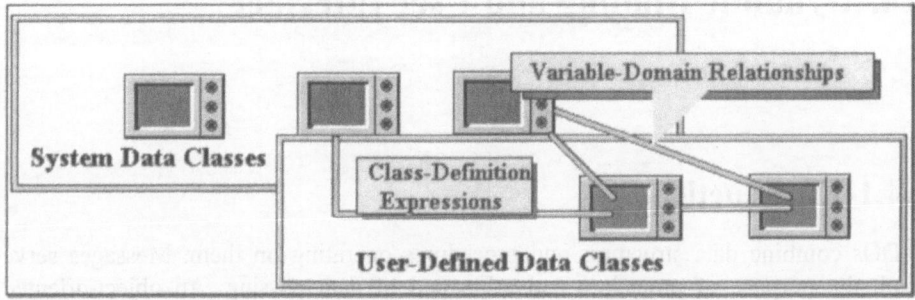

Figure 13-6 Object-Oriented database schema.

A set of data classes therefore defines all possible ADOs that can populate the system. In the context of a database system, such a set of data classes therefore forms an *Object-Oriented Database Schema*. This is illustrated in the figure above. Note that such a schema not only defines the data structures but also purpose-oriented behaviour of the system (ie. operations that can be applied to data objects).

14. Dynamic Binding and User Interface

14.1 Introduction

ADOs combine data structures and procedures operating on them. Messages serve both the purpose of procedure activation and of data passing. An object-oriented database is a collection of ADOs. A user interacts with such a database basically by sending messages to activate processing and receiving data passed back in response. This is depicted in Figure 14-1.

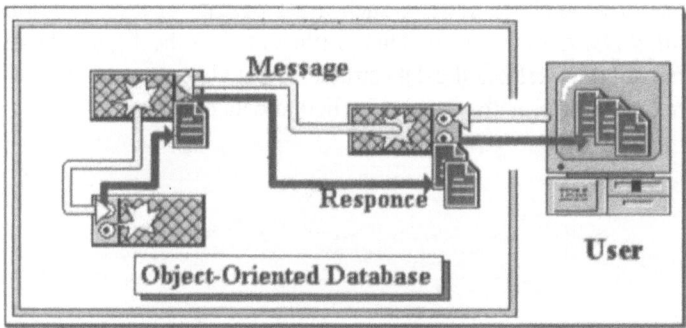

Figure 14-1 A view of an object-oriented DBMS

We have seen that data classes define the meta-structure of an object-oriented database as well as the behaviour of ADOs that instantiate them. Different applications will typically call for different data classes to be defined, ie. the data objects and their associated operations are application dependent. It is not possible, therefore, to have a standard user interface of generalised operations that is application independent. Instead, the user interface for an application must be defined in the object-oriented database schema itself. To facilitate this definition, there are special system data classes that provide some basic building blocks.

14.2 User Interface and System Data Classes

Recall that every object-oriented system includes a number of predefined system classes. A system class is one of

- a Base Class, such as 'Integer', providing base objects upon which the states of objects are eventually constructed

- a primitive Data Item, such as 'String' or 'Numeric'; unlike base class objects, these have states that can inspected or changed

- a Data Structure, such as 'Collection', 'Array', 'Queue', 'Stack', etc, used to combine other data objects into entities with predefined properties

- a User Interface, used to define application-specific user interfaces (in effect, a data manipulation language)

We have seen examples of the first two types earlier and how they are used, and in fact essential, as components of user-defined classes. A user interface system class differs in that they are designed to interact with a user, by visualising data objects or by reacting to user actions or both. Given today's sophisticated visual presentation and interactive input devices, user interface system classes typically include a set of templates for constructing graphical, direct-manipulation interfaces that are visualised on computer screens and provide for interactive user actions through various devices such as a keyboard, a mouse, a touch pad, a touch screen, etc.

For example, it is quite common to find a system class called "Push-Buttons", or something similar. The class represents objects that when visualised presents to the user what looks like a button on the screen, which he/she can then manipulate using interactive input devices like a mouse. We illustrate this in the figure below. As shown, the 'NEW' message brings a number of other objects as parameters. The Push-Button class is assumed to respond by first creating for each parameter an on-screen 3D-look button, with each button labelled with text obtained from the input parameter objects. The method then waits for the user to select one of the buttons, upon which the corresponding object will be returned as the final response.

Figure 14-2 An example of creating and visualising user interface objects

This, of course, is neither a complete nor definitive description of interface classes like Push-Button. It is only intended to outline and highlight that their effects and capability are largely to do with human-computer interaction, viz. visualising information for the user and acquiring information from the user.

The user interface objects created, such as the buttons above, are destroyed once a selection is made. This is typical of the nature of interface objects - they are discarded once they have served their purpose. Interface objects, therefore, have a transitory existence compared to the more persistent data objects in the database.

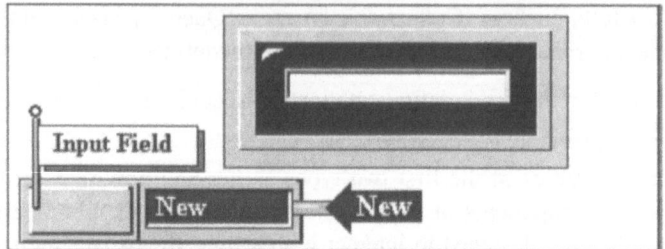

Figure 14-3 Editable fields example

Interface objects, however, may cause instances of other data classes to be created in the course of processing. This is illustrated in Figure 14-3. Here we have an 'Input-Field' interface class that, upon receipt of a (parameterless) 'NEW' message, creates an input field object that is visualised on the screen as an edit box. The field object waits for the user to finish typing text in the box, at which point the text is returned as an instance of 'String', say, while the field object itself is discarded. Note that since the response can be an object, messages to interface objects can be the target of other messages or be passed as parameters in other messages.

There are also system classes used principally for their 'side-effects', ie. their responses to messages are not so much to be found in the objects returned but in changes they cause to the environment, eg. printing information, sending electronic messages, saving information outside the database, etc. Figure 14-4 shows an interface object designed for printing. The response it generates, an 'OK' signal in this case, is largely inconsequential and intended only to inform the message sender of the status of the task.

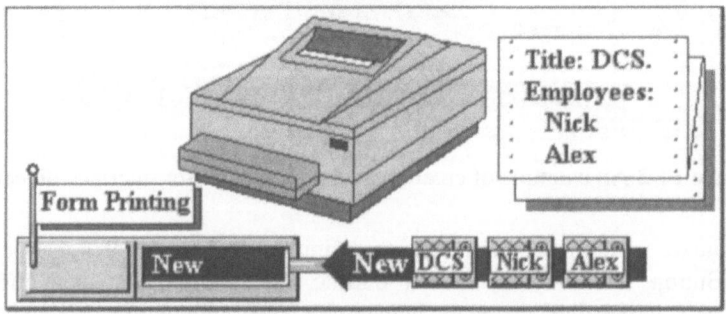

Figure 14-4 System objects with 'side-effects'

We should also note at this point that many system classes, not just user interface classes, can cause side-effects. Printing, especially, is a capability of most system objects, including data structures. That is, their public interfaces include a predefined 'Print' method that when activated will cause information they contain to be printed in some predefined format.

For example, the message

Print(New(String, "Welcome"))

will first create a new string instance containing the text string "Welcome". This new instance will then respond to the 'Print' message, causing "Welcome" to be printed and passing status data back to the message sender.

14.3 Dynamic Binding

In conventional programming languages, the name of a procedure statically defines the code to be executed, ie. it is possible to determine at compile time the code to be activated for any procedure call. Suppose for example, the following procedure was defined:

Print_Person(Name: String, Age: Numeric)
{... code–for–Print_Person ...}

The procedure name 'Print_Person' will be statically bound to

{... code–for–Print_Person ...}.

A call such as

Print_Person("Nick", 40)

will cause a procedure 'jump' to {... code–for–Print_Person ...}, after the procedure's formal parameters Name and Age have been bound to the actual parameters "Nick" and 40 respectively. Any call to 'Print_Person' will in fact activate the same code, differing only in the actual parameters passed to the formal parameters. This is true even for block-structured languages that allow names to be re-used for procedures defined in inner blocks, since scoping rules in such languages allow references to names to be resolved at compile time.

In object-oriented systems, messages play the role of procedure calls and method selectors are analagous to procedure names. In contrast, however, it is not possible to determine statically the code to be executed for a given message. This is because the instance to which a message is directed can only be determined dynamically (at run-time) and the code associated with the specified selector is likely to be different for objects from different classes.

Suppose for example, there were two classes 'Employee' and 'Student', each with the method 'Print' defined in its public interface. Suppose further that "Nick" and "Alex" are instances of 'Employee' and 'Student' respectively.

The messages:

Print("Nick"), and
Print("Alex")

while having the same method selector, will execute different code - that defined in the class 'Employee' for the former, and 'Student' for the latter.

The reader may have noted that the class of an instance expression can be statically determined, eg. a message like 'New(<class>, ...)' clearly identifies the class and thus any message with this expression as its target determines the methods (and code) to be activated. Furthermore, instance variables are bound to data classes, and a message template specifies the data class of its response, again suggesting that we can tell the classes of objects we are dealing with statically. This is true, of course, but object-oriented systems also support inheritance and polymorphism. That is, the actual objects may be instances of derived classes that redefine code for some or all of the methods inherited. It is not possible therefore to determine the method to invoke until run-time. We will treat inheritance in the next chapter, but for now, we will simply re-assert that the binding of a method name to execution code is dynamic.

The dynamic binding property of object-oriented systems increases their flexibility enormously. For example, the definition of a method in a class does not become overly dependent on the domain bindings of instance variables, as long as the specified domains offer (at least) the same public interfaces used in the method body. This is illustrated in Figure 14-5 which shows the definition of a 'Print' method for the class 'Bank-Account'. Note that the body of the definition sends a 'Print' message in turn to the objects in the variables 'Owner' and 'Sum_Available'. As long as these objects can respond to such a message, it doesn't matter what classes they belong to, ie. we can change the domain binding of the variables without having to change the method definition! Eg. the domain of 'Owner' can be changed from 'Student' to 'Employee', and that of 'Sum_Available' from 'Dollar' to 'Numeric', and the 'Print' method will still execute correctly provided that 'Employee' and 'Numeric' can respond to 'Print' messages. Such *object transparency*, afforded mainly through public interfaces and dynamic binding, plays a very important role in object-oriented systems.

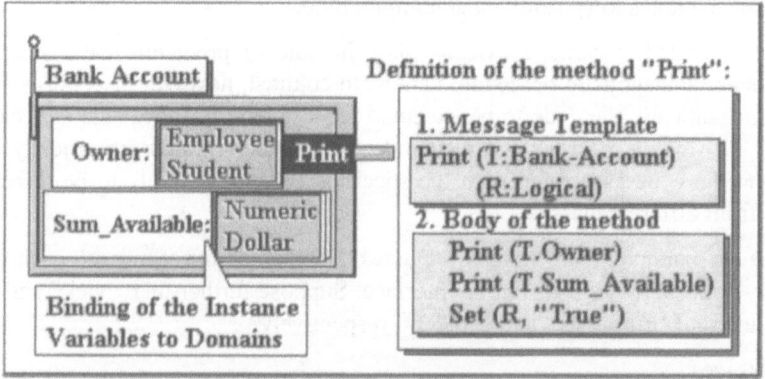

Figure 14-5 Object transparency through dynamic binding

14.4 Summary

Data associations in object-oriented databases are based on the re-use of objects in the private memory of other objects, ie. on the binding of instance variables to data classes. This is in contrast to the relational data model which manifest relationships through foreign keys in relations.

The top half of Figure 14-6 shows the familiar example of a relational schema we have used in earlier chapters. Note that the relationship between the entities 'Customer', 'Product' and 'Transaction' are captured in the latter through the shared attributes 'C#' and 'P#'. These attributes will take on, respectively, values from the corresponding attribute in 'Customer' and 'Product', serving therefore as references (or pointers) to the relevant tuples in those relations.

In contrast, the figure also shows in the bottom half a simple and direct translation from relation definitions to data class definitions - each relation corresponds to a data class and the relation's attributes are represented by instance variables. An instance of a data class then corresponds to a tuple of the corresponding relation. Note, however, that such instances are directly *re-used* in the private memory of 'Transaction' instances instead of being referenced through keys (there is thus no need for the attributes 'C#' and 'P#' in the object-oriented model and so we omit them in our translation from the relational model).

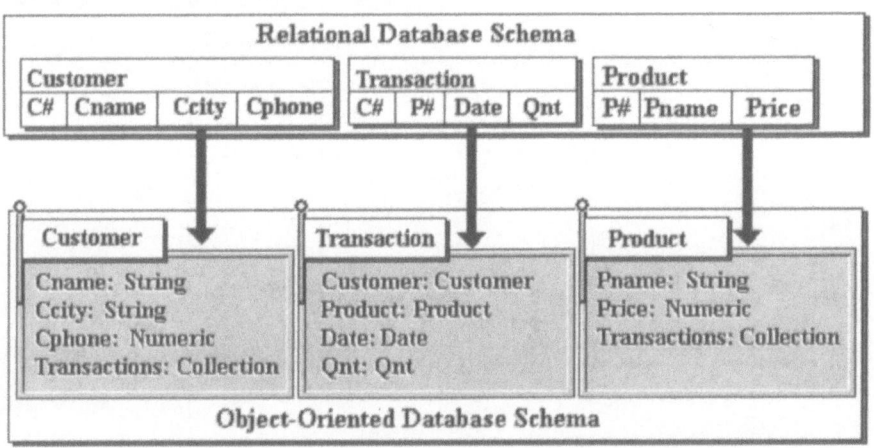

Figure 14-6 Relational vs. Object-Oriented schema

The object-oriented approach to databases offers the following advantages:

1. Level of granularity of data objects:

Methods may be defined for one data class independently of other data classes and of the overall database structure. Dynamic binding of methods provides capability (such as printing) that is object-transparent and that is resilient to changes in object relationships (such as changing variable–domain relations).

2. Re-use of data objects:

The private memories of instances allow the expression of arbitrarily complex associations among them, directly and naturally. The relational model, in contrast, often force the invention of arbitrary key attributes and values to allow relationships to be expressed through foreign keys.

3. Purpose-oriented behaviour of data objects:

Data classes may be designed to reflect the domain entities and their roles or purposes. In a real business, for example, transaction records allow us to compute the profit/loss of each transaction, or to generate invoices. These purpose-orientation is quite simply modelled by methods. The user interface, in particular, will reflect the purpose of the application at hand.

15. Static Inheritance

15.1 Introduction

Thus far, we have seen that data classes define an object-oriented schema. Such data classes are described by users using class definition expressions. A user-defined class will typically use system-provided classes (and other defined classes) to structure its private memory and define its methods. Memory is structured as a set of variable-domain bindings, allowing essentially client-server associations between ADOs, ie. an instance (the client) can call on the services of objects (the servers) that are in its private memory. The resultant database schema, and its instantiations, is therefore a 'flat' collection of objects in that all objects have equal stature and can call on any other object for services published in their public interfaces.

Many applications, however, will have entities that have similar private properties, ie. sharing many private memory structures and public methods. If the only means of structuring available were variable-domain bindings, then the description of such entities as data classes will see many similar definitions with possibly many duplicated parts.

For example, consider the data classes in Figure 15-1. All three classes have in common the instance variables 'Name' and 'Affiliation', and the methods 'Get-Name', 'Affiliation' and 'Print'. But each also has a unique instance variable and method. Given class definition mechanisms discussed so far, these classes will have to be defined separately with the common components duplicated in each definition. This is wasteful and some means of sharing common definitions while still allowing for differences is clearly desirable.

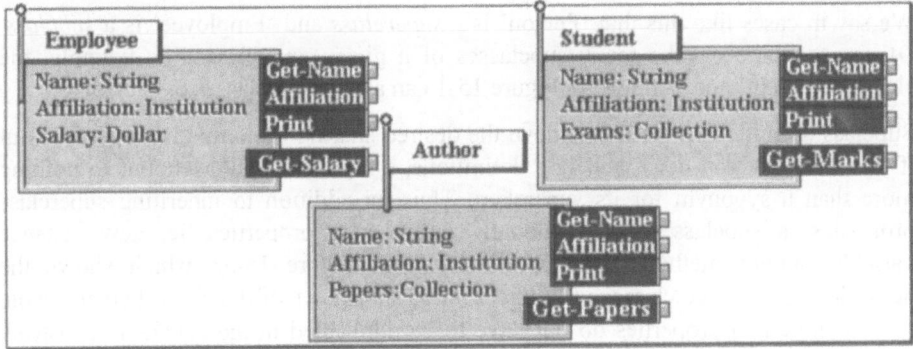

Figure 15-1 Similar classes with some common private properties (variables and methods)

15.2 Static Inheritance of Properties

Such a means is in fact found in all object-oriented systems and is called *static inheritance*. The idea is that a new data class can be defined to *inherit* from an existing class all of the latter's private memory structure and public methods.

Consider for example, the situation in Figure 15-2.

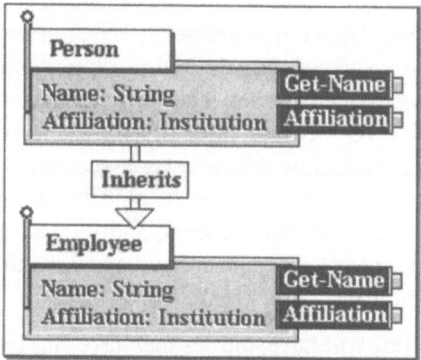

Figure 15-2 Inheritance

Assume that the class person has fully defined its instance variables and public methods. We can extend the class definition expression introduced earlier to include an inheritance specification, eg.

> **class** Employee **inherits** Person; ...

or, equivalently, depict such a definition pictorially as shown in the figure. Then all properties defined in 'Person' becomes also properties of 'Employee', even though the latter's definition makes no explicit mention of instance variables or public methods. That is, if we created an instance of 'Employee', that instance can respond to 'Get_Name' and 'Get_Affiliation' messages.

We say in cases like this that 'Person' is a *superclass* and 'Employee' is a *subclass*. Of course, there can be many subclasses of a given superclass. For example, the classes 'Student' and 'Author' in Figure 15-1 can also be subclasses of 'Person'.

Subclass definitions therefore achieve the desired sharing of common properties. But if this is all we can do in subclass definitions, a subclass would amount to nothing more than a synonym for its superclass. Thus, in addition to inheriting superclass properties, a subclass may additionally define new properties, ie. new instance variables and/or methods. This is illustrated in Figure 15-33 which shows the definition of the three classes in Figure 15-1 as subclasses of the class 'Person'. Note that the inherited properties do not have to be duplicated in the subclasses. Instead, each subclass need only define properties relevant to itself, thus differentiating itself from the superclass and from sibling subclasses.

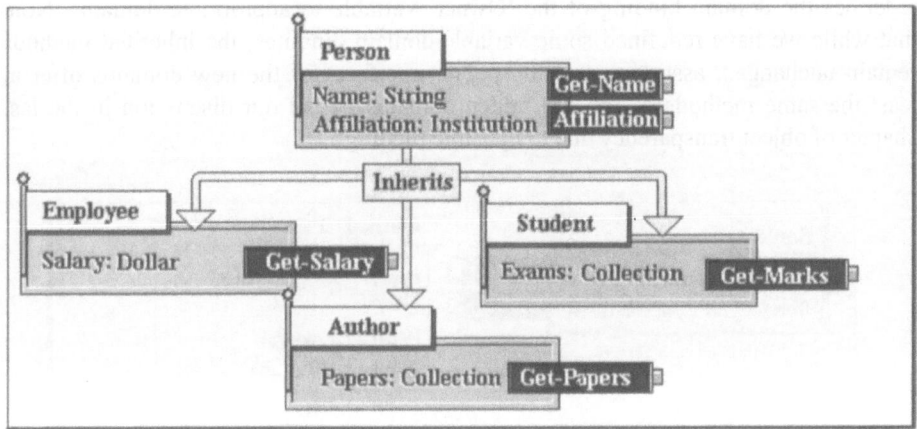

Figure 15-3 Inheritance and specialisation

Subclassing may thus be seen as *specialising* a superclass to a subset of objects that satisfy added properties. But besides adding new properties, specialisation can also involve *suppressing* and *redefining* (or *overriding*) selected properties.

Suppression discards specified properties. Say, for example, that we introduce a subclass for people who have retired and call it 'Retired_Person' (Figure 15-4). A retired person will have no affiliation and the method 'Get_Affiliation' and the instance variable 'Affiliation' are

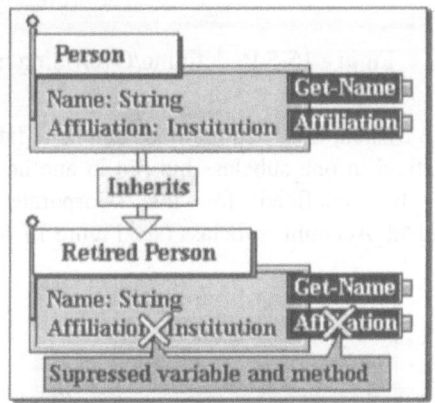

Figure 15-4 Suppressing properties

thus irrelevant, ie. we wish to inherit all properties except these. In the subclass definition, therefore, we explicitly suppress these properties. Instances of 'Retired_Person' will consequently not have 'Affiliation' as a variable nor can they respond to 'Get_Affiliation' messages. They otherwise would behave like instances of 'Person'.

There are also situations when an inherited property is not suppressed but is modified instead, ie. the names of the properties are retained but their attributes are changed. Thus, inherited instance variables may be bound to a different domain, and inherited methods may be assigned different method templates.

Figure 15-5 shows a situation when overriding the domain binding of inherited variables makes sense. For example, a student account is a bank account such that the account owner is a student, and a corporate account is also a bank account but the account owner must be a firm (company or corporate body). Each subclass therefore redefines the domain binding of the 'Owner' variable to appropriate domains. Note that while we have redefined some variable-domain bindings, the inherited methods remain unchanged, assuming that the public interfaces of the new domains offer at least the same methods as the overridden domains (recall our discussion in the last chapter of object transparency due to dynamic binding).

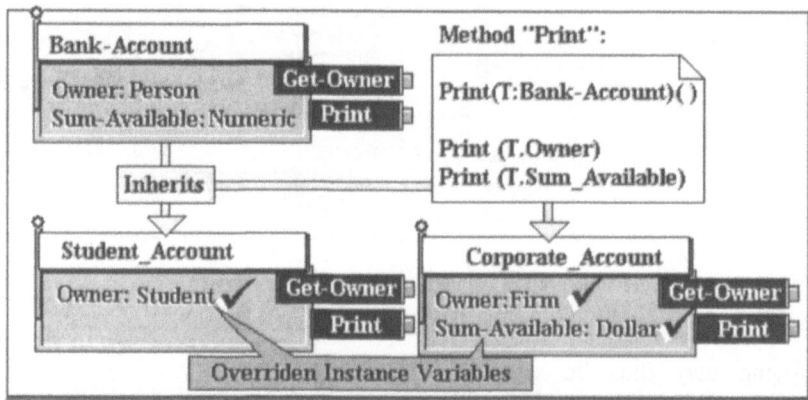

Figure 15-5 Redefining/Overriding inherited variable-domain bindings

If we wished, inherited methods can be redefined too. And we may choose to redefine a method in one subclass but not in another. For example, the 'Print' method above may be redefined for the 'Corporate_Account' subclass but not for the 'Student_Account' subclass (see Figure 15-6).

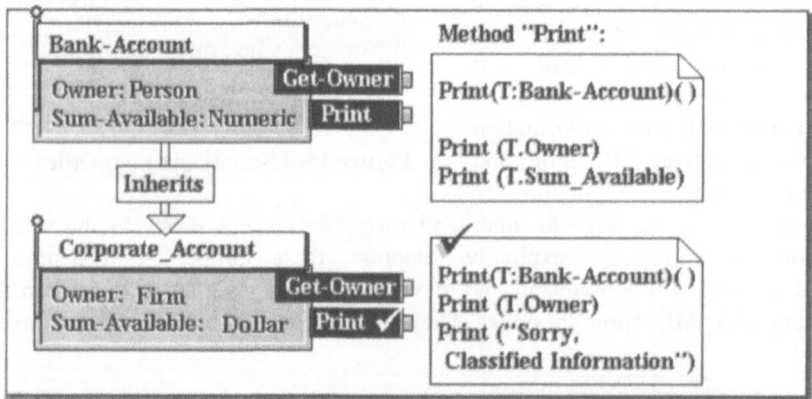

Figure 15-6 Redefining/Overriding inherited methods

Any class can be the superclass for subclass definitions, including system-provided classes. Furthermore, subclassing can be continued to arbitrary levels, ie. a subclass may itself be the superclass of other classes. For example, the 'Employee' subclass in Figure 15-3 may be used as the superclass of two new subclasses, say, 'Permanent' and 'Temporary'. Continuing in this way, an *inheritance hierarchy* of any depth can be constructed. Static inheritance therefore introduces a hierarchical structure to what otherwise would be a flat database schema.

An instance of any class in this hierarchy will have all the properties of that class, including all new properties it defines and all the unsuppressed and redefined properties it inherits from its superclasses.

It is important to realise that while two classes may be related through inheritance, their instances are *separate* ADOs. Thus, if B is a subclass of A, and I_B and I_A are their respective instances, the private memories of I_B and I_A are unrelated. That is, while both can have an instance variable named V, the value of V in I_B is independent of the value of V in I_A. In other words, inheritance is a device for sharing *descriptions* of properties among data classes - *not* the sharing of those properties among their instances.

15.3 Abstract Data Classes

With inheritance defined, a data class can serve two different purposes:

1. As a template, for the creation of ADOs that will populate a database, and

2. As a superclass describing common properties of a number of subclasses

Any data class may in fact serve both purposes within an application. However, there are situations where a data class is created solely for the second purpose above, with no intention of ever creating their instances, or that their instances would be incomplete entities and thus meaningless in the application context. Instead, instances are created only from their subclasses which presumably will describe additional properties that make them meaningful. Such data classes will be referred to as *Abstract Data Classes*.

For example, an abstract bank account can be described as in Figure 15-7. It defines a number of methods and instance variables, but the variables are not as yet bound to any domain. Such incomplete descriptions are allowed in the case of abstract data classes - the intention is for subclasses to specialise it and fill in the gaps. As such, it does not make sense to directly create instances from it.

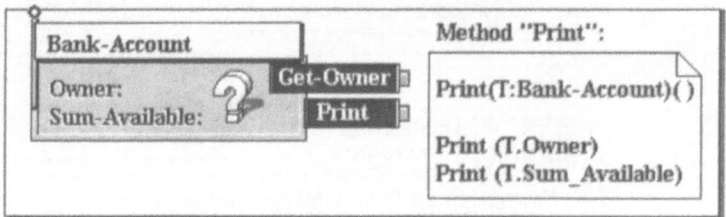

Figure 15-7 An abstract Bank Account class

From such an abstract class, we may derive more complete subclasses, as in:

class Corporate_Account **inherits** Bank_Account;

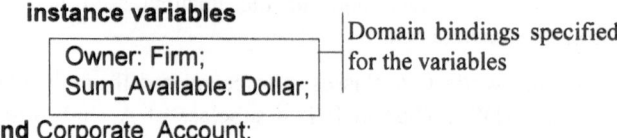

instance variables
| Owner: Firm; | Domain bindings specified for the variables |
| Sum_Available: Dollar; | |

end Corporate_Account;

The missing domains are filled in by this definition (methods are inherited unchanged). This then forms a complete class definition and instances can therefore be created from it.

Recall that a data class represents a set of objects (ie. ADOs) all having the properties and behaviour it describes. A subclass in fact denotes a *subset* of the objects described by its superclass. In other words, an object that is a member of the subclass is also a member of the superclass. We should clarify at this point the distinction between being 'an instance of' and being 'a member of' a data class. When we say that an object is 'an instance of' some class, that object was created by sending a 'New' message to that class. Obviously, it is also 'a member of' that class. Additionally, however, if the class has a superclass, the object is also 'a member of' the superclass, even though it is not 'an instance of' the superclass.

Class membership, rather than instantiation, is the basis for type checking (eg. parameters in messages, values to be assigned to instance variables, etc). In the 'Print' method definition above, for example, the expected parameter is a 'Bank_Account' object. This is actually interpreted to mean any object that is 'a member of' the 'Bank_Account' data class. Thus, any instance of a class that directly or indirectly inherits from 'Bank_Account' is a valid parameter. This is why, when we defined 'Corporate_Account', we do not need to modify the method template.

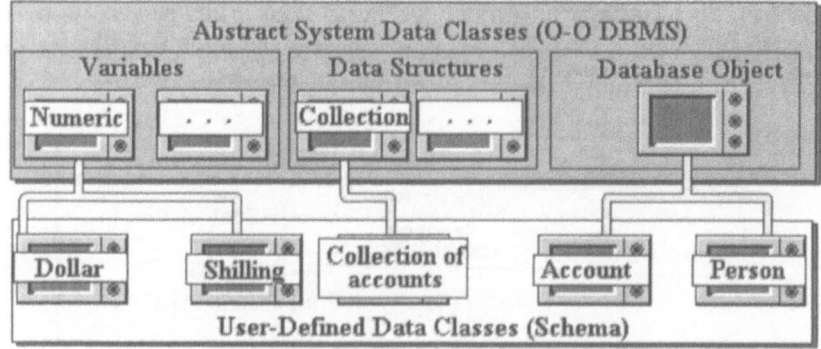

Figure 15-8 Role of abstract system classes in object-oriented databases

Abstract data classes play a very important role in object-oriented systems. Many system data classes, for example, are really defined as abstract classes. Static inheritance then allows users to derive from these abstract classes new application-specific classes. The idea of persistent database objects is in fact abstracted to a special abstract class called 'Database_Object', and all other classes describing database objects inherit properties from it, such as to store/delete an object into/from the database. This is illustrated in Figure 15-8.

15.4 Definition of an Object-Oriented DBMS

We can now define more precisely what an object-oriented DBMS is. Specifically, it is one that:

1. provides a number of system data classes designed for database creation; these include classes to define persistent database objects, to create data structures, and to create application-specific user interfaces for data manipulation

2. supports static inheritance and class definition expressions to create user-defined application-specific data classes

3. allows users to create, modify and access a database through predefined methods of the system data classes

15.5 Summary

Static inheritance allows us to define a new data class N (the *subclass*) from an existing data class C (the *superclass*) by:

a) *adopting* for N all the properties of C (ie. C's memory structure and methods), then

b) (optionally) *suppressing* in N some of the adopted properties, then

c) (optionally) *adapting* (redefining or overriding) in N some of the adopted properties, and finally

d) (optionally) *adding* in N new properties not found in C

Typically, the definition of N will include some suppression or adaptation or addition of properties (although they are optional) - otherwise N would only be a synonym for C.

Static inheritance is basically a descriptive device, allowing several classes to share the same property descriptions. Many applications benefit from this since they usually involve many similar entities that can be organised in an *inheritance hierarchy*. Static inheritance facilitates a concise and natural definition of such entities as data classes.

Some data classes are used only as superclasses, ie. no instances are ever created from them. Such classes are termed *Abstract Data Classes*. They play an important role in object-oriented systems and many system data classes are abstract. In particular, the abstract class 'Database_Object' defines many basic properties needed by persistent database objects. Users define application-specific data classes by inheriting properties from abstract data classes provided by an object-oriented DBMS.

We have largely used, and will continue to use, an informal graphical notation to express object-oriented concepts. This is because our focus is more on the general properties of object-oriented database systems rather than any specific formal system. The main notations for static inheritance are summarised in Figure 15-9.

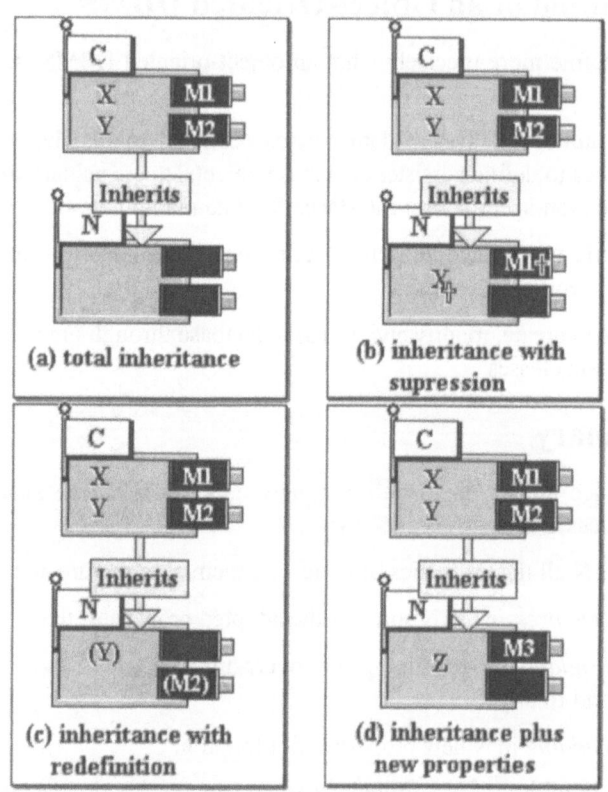

Figure 15-9 Summary of graphical notation for static inheritance

16. Dynamic and Multiple Inheritance

16.1 Introduction

Static inheritance (Chapter 15) is a descriptive device to define new data classes from existing data classes. Recall that a data class is defined by describing its private memory structure and methods (Chapter 13). With static inheritance, part of this description can be achieved by a combination of *adopting*, *adapting* and *suppressing* the memory structure and methods of an existing, similar data class - the superclass. The resultant description may also be extended with definitions of new memory structures and methods not available in the superclass.

Static inheritance extends the class definition apparatus and is orthogonal to variable-domain binding specifications of private memory structure. The latter in fact describes a relationship between instances of data classes. That is, if a data class C binds a domain S (another data class) to one of its instance variables V, it really says that any *member* of C can take any *member* of S as the value for V^1. Different members of C of course have their own private copy of V. In contrast, static inheritance expresses a relationship between data classes only, not between the private memories of their instances. That is, if C were the superclass of S, an instance of S does *not* inherit memory values from an instance of C! Their private memories are in fact independent of each other.

In many database applications, however, inheritance of memory values of one instance by another is a useful feature. Consider, for example, the database of departments and their employees. Let's assume there can be an arbitrary number of departments and each department can have an arbitrary number of employees. Each employee, however, can belong to only one department. To model this in object-oriented terms, we define two data classes: 'Department' and 'Employee'. 'Department' has the variables 'Title' and 'D_Phone' to hold respectively the name of the department and its general line phone number. 'Employee' has the variables 'Name' and 'Phone' to hold respectively an employee's name and personal extension, if any. This is illustrated in Figure 16-1 (a), which also shows some associated methods of each class.

The database itself will therefore be clusters of instances wherein each cluster will have one 'Department' instance and one or more 'Employee' instances that belong to

---

[1] Note that we use 'member of' rather than 'instance of' since this more accurately describes the semantics of variable-domain bindings (in a system that supports static inheritance and abstract data classes). Of course, the member of C, if not also an instance of C, must not have suppressed the variable V.

it (Figure 16-1(b)). Clearly, there is a relationship between an instance of employee and the instance of department. We should, for example, be able to get the department name given an employee instance. Furthermore, if the department name were to change, that change should be reflected in all associated employee instances. That is, we would like employee instances to inherit the value of 'Title' from the department instance. Static inheritance cannot do this (thus the '?' in the relationship drawn in Figure 16-1).

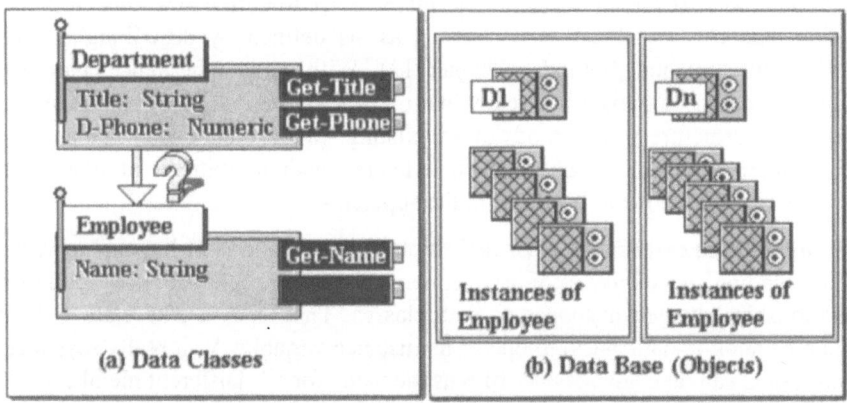

Figure 16-1 A Department - Employee database example

We can actually represent the required relationship above using variable-domain bindings, as follows. Define in the 'Employee' data class a variable called 'Dept' and bind it to the domain 'Department' (see Figure 16-2). The idea is that every instance of employee will re-use the instance of department they belong to as the value of their 'Dept' variable. To get the department name from an employee instance, we must also define a method that relegates the task to the instance held in the 'Dept' variable. Another method will also be needed to set the 'Dept' variable, say, 'Set-Dept' (not shown in the figure).

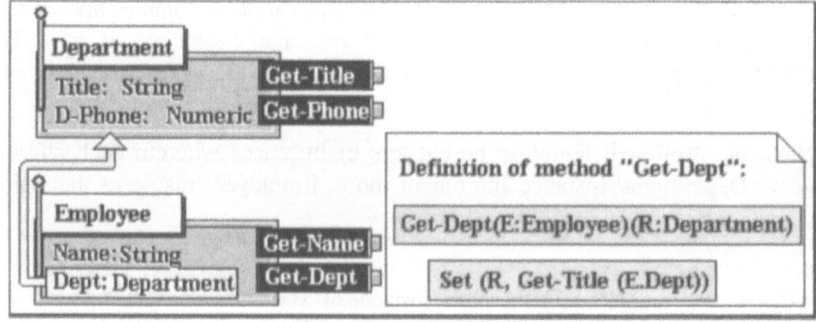

Figure 16-2 Establishing instance relationships through variable-domain bindings

Note that in this solution to the problem, adding an employee to a department is a two stage process: first, create a new employee instance, then send it a message to set its department to a selected instance of department (assuming it already exists in the database).

The solution using variable-domain bindings requires explicit 'programming' on the part of the developer. Alternatively, *dynamic inheritance* provides a way of implicitly establishing instance value and method inheritance among data class instances.

16.2 Dynamic Inheritance

Dynamic inheritance among instances of data classes are still specified at the level of data class definitions. To distinguish between static and dynamic inheritance, we will use the graphical notation as shown in Figure 16-3 to denote the latter (ie. double lines and borders as opposed to single lines and borders for static inheritance).

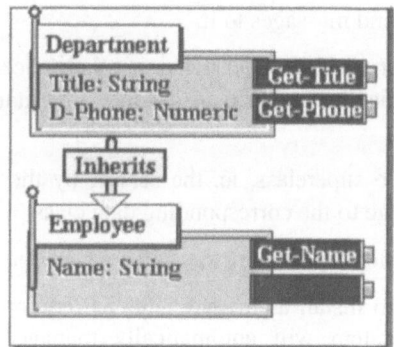

Figure 16-3 Dynamical inheritance notation

When a data class S dynamically inherits from a data class C:

a) Every instance of S will be associated with one, but not necessarily the same, instance of C. Effectively this describes the cluster organisation as shown in Figure 16-1

b) An instance of S will inherit all the private memory structure *and contents* of the C instance it associates with, unless explicitly suppressed or redefined

c) An instance of S will inherit all the methods defined in C, unless explicitly suppressed or redefined (as per static inheritance)

Thus, the definition in Figure 16-3 admits clusters of instances each of which contains a department instance and one or more employee instances. Each employee instance in a cluster will inherit the memory structure and contents of the department instance. Furthermore, each also inherits the methods defined in the 'Department' data class, except for 'Set-Phone' and 'Get-Phone' which are explicitly redefined in the 'Employee' data class.

Inheritance of the memory structure and content is best interpreted as sharing, rather than copying. Thus, if a department instance is sent a 'Set-Title' message, the new value of its 'Title' variable will be instantly available to all employee instances associated with it. In a similar fashion, inheritance of methods is best thought of as an indirection, ie. if a message to an inherited method is received, it is resent to the "super-instance". Thus we can send a 'Get-Title' message to an employee instance and receive in response the value in the 'Title' variable of the associated department instance. Note that we can also send a 'Set-Title' message to an employee instance-the effect will be equivalent to directly sending the message to the associated department instance!

In effect, the super-instance becomes a server of values and their manipulation (through methods) for the sub-instances which constitute its clients. This is similar in principle to the client-server relation established through variable-domain bindings. The difference, however, is that relations through variable-domain bindings must be explicitly installed and managed, ie. methods must be written to install a server in the client's memory and to resend messages to it.

In contrast, the client-server relation under dynamic inheritance is established at client creation time. More specifically, creating an instance inheritance hierarchy involves the following steps:

a) create an instance of the superclass, ie. the server, by the normal mechanism of sending a 'NEW' message to the corresponding data class

b) create an instance of a client by sending the 'NEW' message *to the server*!

Step (b) may be repeated to install as many clients as required for any given server. Having done this, the system will automatically manage all such client-server communication. Note that in step (b) above, the 'NEW' message is sent to an *instance* rather than a data class. This is only defined when dynamic inheritance has been specified. That is, the 'NEW' method of a subclass of a dynamic inheritance definition is relegated to *instances* of the superclass (however, see next section).

Of course, client-server behaviour does not apply to overridden properties. Thus, the message to 'Set-phone' sent to an employee instance will change that instance's memory, leaving the server memory unchanged. Likewise, 'Get-phone' sent to an employee instance will return the value of 'Phone' rather than 'D_Phone'. However, if new or overridden client methods deal with inherited instance variables, messages addressed to such variables will be resent to the server.

In object-oriented systems that support both variable-domain bindings and dynamic inheritance, the user of course has a choice over which method to use to address situations exemplified by the department-employee database. Variable-domain bindings are more general, allowing arbitrary configurations or organisations of instances. Dynamic inheritance forces a particular configuration of instances, but where such configurations are intended, it is more convenient and natural.

16.3 Multiple Inheritance

Simply put, multiple inheritance is the inheritance of properties from two or more superclasses (see Figure 16-4). In the case of static inheritance, the effect of multiple inheritance is the union of properties of the superclasses. Thus, in Figure 16-4, class C will have variables X and Y and methods 1 and 2 defined for its instances.

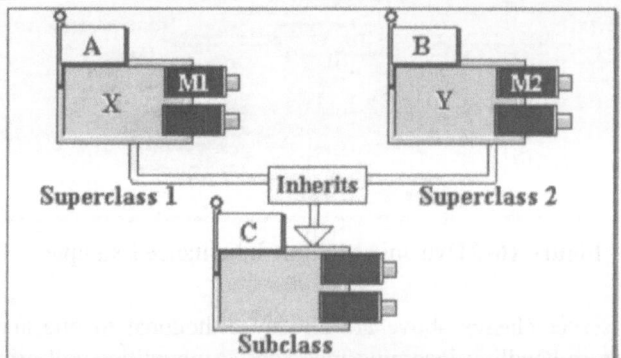

Figure 16-4 Multiple inheritance

There are obviously conditions for this to be a well-defined subclass definition. First, if a variable name appears in more than one superclass, the domain it is bound to in all its occurrences should be the same. Even then, different methods that manipulate the variable must be examined to see that they would not interfere with one another, since in the subclass there will be only one copy of the variable. On the other hand, if the variable is bound to different domains in different superclasses, it suggests they serve different purposes and often renaming the variables will remove the problem (of course, occurrences of the variable in method bodies must also be amended). Second, if a method name occurs in more than one superclass, their definitions must be examined. Even if their definitions are identical, we must ascertain that the variables they use serve the same purpose over the different classes. If not, the variables and the method name should be renamed. On the other hand, if their definitions are different, then renaming the method name may be sufficient.

These are quite complex conditions and are usually difficult to ascertain. The simplest condition to guarantee well-definedness for static multiple inheritance is orthogonality of the superclasses, ie. when they do not have common properties. For these reasons, static multiple inheritance is rarely used in practice.

Dynamic multiple inheritance, on the other hand, turns out to be quite useful and suffers less of the problems mentioned above. An example is shown in Figure 16-5. A 'Person' dynamically inherits from a 'Firm' and a 'Soccer Team'. Intuitively, this models a database of persons and, for each person, the firm he/she is affiliated with and the soccer team he/she plays for. Effectively, such multiple dynamic inheritance sets up multiple servers for a given client, and messages sent to the client will be automatically rerouted to the appropriate server. Thus, the message 'Get-Title' sent to a 'Person' instance will be rerouted to and serviced by the 'Firm' server, whereas the 'Get-Team' message will be rerouted and serviced by the 'Soccer Team' server.

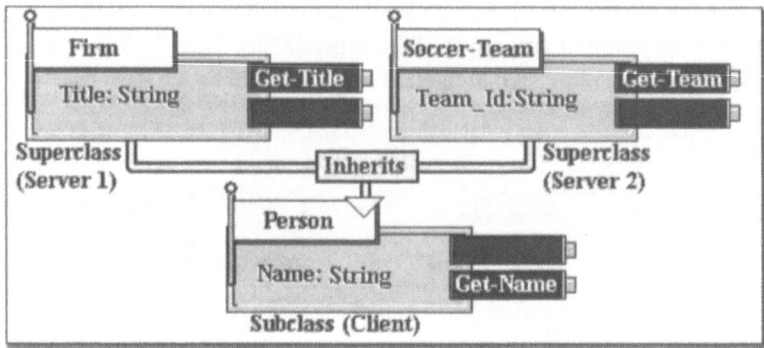

Figure 16-5 Dynamic Multiple Inheritance Example

Of course, the server classes above are already orthogonal to one another and no ambiguities arise in handling incoming messages. Ambiguities will arise only if the different superclasses have methods of the same name. But this is easily circumvented by renaming. Common variable names in the superclasses do not cause problems since they exist in their own memory space, so long as methods that operate on them are not redefined and no new methods that refer to them are defined in the subclass.

There is a slight problem, though, with regard to installing multiple servers. The mechanism of relegating the 'NEW' method of the subclass to superclass instances is not appropriate as there is more than one superclass. Different object-oriented systems may differ in how they handle this, but the essential operation is creating a client object and binding it to one or more server objects. A uniform approach, therefore, is to retain the 'NEW' method with the subclass but to include in the message template parameters that represent the servers of the client object to be created.

16.4 Summary

Dynamic inheritance allows us to describe and establish run-time relationships between instances. The relationship is essentially that of a client (an instance of the subclass) and a server (an instance of the superclass). It differs from variable-domain relationships in that it describes a particular organisation of instances - essentially clusters of clients served by a server (or more, in the case of multiple inheritance) - and that client-server communication (through messages) is automatically managed by the system. Because it deals with instance relationships, it is sometimes also referred to as *instance inheritance*.

Dynamic inheritance and variable-domain specifications of instance relationships may be used in combination. The latter, while general enough to describe any configuration of instances, may be a little too cumbersome for situations that dynamic inheritance naturally models. The choice, however, is with the user.

Multiple inheritance - inheriting properties from more than one superclass - can be applied to both static and dynamic inheritance. The complex conditions of well-formedness for static multiple inheritance, however, makes its use rare in practice. Dynamic multiple inheritance, on the other hand, is useful, offering a means of setting up multiple servers for a client.

17. Object Identity and Database Query

17.1 Introduction

In chapter 15, we characterised an object-oriented DBMS as one that:

a) provides a number of system data classes designed for database creation; these include classes to define persistent database objects, to create data structures, and to create application-specific user interfaces for data manipulation

b) supports inheritance and class definition expressions to create user-defined application-specific data classes

c) allows users to create, modify and access a database through predefined methods of the system data classes

These primary functions are depicted in Figure 17-1, showing particularly a key system data class - 'Database Object'. All database objects derive from it, ie. application-specific data classes defined by users inherit directly or indirectly from it, as do all other system classes including the data structure classes. All database objects therefore inherit from 'Database Object' some necessary methods for database manipulation, particularly the 'Store', 'Delete' and 'Get' methods.

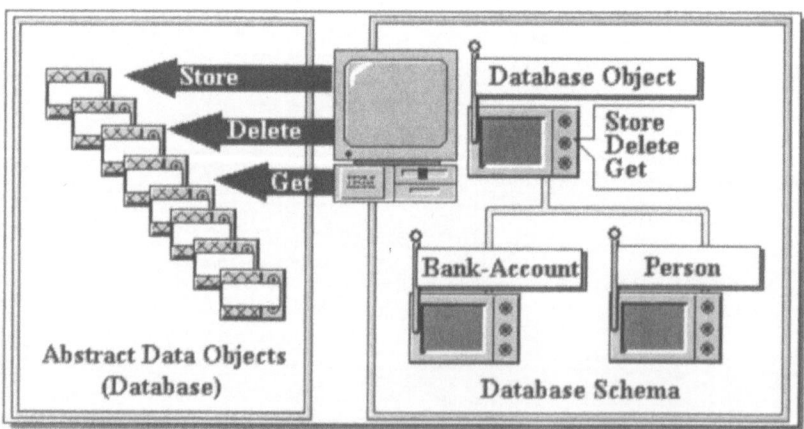

Figure 17-1 Object-oriented database creation and retrieval

It is important to realise that when an object is created, it is not automatically inserted into a database. In other words, objects may be created and manipulated during a user session without ever inserting them into a database. Such objects will be transient, however, and are discarded at the end of a session (user interface objects are mainly of this type). To be part of a database, an object must be explicitly inserted. This is the function of the 'Store' method. Once inserted, objects will persist unless explicitly removed. And this is the role of the 'Delete' method.

The 'Get' method is for non-destructive retrieval of database objects, and thus central to database processing. Its message template is:

Get (Target: Object) Response: Object

'Object' in the template above is an abstract system class that is the superclass of all classes. In other words, any ADO we create will be a member of 'Object'. Thus, the target of a 'Get' message can be any ADO whatsoever. Likewise, the response to a 'Get' message can also be any ADO.

The 'Get' message sent to a database object, returns the target object itself, which can then be manipulated in the usual way (eg. to print, to update its state, etc), and later re-stored into the database if necessary. This is illustrated in Figure 17-2. In the illustration, the target object is specified by its identity. But if we must always explicitly specify the target object identity, 'Get' would be quite uninteresting and somewhat limited in use. Database retrieval capabilities should also include implicit specifications of target objects, particularly involving *predicates over object states*. In other words, we should also be able to retrieve objects based on their (partial) content.

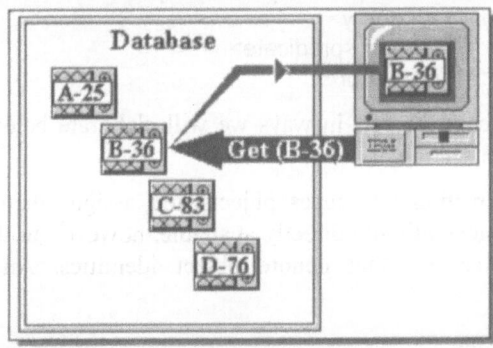

Figure 17-2 Database object retrieval using the 'Get' message

Remember that an object may be a data structure, ie. a collection of other objects. Thus it is also possible for the target and response to 'Get' to be a collection of objects. What we would really like is to send 'Get' to a collection (perhaps the entire database) and receive a response which is a smaller collection satisfying certain predicates over states of the target collection's objects. If we can do this, we can cascade 'Get' messages such that the result of one becomes the target of another, until the desired object is retrieved. This more general query facility is the focus of this chapter.

17.2 Object Identity and Addressability

Let us re-examine the anatomy of a message. Each message comprises three components:

$$S (T, P)$$

where S is a selector (ie. method name), T is the target object to which the message is directed, and P is zero or more parameters. So far in our discussion, we have assumed that T is a name that uniquely identifies some object. In most object-oriented systems, however, T in fact comprises two components:

$$T = [<scope>.] <object\ identity>$$

<scope> is a collection of objects that can potentially receive the message. It is optional and, if omitted, the implicit scope is the entire database. <object identity> specifies an object in the context of the specified <scope>. T, therefore, is a qualification expression in the dot ('.') notation that should be familiar to programmers. A qualification expression, in fact, is the general form for specifying objects, and thus applies to the parameters of a message as well. More specifically, we define qualification expressions as:

```
<qual-expr> ::= <object identity>
<qual-expr> ::= <scope>.<object identity>
<qual-expr> ::= <query>
<query> ::= <scope>.<predicate>
<scope> ::= <qual-expr>
```

<object identity> specify objects in ways we will elaborate below. <query> will be elaborated in the next section.

Recall that object creation introduces objects and assigns them unique identities. These identities are generally not directly available, however, to the user. Users must write, instead, expressions that denote object identities. An <object identity> expression can be:

- a unique global name

- local variable name

- a class name

- a message

Unique Global Name

The identity assigned to an object at the time of creation is an internally generated system identity. Many systems, however, allow users to specify (probably as part of the 'NEW' message) a unique global name/identifier to be associated with the object. User written expressions can then directly use such names to refer to the objects. We have in fact been doing this in our examples, ie. assuming a global name for objects and using them in example messages (such as 'B36' in Figure 17-2).

Local Variable Name

The use of variable names to denote objects have in fact been illustrated in numerous preceding examples, particularly involving method body definitions. By 'local variables', we mean the instance variables *and* the formal parameter names in message templates of a given class. Both types of variables hold at run-time particular object identity values. Their appearance as <object identity> may therefore be interpreted as evaluating to the object identity they hold.

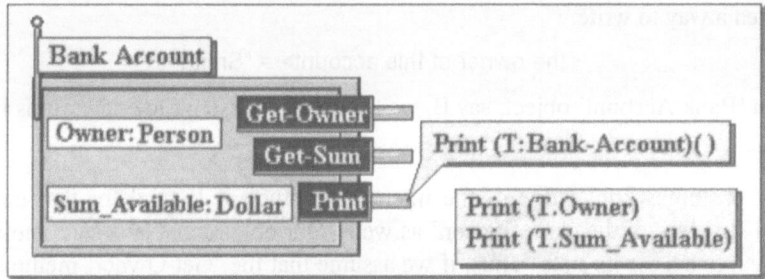

Figure 17-3 Local variable names as object expressions

Figure 17-3 shows a class with instance variables in its memory and a formal parameter variable in one of its methods. Note the target specification "T.Owner" in the method body, which uses the formal parameter variable T as <scope> and instance variable 'Owner' as <object identity>. The object it denotes is determined as follows. First, 'T' is evaluated to the object identity value it holds. Next, in the scope of this object, the instance variable 'Owner' is resolved. This simply means retrieving the value of 'Owner' in that object's memory, which then is the desired object.

Class Name

A data class name of course conceptually denotes all possible objects that fits its description. When used as an <object identity>, however, it denotes the collection of existing database objects that are its members (ie. only those objects that have been stored in the database). Thus given the class 'Bank Account' as in Figure 17-3, we can write:

Get('Bank Account')

Note that as the scope is omitted, it defaults to the entire database. This message therefore serves to select from among all database objects only those that are members of 'Bank Account' and returns them as a collection object.

Note that we say *members* rather than instances, ie. instances of subclasses, if any, are included. This means that abstract data class names can be used as <object identity> as well.

Message

We have already explained earlier how messages, because they evaluate to objects, may be used to denote objects. Thus they can be used as <object identity>.

17.3 Query Expressions

The previous section tells us how objects may be addressed, and to a certain extent we can achieve object selection through the use of class names and method invocations.

More powerful selection facilities, however, must allow selection based on object contents. For example, we may wish to select only those 'Bank Account' objects whose owner is "Smith". This suggests that we must provide comparison operators such as '=', '>', '<', etc., to allow us to write predicates over object states. We will then need a way to write:

<the owner of this account> = "Smith"

Given a 'Bank Account' object, say B, we cannot of course write expressions like

B.Owner.Name

since it presumes knowledge of the internal structure of B (and for that matter the internal structure of the class 'Person' as well). Our only recourse is send messages to the object to access its state. Thus, if we assume that the 'Get-Owner' method returns a string object representing the owner's name, we can write:

Get-Owner(B) = "Smith"

This predication applies to one object and denotes a truth value. This is the form that <predicate> takes. Now we need to apply predicates such as these to a collection of objects (the scope) to cause the selection of only those objects satisfying the predicate. The scope and the predicate together forms a query "<scope>.<predicate>".

The predicate will typically involve messages targeted at objects in scope. Since the target objects are implicit in the scope, messages in the predicate omit specifying them. Thus, selecting bank accounts owned by "Smith" would be written as in the following illustration (note that the 'Get-Owner' message does not have to specify a target):

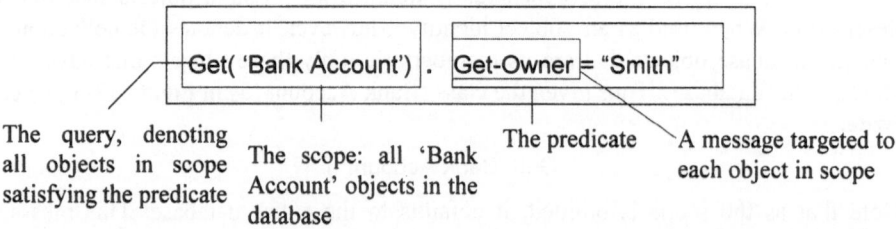

The query, denoting all objects in scope satisfying the predicate

The scope: all 'Bank Account' objects in the database

The predicate

A message targeted to each object in scope

Note that a <query> also denotes an object, specifically a collection object, and may therefore be the target of a message.

For example:

Print(Get('Bank Account'). Get-Owner = "Smith")

As further examples of query construction, assume a database populated with objects of classes in Figure 17-4. Assume further that for each class, there is a method 'Get-X' to retrieve the value of instance variable X.

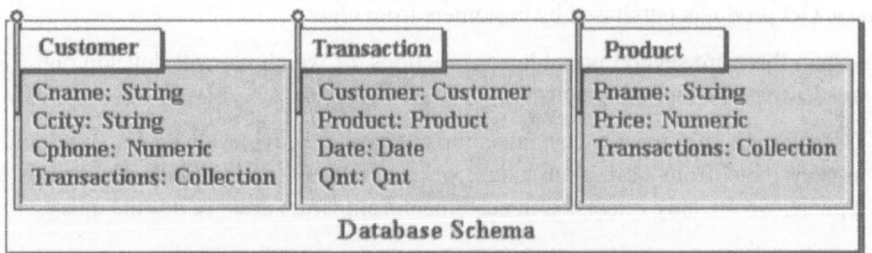

Figure 17-4 Schema for query examples (see text)

Query: Get customers who bought a CPU.

There are several ways this query can be constructed. In one, we observe that the required customer objects can be retrieved from transaction objects of CPU sales. A transaction object T is for a CPU if the following is true:

$$\text{Get-Pname(Get-Product (T)) = "CPU"}$$

The collection of CPU transactions, therefore, is represented by the query:

$$\text{Get(Transaction). Get-Pname(Get-Product) = "CPU"}$$

We can now use this as the scope to get the desired customers:

> (Get(Transaction). Get-Pname(Get-Product) = "CPU"). Get-Customer

Alternatively, we observe that product objects are associated with a collection of transaction objects. Thus, we can retrieve all the transactions for CPU from the product object for CPU. The latter is simply the query:

$$\text{Get(Product). Get-Pname = "CPU"}$$

All the relevant transaction(s), therefore, is given by:

$$\text{(Get(Product). Get-Pname = "CPU"). Get-Transactions}$$

and finally, the desired customer(s) is expressed by:

> ((Get(Product). Get-Pname = "CPU"). Get-Transactions). Get-Customer

Query: Get products purchased by customers from Graz.

Again there are several possible constructions, of which we will develop one. The reader may attempt other constructions as an exercise.

We observe that from a customer object, we can retrieve all his/her transaction objects, and from each transaction we can retrieve the product purchased. Of course, we are only interested in customers from Graz, thus we use the query:

Get(Customer). Get-Ccity = "Graz"

This then becomes the scope to retrieve transactions:

(Get(Customer). Get-Ccity = "Graz"). Get-Transactions

This, in turn, becomes the scope to retrieve the desired products:

((Get(Customer). Get-Ccity = "Graz"). Get-Transactions). Get-Product

The notation used here is not that of any particular object-oriented query language, nor is it proffered as one. We use it here only to facilitate description of the principal concepts of object-oriented queries. Real object-oriented systems frequently use more concise notations. For example, the qualification expression above might be written as:

Customer.Get-Ccity = "Graz".Get-Transaction.Get-Product

Qualification expressions are assumed to be left-associative, so parenthesis may be omitted. 'Get' may be assumed to be performed on object identities whose objects have not yet been retrieved from the database.

Finally, we note that a collection of objects is also necessarily a set (no two objects can have the same identity in the same collection). Thus, conventional set operations can be applied to them and, in particular, to qualification expressions that evaluate to collections. This allows us to handle queries such as "Get products purchased by customers from Graz or Vienna" simply as a union of products purchased by customers from Graz and products purchased by customers from Vienna:

(Customer.Get-Ccity = "Graz".Get-Transaction.Get-Product
UNION
Customer.Get-Ccity = "Vienna".Get-Transaction.Get-Product)

Similarly, queries involving conjunctions can make use of set intersection, negation can make use of set difference, and so on.

17.4 Summary

Ad-hoc query construction is not generally considered a powerful feature of object-oriented databases. The reader can see from the foregoing that queries can be cumbersome to construct and requires considerable understanding of object-oriented concepts.

More often, therefore, queries are anticipated by database developers, built into data classes as methods and provided through easy-to-use interfaces for database users. For example, the 'Customer' class may have the following method pre-defined:

```
Get-Products ( T:Customer ) R: Collection
( Set (R, Get( T.Transactions.Get-Product )) )
```

A user then need only identify a particular customer to see all the products that he/she had purchased. Other similar retrieval methods may be thus embedded into data classes to hide the complexities of database retrieval from the end-user.

Because ad-hoc query facilities are poor, greater onus is on the object-oriented database developer to anticipate uses of the database and to predefine them in user interfaces than if database systems with more friendly end-user query facilities were used.

18. Metalevel Facilities and Database Architecture

18.1 Introduction

In section 14.3 we introduced dynamic binding - the *run-time* binding of execution code to a message. Static binding is not possible because the execution code for a message selector depends on the target object and the latter is only known at run-time. 'Print' messages are good examples of the need for dynamic binding: many objects provide a public method named 'Print' but each object may define them differently; thus the code to execute the message "Print(<target>, ...)" can only be determined once the class that <target> is an instance of is known.

This turns out to be an important and vital feature of object-oriented systems. The power and economy of static inheritance would otherwise be impaired without it. It allows, for example, methods to be inherited unchanged from a superclass while changing the domain binding of some instance variable(s)-so long as the new domain can react to at least the same messages that the old domain could. This is illustrated in Figure 18-1. Note that even though the subclass redefines the domain binding of the variable 'Owner', the inherited method 'Print' remains unchanged since dynamic binding will ensure that the message "Print(T.Owner)" will invoke the right code definition. Abstract data classes, in particular, rely on this property to pass down methods to subclasses.

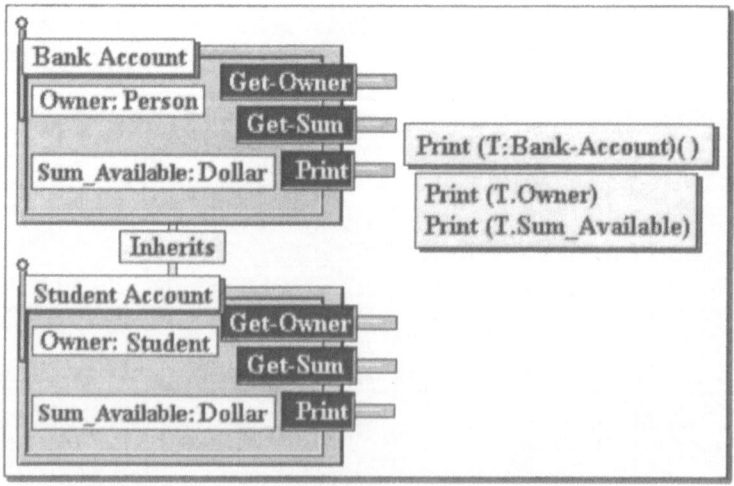

Figure 18-1 Role of dynamic binding in static inheritance

While methods are dynamically bound to messages, note that instance variables are statically bound to their respective domains when a class is defined. There is nothing wrong with this and many object-oriented systems provide little beyond this. Such systems are thus characterised by a static schema, ie. a set of data classes that do not change at run-time; only objects and their states do. When there is a need for a new data class, say a new type of account, the schema must be modified (off-line by a database administrator) by adding a new data class.

For many applications, this suffices. However, there are arguably situations that can benefit from an ability to create data classes at run-time. This would open up, for example, opportunities to write intelligent object-oriented database applications that modify their own schema to adapt to a changing environment. Thus, for the banking example above, it is conceivable that the application includes facilities for end-users to interactively define attributes for a new type of account and cause a new data class representing such accounts to be generated!

The reader might wonder at this point why we should bother with subclassing at all, if all we want to do is redefine a variable's domain, such as in Figure 18-1. Why not just make the 'Object' data class the domain of 'Owner' for example? Then any object will be a valid value and there would not be any need to subclass 'Bank Account' just to change the domain of 'Owner'! This is true of course, but it defeats the purpose of typing and of creating different data classes in the first place. Object-oriented data modelling is intended to structure the universe of objects and this means typing objects through data classes (objects with similar attributes).

18.2 Metavariables and Metaclasses

One approach to the dynamic creation of data classes is to extend the idea of abstraction to data classes themselves. That is, just as a collection of similar ADOs is abstracted or described by a data class, we abstract or describe a collection of similar data classes. Then, we can create a data class from its abstract description just as we can create an ADO from a data class.

In describing things, we distinguish between the description formalism and the things being described. The latter are said to be at the 'object-level' (the objects of description) while the descriptive constructions are said to be at the 'meta-level'. Thus for example, we may use German sentences to describe the English language, ie. German is used as a metalanguage for English. Or, as we have done in this text, we use BNF-like constructions as a metalanguage for various object-level language constructions like relational calculus. It is possible also that a formalism is used as its own metaformalism, eg. using English to talk about English sentences.

Making use of this distinction, we could have called data classes "metaobjects"-objects that exist at the meta-level and which describe ADOs. In like manner, we will call the objects describing data classes "metaclasses" (we could use "meta-metaobjects", but this gets a bit awkward!).

The particular form of metaclass we will discuss here looks very much like a data class except that the domain of an instance variable can be an identifier other than an existing data class name and interpreted as a variable that can take data class names as its value. Note that such an identifier is a variable only at the meta-level and, to avoid confusion with object-level variables, we will refer to it as a "metavariable". Given a metaclass with metavariables, the idea then is to derive from it a data class definition by dynamically binding metavariables to data class names. This approach therefore introduces a dynamic binding of instance variables to domains.

The creation of a data class from a metaclass, just like the creation of an ADO from a data class, is an instantiation process. That is, data classes are instances of metaclasses and are created in response to 'NEW' messages sent to metaclasses. Thus, just as data classes are viewed as cookie cutters or factories for ADOs, metaclasses are factories for data classes.

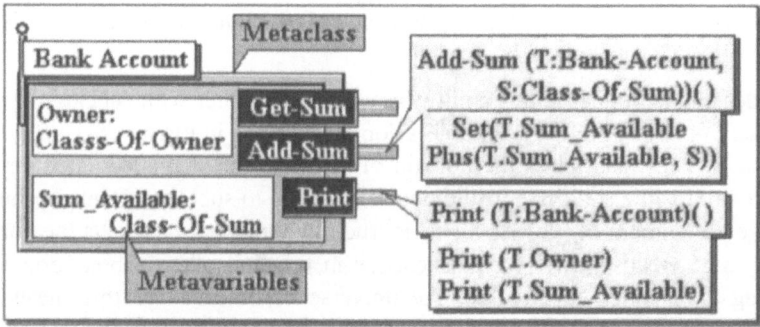

Figure 18-2 Metaclass definition

Defining a metaclass is very similar to defining a data class:

1. Define a unique name for it

2. Define its private memory structure

3. Define its public methods

This is illustrated in Figure 18-2 (assume that we have decided to make 'Bank-Account' a metaclass instead). Note two points of difference compared to a data class definition. First, the use of metavariables-'Class-Of-Owner' and 'Class-Of-Sum' are metavariables that can take existing data class names as values. Second, such metavariables and metaclass names can also be used in message templates as the type of formal message variables.

The 'NEW' message template for a metaclass specifies the binding of metavariables to class names. For example, the 'NEW' template for the metaclass 'Bank-Account' above would be:

'NEW'(Bank-Account, Class-Of-Owner: Class, Class-Of-Sum: Class, ...)
...

where 'Class' is a system-defined abstract class of classes. A 'NEW' message must therefore provide names of existing data classes as parameters. The result will be a data class definition with all occurrences of metavariables, including those in method definitions, replaced by corresponding class names in the message. For example, to create the 'Student-Account' data class, issue the message:

'NEW'(Bank-Account, Student, Numeric, ...)

The result is illustrated in Figure 18-3. Note that occurrences of metanames are replaced by data class names.

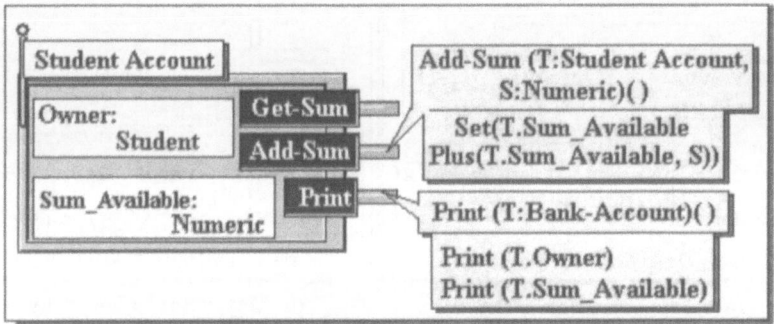

Figure 18-3 Data class created from the metaclass 'Bank-Account'

In defining metaclasses, we can use static inheritance. A sub-metaclass will inherit the super-metaclass' memory structure and methods, unless overridden, and can add new instance variables and methods. This is illustrated in Figure 18-4.

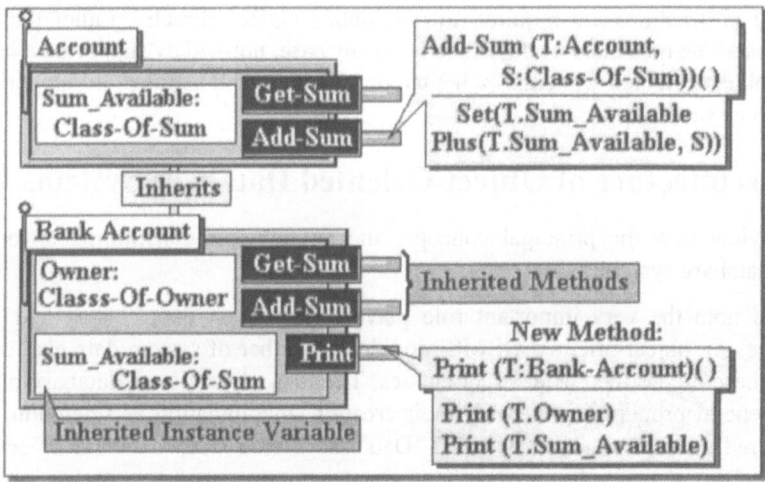

Figure 18-4 Static inheritance applied to metaclasses

Thus, an object-oriented system supporting static inheritance and metaclasses have two parallel inheritance hierarchies: a metaclass hierarchy and a data class hierarchy, as illustrated in Figure 18-5. All metaclasses inherit from the super-metaclass 'Class'. Instances of metaclasses, ie. data classes, are therefore members of 'Class' (thus the use of 'Class' as the type of metavariables in 'NEW' message templates). And as we have seen earlier, all data classes inherit from the superclass 'Object' and their instances, ie. the ADOs, are thus members of 'Object'.

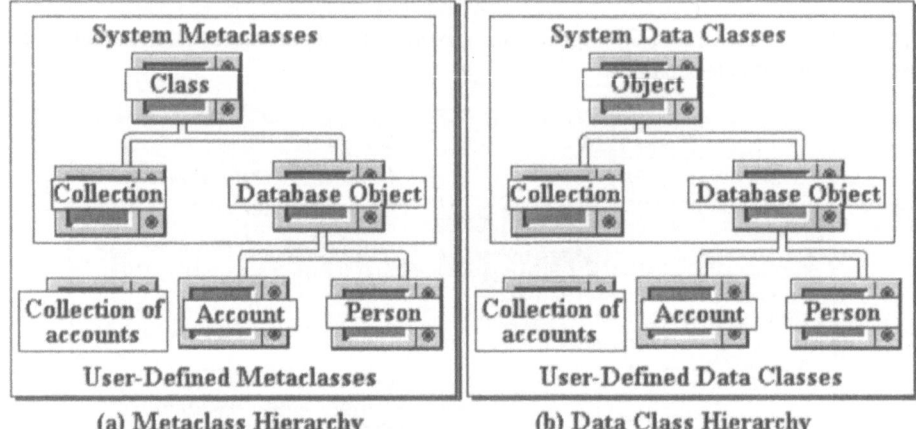

Figure 18-5 Parallel static inheritance hierarchies

In such systems, users have a choice of either creating a data class explicitly using data class expressions or creating a data class by sending a 'NEW' message to a metaclass. Generally, however, explicit definition of data classes are sufficient for most practical purposes. Metaclasses tend to be used in specialised applications where meta-level abstractions are required to manipulate classes directly, rather than just their objects. The metaclass as described is, in any case, not widely supported amongst existing object-oriented systems. Whether or not they will gain wide support still remains to be seen.

18.3 Architecture of Object-Oriented Database Systems

Let us review now the principal concepts and components constituting an object-oriented database system.

First is to note the very important role played by abstract data classes and static inheritance. An object-oriented DBMS provides a number of system data classes and many of these are defined as abstract classes. The idea of persistent database objects and the general properties governing their creation, manipulation and deletion, is in fact captured as an abstract class called 'Database_Object'. All database objects are members of this abstract class.

Users can also define abstract data classes to organise their description of an application domain. Through the power and economy of static inheritance, hierarchies of data classes leading to application-specific data classes may be defined. This is illustrated in Figure 18-6.

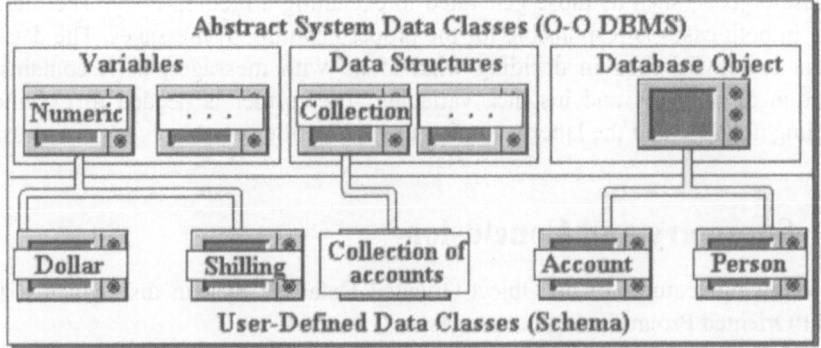

Figure 18-6 The role of abstract data classes in Object-Oriented databases

The architecture of an object-oriented database system is depicted in Figure 18-7.

The database schema defines data classes and their associations with one another. Associations may be expressed through variable-domain bindings and through inheritance (both static and dynamic). The database is the set of persistent data objects that are instances of data classes in the schema. Thus, the schema determines all possible objects that can populate the database.

Users interact with the system by sending messages to data objects and receiving their responses. The types and structure of messages and responses are predefined in the database schema, ie. the public interfaces of data classes (and their instances). The set of public interfaces therefore constitute the Data Manipulation Language (DML) of the system.

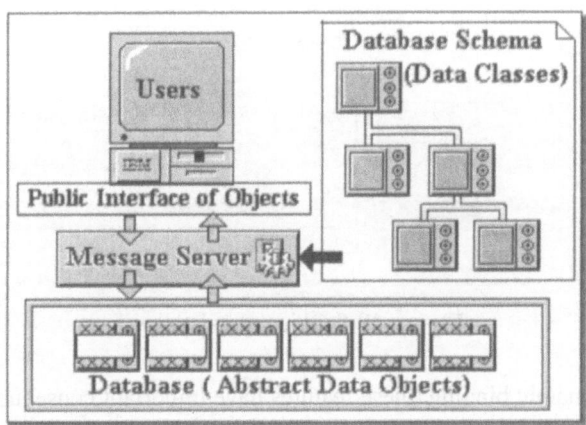

Figure 18-7 Architecture of an Object-Oriented database system

The *message server* is the component of the database system that handles external and internal messages. External messages are those that come from or go to the user, such as a query and its response. Internal messages are those generated and passed between database objects, such as those generated in executing a method body. The message server in both cases is responsible for the proper handling of messages. The database schema is heavily used in deciding what to do with messages, as it contains the definition of methods and instance variables. The former is needed to execute an incoming message and the latter is needed to get identities of objects to pass messages to.

18.4 Summary and Conclusion

The following features of an Object-Oriented Database System distinguish it from Object-Oriented Programming Languages:

1. Data Objects are persistent, exist independently of user sessions and can be shared between users (Figure 18-8 (a)).

2. Data Objects have states that can change over time and may thus react differently to the same message at different times. Figure 18-8 (b) shows an object's response to the same message, returning 'X' before and 'Y' after a state changing transaction has been applied to it.

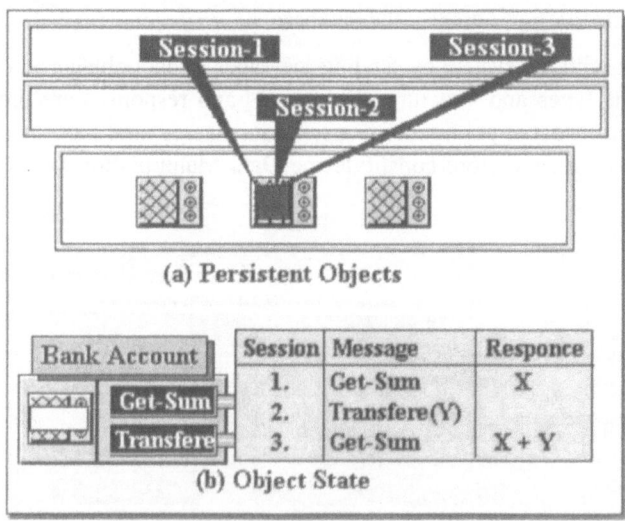

Figure 18-8 Object persistency

Coupled with dynamic binding, these features have important consequences in respect of error detection and database recovery (from interrupted or failed transactions). In databases with complex inheritance hierarchies, and particularly when those hierarchies evolve over time in response to changing or new user requirements, it is extremely difficult to fully 'debug' database behaviour. The most common fault arises from secondary messages.

For example, suppose we had the following data class:

```
class Bank-Account;
    instance variables
        Sum-Available: Numeric;
    methods
        Transfer( To: Bank-Account, Sum: Numeric, From: Bank-Account ) R:
        Logical;
        [    +( To.Sum-Available, Sum );
             −( From.Sum-Available, Sum);
             Set( R, true )
        ]
end Bank-Account;
```

A primary message such as "Transfer(A1, 50, A5)" generates secondary messages as a result of executing the body - specifically, the "+" message directed to the object "A1.Sum-Available" and the "−" message directed to the object "A5.Sum-Available". The problem is that the actual objects receiving them are only known at run-time and there is no guarantee that they can handle the messages. An object-oriented run-time system, in general, must therefore be able to detect cases where an object cannot handle a message directed to it and deal with the error appropriately.

For general programming systems, it may be sufficient to just flag the error and terminate execution or return an error code for the program to act on. For a database system, however, this is not enough. In the above example, it may have been that the "+" message was successfully executed but the "−" message failed. Just flagging the error will clearly leave the database in a logically inconsistent state! Thus, the run-time system of an object-oriented database should also have mechanisms to recover from failure and reinstate objects to their states before a failed transaction. The exact nature of such mechanisms is not within the scope of this book, but suffice it to say here that they would be similar in principle to those described for relational databases.

18.5 Further Reading

Those of you wanting a more detailed introduction to Object-Oriented databases, are strongly recommended to read [Ullmann & Widom1997]. The book is written in a tutorial style with many of the Object-Oriented issues presented through a progressive series of examples. Other books presenting Object-Oriented databases in a tutorial fashion, are [Parsaye 1989] and [Delobel 1995]. These books provide a comprehensive and cohesive presentation of object database technology that is accessible to undergraduate students. [Parsaye 1989] contains also a useful comparison of Object-Oriented and Deductive technologies.

The book [Date 1995] is very well written and presents main Object-Oriented concepts in an easy-to-comprehend fashion, but the author is a bit biased in comparison of object-oriented databases with so-called extended relational database systems which he considers to be a main stream of the current database development practice.

The books [Chorafas & Steinmann H. 1995] and [Kim & Lochovsky 1989] are not written with the novice in mind, they are more useful for people having a solid background in database systems. Actually, the books provide reviews of the various ODBMS and of current trends in object-oriented data modelling.

References:

[Chorafas & Steinmann H. 1995] Chorafas, D.N. and Steinmann H. *Object-Oriented Databases,* Prentice Hall (1995).

[Date 1995] Date, C.J. *Introduction to Database Systems* (6th Edition), Addison-Wesley Publ. company (1995).

[Delobel 1995] Delobel, K. *Databases: from Relational to Object-Oriented Systems*, Chapman Hall (1995).

[Kim & Lochovsky 1989] Kim, W. and Lochovsky, F.H. *Object-Oriented Concepts, Databases and Applications,* Prentice Hall (1989).

[Parsaye 1989] Parsaye, K. et.al. *Intelligent Databases. Object-Oriented, Deductive, Hypermedia Technologies,* John Wiley & Sons (1989).

[Ullmann & Widom1997] Ullman, J.D. and Widom, S. *A First Course in Database Systems*, Prentice Hall (1997).

Part III
Hypermedia

19. Introduction to Multimedia

19.1 Introduction

Hypermedia is an acronym which combines the words '*hyper*text' and '*multimedia*'.

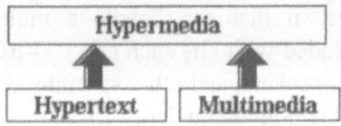

The human mind does not operate in a strictly linear manner. Our train of thoughts tend to form associations - when we think of something, we will also think of something else that is related to it. We thus jump quickly from one topic to another related piece of information. This what the hypertext paradigm offers. It attempts to model this non-linear association with information repositories. Self-contained pieces of information are linked together by natural or topical association rather than organising them in the familiar paper-based book sequential structure.

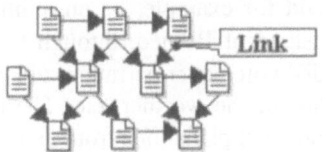

Figure 19-1 Hypertext

A book or encyclopaedia nevertheless still allows the reader to 'jump read' to the references or related topics section to find out more about a particular topic. Likewise, the hypertext technology allows the reader to move from one location to another by following the links that connect the topic of interest, only that it is much easier and faster to browse through the electronic excerpts of hypertext documents than it would be with a paper-based book. A word in an electronic document may be highlighted and when the user selects the particular word, other documents containing the related text are made immediately available to the user. More in-depth explanation about that particular topic or an associated topic will be displayed. The term hypertext however suggests that all information are in the form of basic *text*.

Multimedia, on the other hand, allows the use of information in other forms, such as graphics, pictures, sound, animation, video, etc. It unites the different media to create a single multisensory experience.

Figure 19-2 Multimedia document

A multimedia computer system that can handle a multimedia document would normally be a PC that is upgraded with kits such as a CD-ROM drive, a sound card, a video card, microphones and speakers, and other specialised devices which are needed for the computer to read CDs containing large files, produce high quality sounds, capture and replay full motion pictures, etc. The system may be attached to scanners, music keyboards, VCRs and other peripheral equipment. Multimedia technology spurs many exciting applications in the home, education, entertainment, business, government and industry.

Hypermedia has its roots in hypertext. It is an augmented (or generalised) hypertext because it incorporates multimedia. Hypermedia thus enables the user to selectively navigate through not only text, but virtually any kind of information that can be electronically stored, such as digital pictures, graphics, sound, animation and video.

A hypermedia document, could for example, be an animated tour starting from an image of a map, say of the island of Borneo, through to pictures of the rainforests there. There could be a recorded voice-over narration, video clips on places, people or animals of interest, simulations of the weather, etc. The user may click to different parts of the display to get in-depth explanations from annotated text or track a subject through a variety of topics via the links. All in all, it provides a very rich and visually compelling presentation.

19.2 Media Object

Electronic documents are increasingly being written, read and disseminated. Multimedia documents are composed with components such as music, photographs, clip art, video clips, fractals or holograms. These components are the visible manifestations of some type of data. Generally speaking, multimedia systems operate with 'media objects' which have some basic data type, i.e. a multimedia object is a homogeneous chunk of information (which we can see as a file of some file type residing in the computer's memory). The basic types being text, image, audio and full motion video, and each type will have its own way for data handling, processing, storage and retrieval. Standardisation for multimedia is very important and there exist standards (as well as propriety) for data/file formats, file interchange and video processing standards. Standards such as RTF, TIFF, MIDI, PAL, AVI, MIDI, JPEG, MPEG etc. are part of the vocabulary of multimedia developers.

Media objects can be visualised (i.e. displayed) on the user's screen using a particular procedure of *visualisation*. Very often, software packages implementing such procedures are called 'viewers'. Thus one may have a viewer to read the text of a document created by a certain word processor, or a viewer to display a facsimile transmission, or a viewer to watch the playback of a video. An object's visualization or representation may also have controls to dynamically change the object's rendering. These may include VCR-like buttons to rewind, play, fast-forward, pause or stop or sliders for the volume control of sounds.

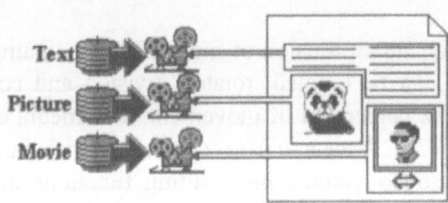

Figure 19-3 Different viewers for different media object types

Media objects are created using editing systems. The media editor is an application software to create and edit the object. Preparing a multimedia document is a non-trivial task. It is very difficult, if possible at all, to find a single system capable of creating all media objects which are needed for a more or less complex multimedia application. Normally, different media objects are created by means of different editing systems. Each editing system essentially allows the user to perform operations to create, cut, copy, paste, delete, format, merge, move and save.

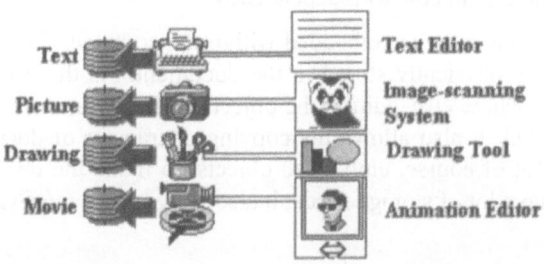

Figure 19-4 Different editors for different media object types

We are familiar, for example, with the use of a text editor such as a word processor which have features to format or style paragraphs (e.g. left justify, center, single space), style characters (e.g. font, bold, italics, underline), or even check the spelling and grammar of our text document.

There are also document image-scanning systems which allow image objects (i.e. not coded text and not with temporal properties) to be captured and then allow operations such as image scaling, zooming, rubber banding, panning, enhancement, etc. Images may also be created from drawing or bitmap paint editors that allow line or circle creation, rectangle filling with colours or texture patterns, pixel processing, histogram sliding,, spatial filtering, etc. to produce simple clip art right up to impressive works of (electronic) art. Still pictures may be captured from digital cameras or from grabbing still video frames.

Voice, music and sound may be captured from microphones, musical keyboards, cassette tapes or CDs, or WAVE file inputs. Analogue signals are converted to digital formats where they can be sampled, edited, added with special effects, or changed to a different instrument.

Animation editors can create an illusion of movement by creating a sequence of still image frames. Objects can be toggled, rotated, twisted and colour palettes can be manipulated to create the perception of movement. The media editor for full motion video usually have a TV/VCR-metaphor user interface with functions such as video capture, channel play, sound volume plus editing functions mimicking the cutting floor of a movie (e.g. multiple film strip viewed at user-selected frame rates, audio/video indexing and marking, frame level splicing, soundtrack splicing, automatic scene change detection, etc.) to produce the desired or special effects.

Having created the media objects using the various specialised media editors, these components can then be put together to compose a multimedia document.

19.3 Multimedia Documents

A multimedia document is a compound semantical unit consisting of a number of different media objects within it. Each multimedia document has an internal structure which defines a combination of media objects in it. These media objects presumably have been precaptured (and edited) independently.

The multimedia objects may be embedded within the container document itself, i.e. a copy of the object is physically stored in the document. As the original copy of the object may be somewhere else, editing the object within the container document does not affect the original. It also allows the copying or transfer of document to another computer easier. But of course, embedded objects do make the document larger and this not only uses up a lot of storage space, it also slows down retrieval.

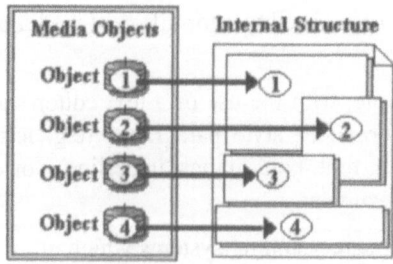

Figure 19-5 Internal representation of a multimedia document

Alternatively, a multimedia object can be associated with a document via linking,. The multimedia object itself can reside in another database, presumably a database optimised for the object's particular data type (e.g. an image database, an optical jukebox or a video server) and a link is established between the object and the document. The link reference would be a pointer to the file containing the media data object plus other information needed for object editing, display, playback, etc. This way, a multimedia object can also be shared by a number of different multimedia documents and storage use is minimised.

We shall now look at the different ways in which we can construct the structure of documents that contain multimedia data objects within them.

19.3.1 The Layout Metaphor

In the most simple case, the internal structure of a multimedia document can be defined using a 'layout metaphor' similar to pages of an ordinary book. A background text can be extended with 'tags' which mark particular places where the media objects should be displayed within the text.

Figure 19-6 Tag placements in a metaphor layout

Upon retrieval, the multimedia document is converted into a resultant image that combines all the source media objects with the specific objects displayed at the tag locations. Since the resultant document may be too big to display on the user's screen, a scrollable window is normally used to visualise such multimedia documents.

The layout metaphor has a number of obvious disadvantages. Truly dynamic media objects such as movies, sound and animation cannot be easily incorporated into a layout. It should also be noted that the layout metaphor does not provide a satisfactory user interaction interface.

19.3.2 The Scripting Metaphor

Another very popular way of defining the internal structure of multimedia documents is called a 'scripting metaphor'. A script consists of a sequence of operations and is interpreted by a multimedia system in a way that is similar to an interpretation of an ordinary computer program. The operations in the script are executed accordingly; for example, clicking on a poster frame would start a video clip.

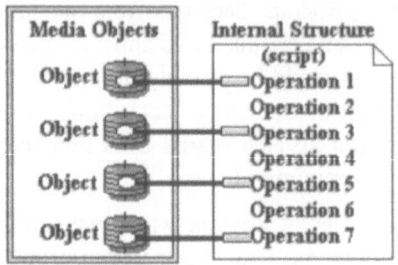

Figure 19-7 Scripting multimedia objects in a document

The script metaphor does not handle a time factor which is often involved in the presentation of multimedia materials. It does not provide a convenient way to handle two or more media objects that are operating simultaneously on the screen.

19.3.3 The Cast/Score Metaphor

Consider for instance, a simultaneous animation of a number of media objects provided with a background sound. The 'cast/score paradigm' considers all media objects to be 'actors' playing in a 'scene' or a stage. The scene is a user's screen with some background picture. The cast/score paradigm uses a *music score* as its primary authoring metaphor - the actions to be performed by actors are shown in various horizontal 'tracks' with simultaneity shown via the vertical columns. For example, a music jingle may be timed to synchronise with an animation.

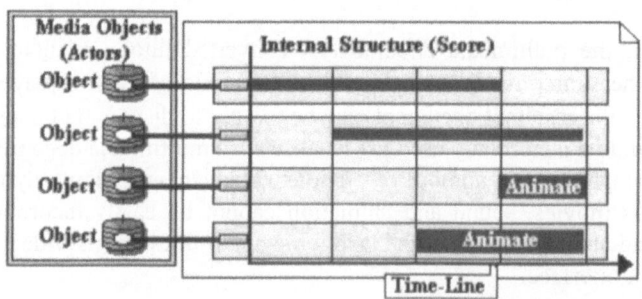

Figure 19-8 Positioning objects according to a 'score'

It is timeline-based where a specific media object is positioned on the timeline. The timeline of each object shows its start point and its duration. When played back, the objects or actors begin to 'act' according to the score. The true power of this metaphor lies in the ability to script the behaviour of each of the actors. This paradigm is best suited for animation intensive or synchronised media applications.

19.4 Multimedia Authoring

Multimedia applications, whether it is an information kiosk or an interactive game, are put together by combining and controlling the flow of the multimedia components. This is the process of *authoring*. Authoring multimedia systems can be quite complex given the variety of data objects and the degree of integration. The author, in putting together the application, must determine its scope, functionality and user interface. The author (or the group of people authoring) must plan for the overall structure of the application, create its content, design its interactive bahaviour and implement the user interface or look-and-feel of the application. Any user interface must of course be perceived by the end user to be efficient, intuitive, easy to use and responsive to the user's needs.

An authoring system is a development tool used to organise multimedia objects for end-user applications. It is a program which has pre-programmed elements for the development of interactive multimedia documents. Many authoring systems are available in the market and these vary widely in orientation, capabilities, and learning curve. How complex the system is depends on the functionality it must support and, as previously discussed, the metaphor for the representation of an internal structure of multimedia documents. The structuring metaphor can be seen as a methodology by which an authoring system accomplishes its task.

Figure 19-9 Deciding on multimedia authoring systems

Recollect that the following structuring metaphors exist:

1. Layout
2. Scripting
3. Cast/score

Dedicated authoring systems are the simplest, designed usually for the single author working on documents structured along the layout metaphor. Familiar real-world interfaces, like a VCR interface, are used and the authoring is performed on precaptured multimedia objects. However, combining different media objects can prove difficult to implement. Writing scripts provide greater power and flexibility to the authoring process. Cast/score metaphors further allow structured timeline-based authoring for more complex presentations with detailed timing constraints. Thus a multimedia authoring system should be considered for a particular application if it supports a suitable structuring metaphor, at least. Of course, there exists a number of implementations of each metaphor which varies in syntax and user-interface, nevertheless general facilities available in a particular authoring system are defined by the document structuring metaphor.

Remember however that the actual content creation of the multimedia objects themselves (graphics, text, video, audio, animation, etc.) is not generally made by an authoring system, i.e. the authoring system does not manipulate the media objects directly. For more professional output, software packages (media editors) dedicated to the creation and editing of that medium should be used. The authoring system then coordinates the sequence (navigation) in which the application progresses and which objects should be used and when to meet the user requirements of the system.

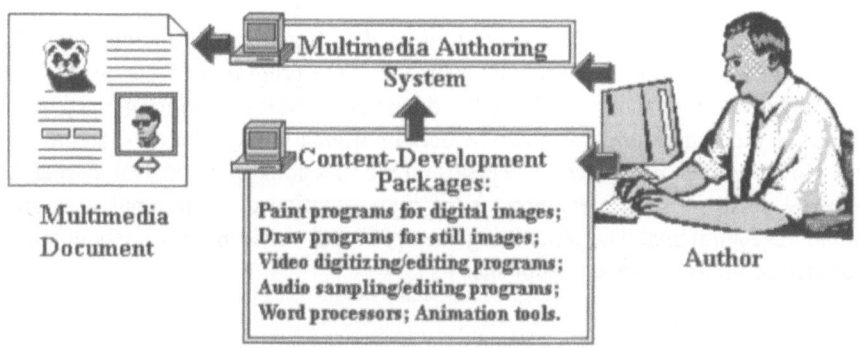

Figure 19-10 Development tools for multimedia applications

19.5 Multimedia Databases and Hypermedia

Multimedia objects are characterised, amongst others, by their large storage volume, complexity in object relationships and temporal retrieval requirements. Large multimedia objects require mass storage devices that are online (high-speed magnetic disk systems), near online as well as offline (e.g. optical disk platters/jukeboxes or tapes) to serve as repositories. Storage is often best organised to consist of servers designed for specific data types as certain storage media technologies are more suited to certain data types. For example, video objects require constant playback speed and fast caching and video servers using magneto-optical technology may be more suitable. Other servers include image servers, audio servers, voice-mail servers, database servers, etc. Objects of similar characteristics and usage pattern may of course reside on the same physical server.

Additionally, flexible access requires a high degree of data independence (i.e. insulation between the data object and the application using it). A multimedia object may contain other linked objects, (e.g. a video presentation may be a component of another multimedia document) - adding to the complexity in retrieval. Transaction management is very complex given the different media types to be handled, compounded by their distribution over multiple data servers and simultaneous access by many users. Clearly, issues of standards, data compression/decompression, document indexing, retrieval and management are issues of continuous challenge and progress.

One significant challenge is the need to organise and manage the large, complex often distributed repository of multimedia documents. Flexibility and performance are prime concerns. A number of different technologies are available, the two common ones being:

1. Multimedia databases

2. Hypermedia databases

Repository of MM Documents

Management System

Figure 19-11 Database management systems for multimedia systems

A number of existing relational database management systems (RDBMSs) now provide extensions to support multimedia data types. In addition to the standard alphanumeric data types to support textual fields(plus some limited binary types to handles date fields, etc.), RDBMS now have data items called *Long Binary Streams* (LBS) or *Binary Large Object* (BLOB) to handle binary and free-form text. The media objects can be simply embedded into the relations as data items which store the location information for the LBS or BLOB. The LBS itself would be stored on a separate image server or video server. Generally such multimedia databases are used if a structure of multimedia documents can be separated from an actual content (i.e. from the media objects).

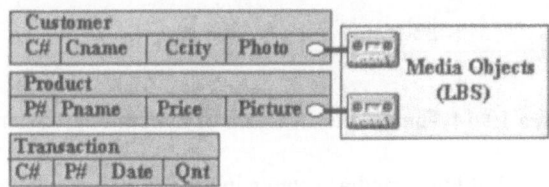

Figure 19-12 Schema of a multimedia database extended to support LBS

In other words, multimedia documents are considered to be instances of a predefined document types (i.e. templates).

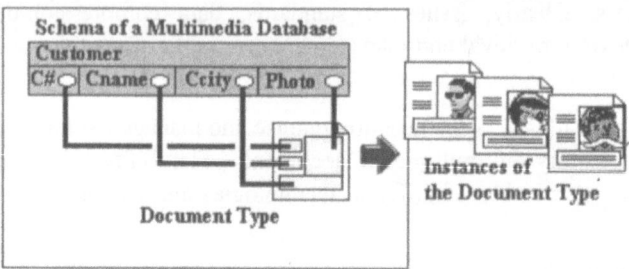

Figure 19-13 Schema, document type and instances of a multimedia database

Extended RDBMS have the advantage of the strengths of the database management systems, as in it rigorous security and integrity maintenance as well as its powerful concurrency and transaction control. However, there are shortcomings in the inability of standard SQL to manipulate the multimedia objects.

Multimedia systems utilising relational systems cannot satisfactorily handle the complexity and richness of multimedia data. These objects are not only large, but they are also created and presented in different ways and cannot be interpreted or handled as alphanumeric data, upon which relational systems were initially designed for. For example, simple attributes like the seating capacity of a car may be easily stored as a database attribute, other attributes as found in an image of the car cannot be easily represented as database attributes.

Clearly, hypermedia documents require an information model that is more complex to define the components, meanings and relationships together with the representation in the various data types. The systems must operate with multimedia documents that have their own, unique internal structures.

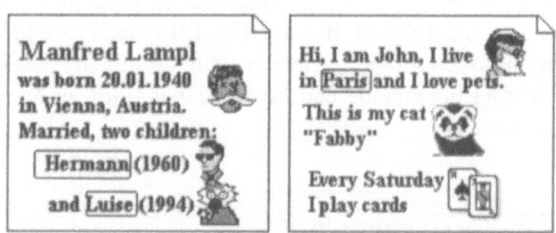

Figure 19-14 The unique structure of hypermedia systems

More will be discussed of hypermedia systems in the following chapter.

20. Basic Node-Link Paradigm

20.1 Introduction

As we have seen in the previous chapter, hypermedia allows multimedia information to be connected to one another via associative links. In a most general sense, hypermedia can be seen as a special technology dealing with big repositories that hold multimedia documents. More precisely, hypermedia deals with data structures imposed on a collection of multimedia documents.

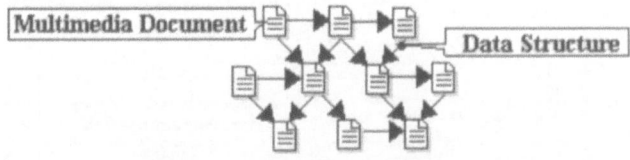

Figure 20-1 Associative links in documents

Thus, hypermedia is a special type of database. The database is not simply a bucket full of multimedia documents, but is structured, and also large, much like the information stored in most databases.

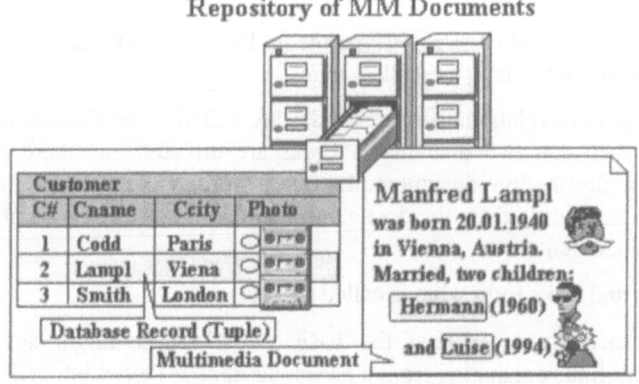

Figure 20-2 Repository of multimedia documents

Despite the fact that we consider hypermedia to be a special kind of database application, there exist a number of special features which distinguish a hypermedia application from other database applications. Thus hypermedia deals with multimedia documents which cannot be seen as normal database records or tuples having a predefined meta-structure.

Multimedia documents have their own unique, internal structure. The author of such documents controls the exact structure of the document. Thus:

1. The first important difference is that hypermedia technology does not separate structure and content of multimedia documents.

2. The second important difference between conventional databases and the hypermedia technology is that hypermedia technology does not utilise the concept of predefined meta-structure (i.e. the concept of database schema).

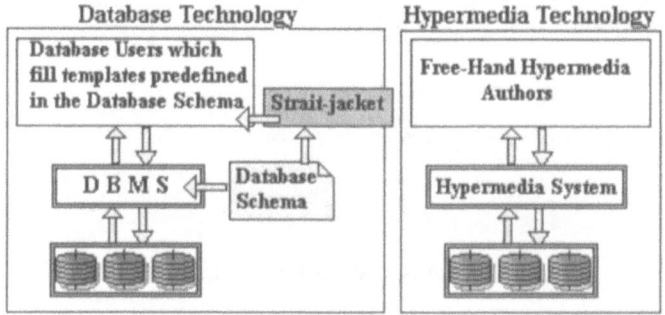

Figure 20-3 Differences database and hypermedia technologies

20.2 Node-Link Model

In accordance with a so-called 'Basic Hypermedia Paradigm', multimedia documents (i.e. chunks of multimedia data) are called *nodes*.

The cross-references or relations between nodes are called *links*. Conceptually, a link is a connection between two documents. Links are directed, i.e. there is a source document and a destination document. In other words, a document may have a number of links emanating from the document, and there may exist a number of links pointing to the document.

Together, nodes and links form what is called a *hyperweb*.

It should be especially noted that the basic node-link paradigm supposes that information on all links emanating from a particular node is stored into a database as a part of such node definition. This situation is termed as *embedded* links.

The concept of embedded links has a number of important consequences:

1. Links are unidirectional, i.e. can be traversed only in forward direction (i.e. from a source document to a destination document)

2. All links emanating from a particular node cease to exist when the node is deleted.

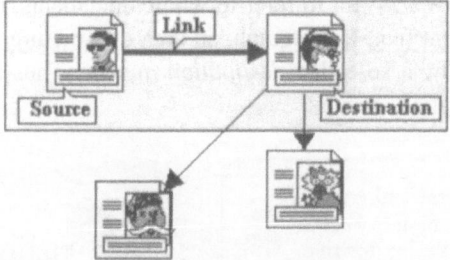

Figure 20-4 Hyperweb

20.3 Anchors

All links are therefore directed - they have a source node and a destination node. Usually the link is connected to a small portion of the source node - a word, a phrase, a picture, etc. This part is called the *source anchor* of the link.

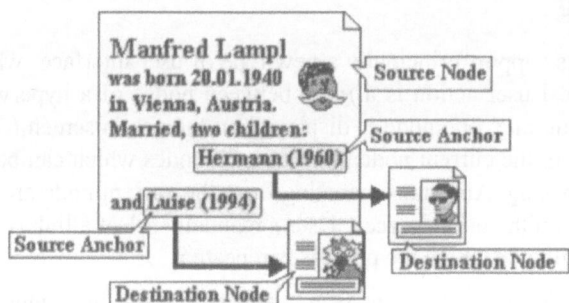

Figure 20-5 Anchors of links

Technically speaking, we can see source anchors as being human-computer interaction primitives (i.e. hot words, hot areas, etc.) embedded into a source node. Source anchors provide users with a possibility to select one of the links emanating from a node.

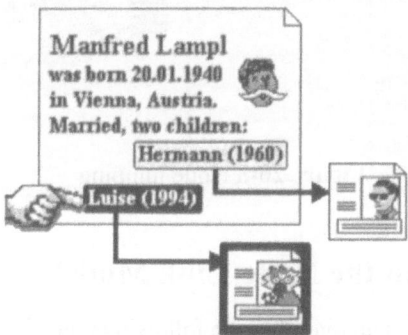

Figure 20-6 Source anchors

However, we do not always want to refer to whole documents, but rather to a part of the destination document (e.g. a paragraph, an area of a picture, etc.). This document part can be described by a so-called *destination anchor*. Thus a particular link may have source and destination anchors.

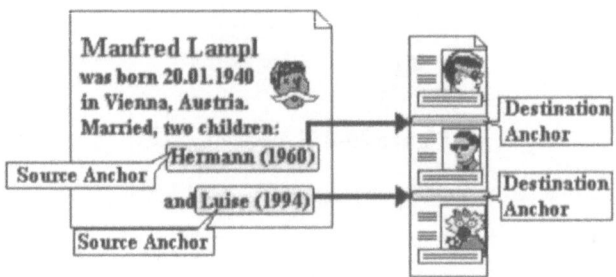

Figure 20-7 Destination anchors

20.4 Browsing

Hypermedia systems support principally a new type of user interface which is called *browsing*. The typical user action is a *jump* between nodes of a hyperweb. Thus on each step of browsing one, one node is displayed on the user's screen (current node). Links emanating from the current node point to such nodes which can be accessed on the next step of browsing. All links emanating from the current node are visualised in the form of anchors on the user's screen. User s manually select a link (i.e. anchor), to jump to a destination node where the process is repeated.

Note that browsing is rather different from typical database use, which consists of making queries that gather information elements from different parts of the database and present them together.

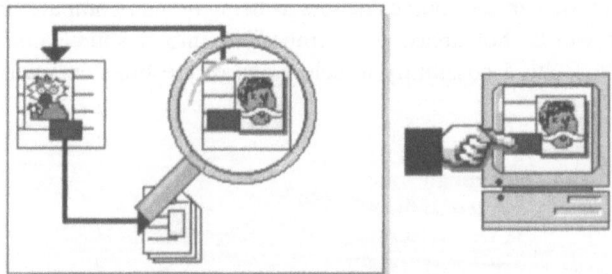

Figure 20-8 Node jumping

20.5 Problems with the Node-Link Model

Thus, the basic Node-Link paradigm has the following main features:

1. A hypermedia database is called a hyperweb which consists of multimedia documents (i.e. nodes) interrelated by means of computer navigable links.

2. Links are unidirectional, and are embedded into a source document

3. So-called source anchors are interactive elements which are also embedded into the source document

4. Source anchors are used for link visualisation and selection.

There are a number of well-known problems resulting from the simplicity of Node-Link Data Model. We can identify at least the following problems which are discussed in this section:

1. Editing of links is tedious

2. Logical integrity is not supported

3. Links are not context-dependent

4. The presence of links rapidly leads to reader disorientation ("Getting lost" syndrome)

5. The reuse of hypermedia materials is unsatisfactory

Link Editing

Consider a tiny part of the whole hyperweb dealing with an alphabetically sorted list of persons (Fig. 20-9). The documents can be accessed directly or browsed sequentially. Suppose, a new document ("information on Lampl") has to be inserted into the list. The sequence of operations are:

1) Insert document Lampl

2) Edit document List

3) Edit Next in Codd

4) Edit Next in Lampl

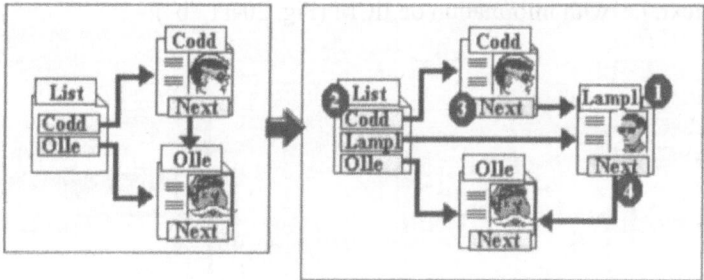

Figure 20-9 Editing Hyperweb

Logical Integrity and Dangling Links

Consider the same part of a whole hyperweb representing an alphabetically sorted list of persons. Suppose the document Lampl is deleted for some reason. All references to such a non-existent document becomes so-called 'dangling links' which point to nowhere.

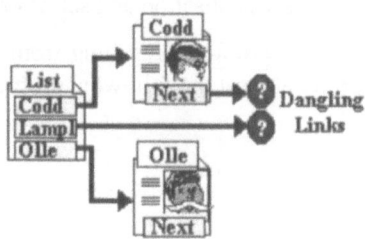

Figure 20-10 References to non-existent documents

Non Context-dependence of Links

All links of a document are present all the time. Consider two lists of persons. The documents in the first list present employees of an institution called IICM. The second list presents members of a soccer team 'Lions'. Note that two links emanating from the document 'Codd' belong to two different contexts, (i.e. 'Employees of IICM' and 'Members of the 'Lions' team) but that are presented to a user simultaneously.

The presence of links completely unrelated to the current context rapidly leads to user disorientation. Consider browsing of the previously discussed fragment of a hyperweb.

Suppose a user starts browsing from the document IICM and further accesses the 'first' employee, 'Codd' (Fig. 20-11 "a"). Now the user may well jump to the document 'Lampl' by clicking on the corresponding anchor 'Next'. It immediately leads to user disorientation since the document 'Lampl' has nothing to do with the current context, i.e. with information on IICM (Fig. 20-11 "b").

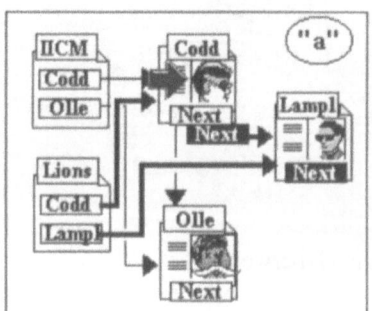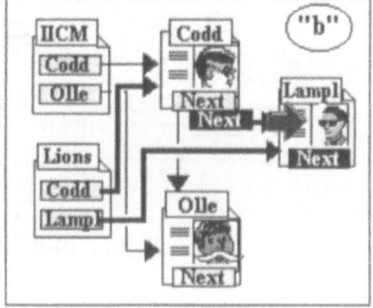

Figure 20-11 Context dependency

Unsatisfactory Reuse of Materials

The reuse of hypermedia materials is unsatisfactory because an author can refer to other documents but cannot embed them locally with possibly new or different hyperlinks. Consider the same links of persons employed by IICM. Suppose these three documents were employed by a first author, 'A'. Suppose also that another part of the database is also prepared by another author, say by author 'B'. Note that author B can refer to the documents prepared by author A. But he/she cannot reuse them as in providing with new links as desired.

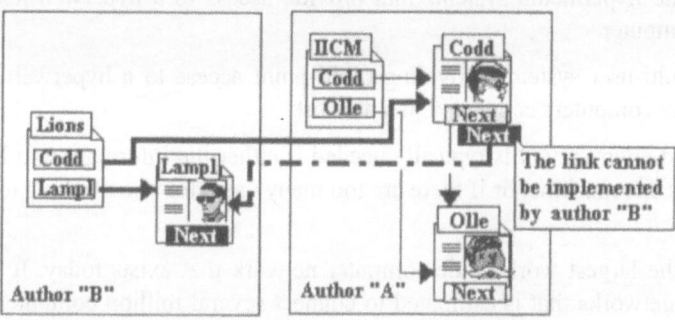

Figure 20-12 Limitation on reuse of material

21. Internet and Hypermedia

21.1 Introduction

Today's hypermedia systems can roughly be divided into two groups:

1. Standalone hypermedia systems that provide access to a hyperweb residing on a single computer

2. Large multi-user systems providing multi-point access to a hyperweb distributed over many computers connected in a network

A distributed environment is typically needed if either the information to be stored is too large for one machine, or if there are too many users for one machine to handle, or both.

Internet is the largest world-wide computer network that exists today. It is in fact a network of networks that is estimated to connect several million computers and with over 50 million individual users around the world - and it is still growing rapidly (exact figures are difficult to determine and the user would do best to use the Internet itself to find out the latest statistics about it)! Its popularity is understandable when one realises its capability for practically instantaneous communication and for sharing information across national borders and time zones. Already, it is the platform for information services covering a broad range of individual, social and economic interests from entertainment to electronic commerce. We're only beginning to exploit its potential , however, and we may expect to see it radically changing the way we work and live, perhaps in ways yet to be imagined.

Everyone on the Internet is potentially an information provider, and unless we have effective means of handling information explosion on the net, it may be turn out to be more harmful than it is useful! A number of systems and conventions have of course grown over the years, catering to specific needs and functions. Electronic mail and file transfer systems are examples of such systems which are more or less stable. The need, however, for more general mechanisms to store, organise and retrieve information and to integrate different services is becoming more pressing, particularly with multimedia entering the scene. Hypermedia systems that organise multimedia resources distributed on the net is one of the responses to the challenge.

A notable feature of the Internet is that it brings together multiple hardware and operating system platforms from dozens of different manufacturers. Clearly, communication between these different platforms would not be possible unless they agree to some way of exchanging data. The *Internet Protocols* define such data exchange schemes, comprising two kinds of standards.

First is *TCP/IP*, which is an acronym for Transmission Control Protocol/Internet Protocol. TCP/IP specifies the *data transport layer* of communication, which treats a data transaction between two computers as a stream of bytes referred to as a *transport data unit*. Simply put, data exchange between any two computers on the net is supported by TCP/IP if the data is sent in one or more transport data units (see Figure 21-1).

Figure 21-1 Transport Data Unit of TCP/IP

To TCP/IP, a transport data unit is just a parcel of bytes. The internal structure and semantics of a data unit is not its concern but that of *Internet Data Service* protocols, the second kind of Internet protocols. There are a number of such protocols, each designed for some particular purpose. There are special protocols, for example, to support distributed collaborative hypermedia systems (HTTP), Internet News System (News) and File Transfer Systems (FTP). These protocols allow the contents of messages transported in data units to be interpreted (see Figure 21-2).

Figure 21-2 Internet protocols

21.2 TCP/IP Protocol

TCP/IP was developed to connect a number of different networks designed by different vendors into a network of networks (the Internet). Thus, individual machines are first connected in a local area network (LAN). Then each LAN is connected to other LANs through one of the machines, acting as a *gateway* for incoming and outgoing messages, using TCP/IP (see Figure 21-3).

As with all other communication protocols, TCP/IP is layered:

- The IP layer is responsible for moving data packets from node to node, and

- The TCP layer is responsible for verifying the correct delivery of data

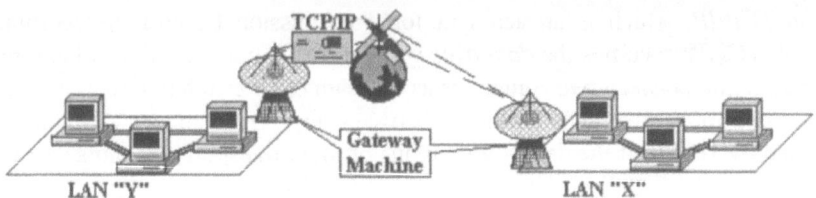

Figure 21-3 LAN Gateways

IP Addresses and Routing

TCP/IP forwards each data packet based on a 4-byte destination address, also known as the IP number. This is a globally unique address, ie. every node on the Internet is assigned a unique IP number. Of course, TCP/IP may be used in a standalone LAN - IP numbers are still required for each node in this case but they need only be unique within the LAN. More importantly, TCP/IP can coexist with other LAN protocols that may be vendor specific. In this case, IP numbers are assigned over and above any other vendor-specific network address. This allows users to have access to vendor-specific network services as well as TCP/IP-based services.

The IP number, by convention, is written as a sequence of four decimal values separated by a period ('.'). Each value is the decimal value of the corresponding byte in the address and is therefore between 0 and 255. For example, '161.142.84.168' would be a valid IP number. LANs intended to be on the Internet must apply to Internet authorities for an allocation of IP numbers. This is to ensure that IPs used are globally unique. Once allocated, the LAN owner may assign subgroups of numbers to subLANs and eventually assign individual numbers to individual nodes.

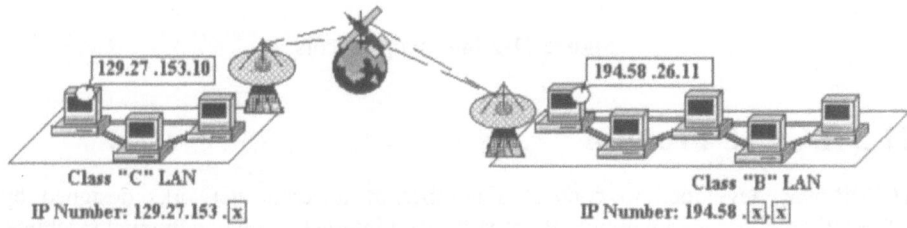

Figure 21-4 LAN classes

The structure of an IP address allows over 4 billion unique addresses. While this may already seem enormous, the Internet world is already faced with the prospect of running out of address space! This reflects, of course, the almost exponential growth of nodes on the net, particularly in parts of the world that are just discovering its potential. But the main reason is that the address space is organised into a hierarchy of domains and each domain is allocated a block of consecutive numbers. And while many numbers may not actually be used within a domain, it cannot be reassigned to other domains.

Internet authorities assign a block of numbers based on the size of a LAN. Thus, for a small so-called "class C" network, the first three bytes identify the network and the last byte identifies the node in the network, allowing for up to 256 individual nodes in the network. Larger organisations may qualify for a "class B" network, where the first two bytes identify the network and the last two allows for 65,536 individual nodes. Still larger classes are possible, for example, for an entire country.

Individual nodes, such as a personal computer or a workstation, can install TCP/IP with little knowledge of the local or regional network as a whole. First, it needs to install a TCP/IP socket, a piece of software that provides TCP/IP access (this software is available on most platforms). Next, it needs to be set up such that it is assigned:

a) a unique IP address (e.q. "129.27.153.10"),

b) a subnet mask (e.q. "255.255.0.0"), and

c) an IP address of a router (e.q. "129.27.153.1").

Once this is done, any internet application can be run on the node. Such applications will simply gain access to the net through the socket. This is illustrated in Figure 21-5.

Figure 21-5 Individual node connection

The subnet mask is used to determine if the destination of an outgoing message is intended for a machine within the LAN to which the node is connected. If so, the message is sent to it directly. Otherwise, the message will be sent to the router (which is on the same LAN) that connects this LAN to the rest of the world. It will be the router's responsibility to forward the message to the destination.

In Figure 21-5, for example, the subnet mask tells us this is a class C network (a class B network would have a mask of '255.255.0.0', but details of subnetting need not worry us here). Thus, if the destination of a message begins with a value different from '129.27.153', it is intended for a machine outside this LAN and would be sent through the router. Note that the router is part of the LAN (its IP number begins with '129.27.153').

Local, regional and central Internet routers locate destination networks by looking up a table of network numbers. There are potentially thousands of class B networks and millions of class C networks. But computer memory costs are relatively low, so the table lookup approach is acceptable. Also, not all routers need to keep the complete table - a range of entries may be entered instead for forwarding to another router that has more detail entries for that range. Thus a message can go through a number of routers before reaching its destination.

Domain and Node Names

Names would almost certainly be easier to remember than 32-bit numbers. Thus, any Internet node that has been assigned an IP number may also be assigned an official name. Names are assigned in accordance to a hierarchical schema of domains. More specifically, a domain is a collection of elements each of which is either another domain (a subdomain) or a node with an IP address. The domain as a whole therefore is a collection of IP addresses. Elements of a domain (subdomains and individual nodes) are assigned names unique within the domain. The official name of a node is the path from the node to the root of the hierarchy, written as the sequence of names on the path separated by '.'.

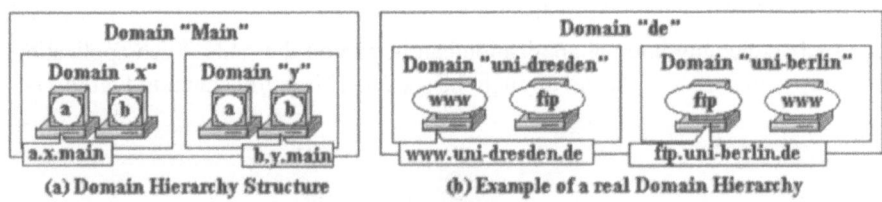

(a) Domain Hierarchy Structure   (b) Example of a real Domain Hierarchy

Figure 21-6 Domain hierarchy

Figure 21-6(a) illustrates the hierarchy structure, showing the path from one node to the root and the corresponding official name the node would therefore take. Figure 21-6(b) shows part of a real domain hierarchy. The root "de" is the domain of all nodes in Germany. Its two subdomains, "uni-dresden" and "uni-berlin" are respectively the domain of nodes in Dresden University and Berlin University. Under each of these subdomains are individual machines named "www" (presumably a WWW server) and "ftp" (presumably an FTP server). Note that uniqueness of individual node and domain names are only required within the next higher domain. Thus it doesn't matter that machines in different domains are assigned the same name. Their full official names remain unique.

Internet Name Translation

While internet names as described above are easier for us to remember and use in applications, they must be translated to IP addresses before messages can be sent out. But since names are arbitrary (often with "pet" names requested by individual users!) rather than derived according to some functional formula or algorithm, no inverse function exists to compute an IP address given a name. Names must therefore be officially registered in special tables together with their IP addresses, and the translation process must involve looking up names in such tables.

Typically, a given domain will have a machine designated as its domain name server (DNS). The table will be maintained on that machine, which will also have special software that resolves names given to it into IP addresses. The table in the DNS is usually set up such that names within the domain(s) it serves will have appropriate table entries. Such names can be resolved directly. For names outside its domain(s), the table must be set up to point to other name servers that could have the necessary information. Thus any name it can't resolve will be delegated to other DNSs to resolve. Such delegation of work is, however, transparent to the DNS client. As far as the client is concerned, it sends a name translation request to one DNS and waits for a response (see Figure 21-7).

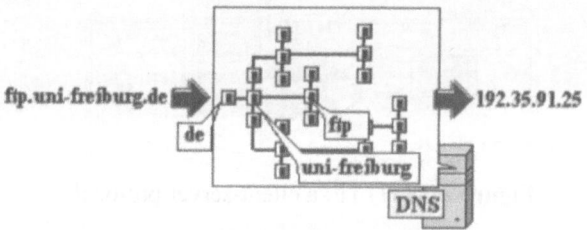

Figure 21-7 Name translation

An organisation connects to the Internet by subscribing to one of many network operators. Network operators are responsible for maintaining routing data and domain name tables in their own machines. They must also coordinate with other major network operators so that new routing and domain name data become globally known.

The following important points, however, must be remembered:

- parts of a domain name do not correspond directly to parts of an IP address; thus 'info.tu-graz.ac.at' and 'iicm.tu-graz.ac.at' may be on different networks!

- the top-level domain does not necessarily tell you where the machine is located; the domain 'www.websoc.org', for example, is in Austria

- a machine may have several names (aliases); the domain name table in this case will map all aliases to the same IP address. Names are not necessary for communication - only IP addresses

- while names are not strictly necessary for communication, it is better for users to remember names rather than IP addresses; this is because a machine or a particular service may move and change its IP address but will probably retain its name. Thus, an email server may be named 'mailhost.unimas.my' but the service may be moved to different machines over time. As long as the domain name table is kept current, a user that refers to the service by name will always access the correct machine.

21.3 HTTP Protocol

The HyperText Transfer Protocol (HTTP) was cited above as an example of an Internet Data Service protocol. It is designed to support communication between clients and a hypermedia information server. In client-server processing, clients send requests for certain services to a server. The server, assuming it can honor such requests, will typically respond by sending back relevant data to the clients. Some requests can also cause side effects in the information maintained by the server, such as addition or deletion of certain documents.

HTTP basically defines the internal structure of supported requests and responses. Thus, from the client's point of view, the capabilities of the server are completely captured by the description of message exchanges (requests and responses) the protocol allows (see Figure 21-8).

Figure 21-8 HTTP: a client-server protocol

An interesting view of HTTP (and other similar protocols), particularly in light of earlier discussions on object-oriented systems, is that it defines a class of servers whose public methods define (in their message templates) the internal structures of requests that clients can send it and the data it will generate in response. A particular HTTP server running on some machine is then an instance of this class! However, this is only a conceptual view intended to clarify the idea.

On the Internet, the client-server communication of course takes place over a TCP/IP connection. In other words, the request and response structures are mapped onto the transport data units of TCP/IP (see Figure 21-9). In discussing HTTP messages, however, we may ignore the TCP/IP layer and assume that the necessary mapping will take place.

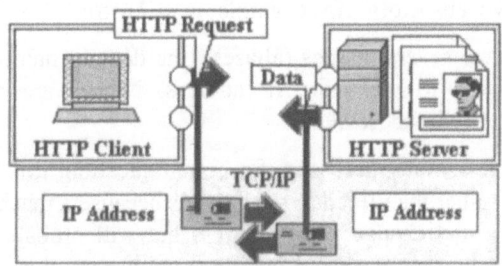

Figure 21-9 HTTP over TCP/IP

Uniform Resource Locator (URL)

The URL is one of the most important Internet concepts. It may be viewed as a means of uniquely identifying resources on the net. In HTTP, URLs identify the data to be transmitted. In fact, a URL is a vital part of any HTTP request. Figure 21-10 illustrates a request specifying a URL, to which the server responds by returning the data resource it identifies.

Figure 21-10 URL in HTTP request

A URL is made up of four parts, as shown in the example below:

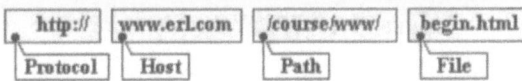

- the '**Protocol**' part must identify the service protocol to be used to retrieve the resource (note, therefore, that URLs are not specific to HTTP but used in other protocols as well, eg. ftp);

- the '**Host**' part must be a complete internet address or official name of the host machine on which the data resides;

- the '**Path**' part must specify the complete path through the server's directory hierarchy; and

- the '**File**' part must name the file containing the required data

Given a URL, a client can therefore determine the protocol to use and the target server of the desired document/resource. The appropriate communication can then be established, with the client forwarding the complete pathname of the resource and the server responding by transmitting back the contents of the resource.

21.4 World-Wide Web (WWW)

The World-Wide Web (WWW) was started at CERN, the European Laboratory for Particle Physics in Switzerland. Essentially, the aim of the WWW project is to build a distributed hypermedia system.

The WWW is a globally distributed collection of so-called *WWW pages*. These are in fact documents written in a mark-up language called a *HyperText Mark-up Language* (HTML). The pages residing on some particular host machine are made accessible over the net through HTTP. In other words, the WWW architecture is essentially that of multiple HTTP servers on the Internet serving WWW pages to HTML clients (see Figure 21-10).

HTML allows for URLs to be embedded in its pages. This is the basic linking mechanism in WWW: the embedded URLs typically point to other HTML pages or multimedia resources (eg. audio file, movie file, graphics file, etc). Embedded URLs are thus like hypertext links, but because they can generally lead to multimedia resources, the set of all these linked resources is more aptly called a hypermedia collection (see Figure 21-11).

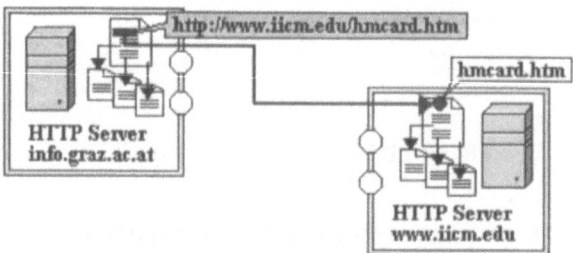

Figure 21-11 WWW Architecture

HTML is the standard ASCII mark-up language for WWW. We will cover the details of this language in a later chapter. For now, it should be sufficient to note that mark-ups are special coded sequences inserted amongst text we wish to display. Most mark-ups describe how the text they apply to should be displayed (eg. centered, bold, colour, etc). Thus, given a software package that can read an HTML page and interpret the mark-ups, text may be formatted for display on the screen. Such software is what is commonly referred to as a WWW browser or a HTML browser (see Figure 21-12). Additionally, as HTML can contain embedded URLs, the browser must also be able to 'follow' such links, ie. retrieve the resource with the given URL.

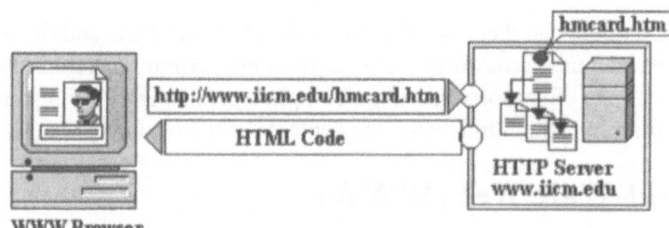

Figure 21-12 WWW Browser

In short, to access the WWW, users must run a browser program that is:

- an HTML browser, ie. capable of interpreting HTML codes including embedded URLs;

- an HTTP client, ie. capable of communicating with different HTTP servers to retrieve resources identified by URLs (embedded or user-specified)

22. HyperText Mark-up Language (HTML)

22.1 Introduction

HTML, HTTP and the URL addressing/naming scheme are the three principal concepts behind WWW (see Figure 22-1). The latter two have been discussed in the preceding chapter. Here, we will focus on HTML.

HTML plays a very important role in web document creation and, through embedded URLs, provide hypertext-style links between web documents. It is important therefore to have a working knowledge of its capabilities and limitations. At the time of writing, HTML provides three primary facilities dealing with:

a) how information within a document should be presented/displayed;

b) inclusion of other forms of data, including non-textual data (eg. images), in designated parts of the document; and

c) links or references to other documents

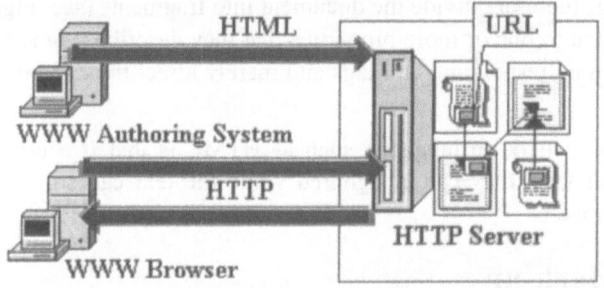

Figure 22-1 Components of the World-Wide Web

An HTML document is just ASCII text. But through its facilities to include other forms of media data, HTML in fact describes a multimedia document. And through facilities to include links to other information resources, it becomes a hypermedia document. Additionally, links come with implicit behaviour: when "selected" by the user, the associated document is accessed. Other capabilities, such as forms handling, can be viewed as extensions of these three primary facilities.

The fact that HTML is the WWW de facto standard for describing how information is structured and displayed underlines its importance to the web architecture. It allows different vendors to develop browsers that, while running on different hardware and software platforms, still display web pages in approximately the same way. There are WWW browsers in fact for most hardware and software platforms, making access to

WWW almost universal and further reinforcing HTML as a standard. However, being an industry standard comes at a cost and its features limited by compromise. It is currently very limited, for example, in its formatting capabilities - far more so than what users have come to expect from their word processing and desktop publishing systems.

A mark-up code is simply an ASCII character sequence distinct from the text. Typically, text is bracketed by a start code and an end code, and the text thus enclosed is subject to the properties that the code describes. HTML mark-up codes are called HTML *tags* and are distinguished from text by adopting the following notation:

- a start tag is written as "< tag-X >" where tag-X is some reserved code identifier

- the corresponding end tag is written as "</ tag-X >"

<TAG-X> Text bracketed by TAG-X</TAG-X>

<TAG-Y> Text bracketed by TAG-Y</TAG-Y>

Figure 22-2 HTML tags

Start and end tags therefore divide the document into fragments (see Figure 22-2) and bind each fragment to one or more properties that they describe. Some tags, however, are not used with corresponding end tags and merely affect the document where they occur.

An advantage of a mark-up language such as HTML is that if a browser does not support particular tags, they can be ignored while the text can still be displayed in some default format.

22.2 Text Mark-up

Document Definition Tags

An HTML document begins with the tag <HTML> and ends with </HTML>. More generally, the <HTML> tag announces that whatever follows up until </HTML> is subject to HTML mark-up. Within these tags, the document is further divided into two nonoverlapping sections: a *header* and a *body*. The header is defined between the <HEAD> and </HEAD> tags, while the body is defined between the <BODY> and </BODY> tags.

Information in the header is often used by some search engines to determine if a document is relevant to some user query before downloading it to the user. A typical entry in the header is the title of the document enclosed within <TITLE> and </TITLE> tags. Information in the body is the actual text of the document, which will typically contain other mark-ups we will describe below.

Thus, an HTML document will have the following general structure:

```
<HTML>
    <HEAD>
        <TITLE> ... the title text goes here ... </TITLE>
    </HEAD>
    <BODY>
            ... the document text goes here (plus other mark-ups) ...
    </BODY>
</HTML>
```

Multiple spaces, indentations and line breaks are generally not significant in HTML and can be used to facilitate reading, as we have done in the above example.

Tag Attributes

In addition to the tag identifier, a tag can also include explicit assignment of values to attributes. Such assignments remain in force until the corresponding end tag is encountered. For example, the <BODY> tag may optionally specify some general properties of the document, such as background colour, font colour, etc:

<BODY bgcolor="#000000"   text="#ffffff" ... >

Attribute–value assignments generally take the form

attribute-id = attribute-value

where *attribute-id* is a reserved identifier denoting some particular property, and *attribute-value* is some value appropriate for the attribute in question. Thus 'bgcolor' is an *attribute-id* denoting the background colour of the document. Valid values it can take are 6-digit hexadecimal numbers written as '#rrggbb', representing the red, blue and green components of a 24-bit colour specification. 'text' is an *attribute-id* denoting the text colour and can take on values that 'bgcolor' can. The above example therefore describes white (#ffffff) text over a black (#000000) background.

Another common attribute used in <BODY> tags is the background image attribute, 'background'. Its value is typically an image file, ie. a file name. If specified, its intended effect is that the document will be visualised with the specified image as its background, eg.

<BODY background = "picture.gif" text = "ff0000">

specifies a red text over the image in the file 'picture.gif'.

Of course, it may not make sense for some attributes to be specified together. For example, specifying 'bgcolor' and 'background' together results in an ambiguity: which property should the browser use for the background? If they do appear together, perhaps inadvertently, most browsers adopt the convention that a later specification overrides an earlier one[1]. Also, not all attributes are applicable to all tags. We will highlight relevant attributes as we discuss various tags (if inappropriate attributes are specified for a tag, most browsers will ignore them).

Header Tags

These tags are used to mark headers in the body of a document and take the general form

<Hn> … header text … </Hn>

where n is an integer indicating the header level ($n \geq 1$).

<H1>Header 1</H1>	Header 1
<H2>Header 2</H2>	Header 2
<H3>Header 3</H3>	Header 3
<H4>Header 4</H4>	Header 4

Figure 22-3 Possible visualization of Header text

Generally, browsers will visualise lower order n more prominently than higher order ones, ie. higher values of n are normally interpreted as subsections of the next lower value. The actual formatting of header text (eg. position, font size and style, colour, etc) are controlled by other tags (see later), but if these are not specified, browsers will use default settings. Defaults may differ from browser to browser, but there are also fairly standard 'style sheets' - files that provide defaults for most visualisation attributes - that most browsers use. Figure 22-3 shows a possible visualisation of four different header levels.

Line Breaks

As mentioned above, carriage returns and line breaks in the source HTML document are generally not significant, ie. browsers will ignore them. If a carriage return/line break is desired in the final display, the <BR> tag must be used. Note that this is one of the tags that appear without a corresponding end tag. Its effect is to insert in the final display a carriage return/line break at the point specified (see Figure 22-4).

---

[1]Most browsers are written to ignore errors and codes they don't recognise rather than to report errors and abort document visualisation. So while documents are almost always visualised (perhaps not the way intended), it makes 'debugging' mark-up errors somewhat difficult!

First line 	First line
Second line	Second line
Please note: 	Please note:
First line	First line Second line
Second line	

Figure 22-4 Effect of <BR> tag

Paragraphs

For the same reasons as above, paragraphs must be explicitly marked. The tag <P> is used to mark that a new paragraph is to begin. There is no corresponding end tag. This is normally visualised by a browser as adding a carriage return and line break as well as some vertical spacing to visually separate it from preceding text. Optionally, the 'align' attribute can be specified to align the paragraph 'left' (the default, if not specified), 'center' or 'right' in the display window (see Figure 22-5).

<P>	New Paragraph
New Paragraph 	Some text ...
Some text ...	
<P align=center>	New Paragraph
New Paragraph 	Some text ...
Some text ...	
<P align=right>>	New Paragraph
New Paragraph 	Some text ...
Some text ...	

Figure 22-5 Effect of <P> tag

Horizontal Ruler

The <HR> tag displays a horizontal line across the display window and starts a new paragraph (see Figure 22-6).

First line	First line
<HR>	
Second line	Second line

Figure 22-6 Effect of <HR> tag

There is no corresponding end tag. Some relevant attributes are:
- 'size': the width of the line in pixels
- 'width': the length of the line in pixels
- 'align': 'left', 'center' or 'right' (as per the <P> tag)

eg. <HR size=5 width=200 align=center>

Text emphasis

Text may be emphasised using the following tags:

- <B> ... </B>:   display enclosed text in **bold** typeface

- <I> ... </I>: display enclosed text in *italics* typeface

- <U> ...</U>: <u>underline</u> enclosed text

- <FONT size=*n*> ... </FONT>: display enclosed text in font size *n*

The value *n* for the size attribute is an integer in the range 1 to 7 (the default is 3). However, *n* may also be specified as an offset, '+*i*' or '-*i*', to respectively increase or decrease the current font size by *i*.

These tags may be used in combination to achieve multiple text emphasis effects: eg.

> <B> <I> bold and italics <U> and underlined; </B> </I>
>
> <FONT size=+2>
> but this line is only underlined and 2 sizes larger;
> </FONT>
> </U> and this is back to normal, unemphasised text

will display something like the following:

> *bold and italics <u>and underlined;</u>*
> <u>but this line is only underlined and 2 sizes larger;</u>
> and this is back to normal, unemphasised text

Preformatted Text

Sometimes, we may wish to manually format text using carriage returns and multiple spaces or tabs between text, eg. to arrange text in a table-like format. This poses a problem, of course, because multiple spaces, tabs and carriage returns/linefeeds are ignored by default when the document is visualised. To allow for this, HTML provides the tags <PRE> and </PRE>. Between these, text will be displayed "as is" (see Figure 22-7).

Manually formatted text	Manually formatted text
\<HR>\<PRE>	
I1 I2 I3	I1 I2 I3
a b c	a b c
x y z	x y z
\</PRE>	

Figure 22-7 Preformatted text

Centering

Any text and/or image, with or without mark-ups, may be centered on the display by putting them between \<CENTRE> and \</CENTRE>. While centering can also be specified as an alignment attribute in many tags, these centering tags provide greater control. For example, we may wish a paragraph to be left aligned except for a particular line somewhere in the middle that we wish centered. These tags will do the job. They are also more convenient when a number of consecutive fragments all need to be centered, eg. a run of a several paragraphs. Thus, instead of specifying center alignments for each paragraph, we simply place all the paragraphs between the centering tags.

22.3 Lists and Tables

Lists and tables are probably the most common ways of displaying information. We could of course use preformatted text, as we did above, but HTML also provides mark-ups for them.

Definition List

A definition list is like a dictionary, ie. an entry in the list is an item (eg. a term or phrase) and its definition. It takes the following form:

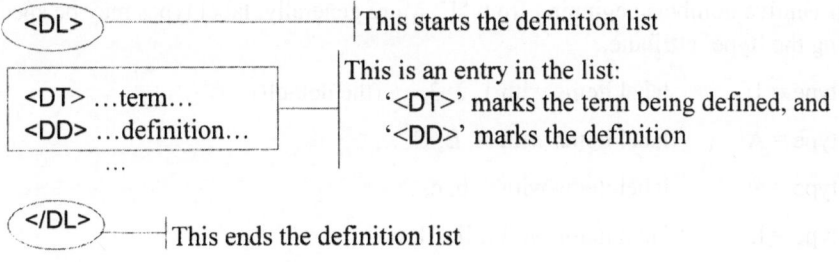

A possible visualisation of a definition list is shown in Figure 22-8.

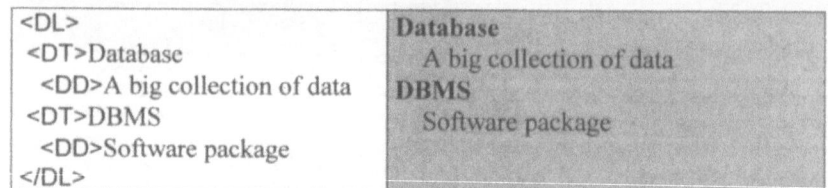

Figure 22-8 Definition list

Ordered List

Text may be organised into an ordered list using the following form:

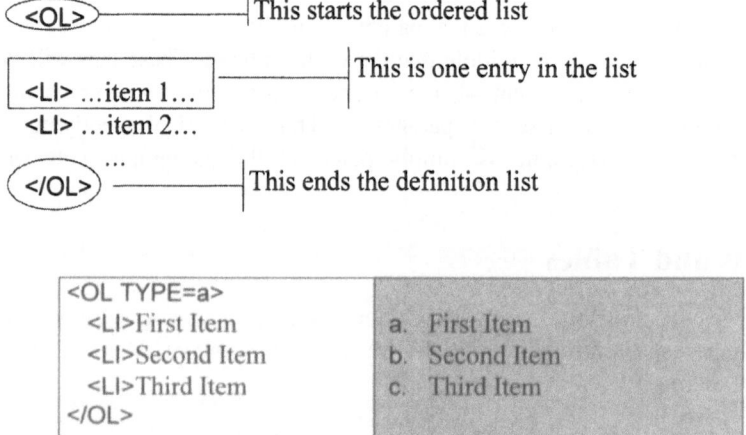

Figure 22-9 Ordered list

When displayed, list items are automatically labelled. By default, labels used are consecutive numbers beginning from '1'. More generally, label types may be specified using the 'type' attribute:

- type = 1:   label items with 1, 2, 3, ... (the default)
- type = A: label items with A, B, C, ...
- type = a: label items with a, b, c, ...
- type = I: label items with I, II, III, ...
- type = i: label items with i, ii, iii, ...

Figure 22-9 illustrates an ordered list and its possible visualisation.

Unordered List

An unordered, or 'bulleted', list is like an ordered list except that:

a) the tags <UL> and </UL> replace the ordered list start and end tags

b) when the list is displayed, items are labelled with a 'bullet' symbol (see Figure 22-10)

The solid disc ('•') used in the above example is the default unless a 'type' attribute is specified. The valid values for 'type' in this case is different from those in ordered lists:

- type = disc: label items with '•'

- type = square: label items with ' ■ '

- type = circle: label items with ' O '

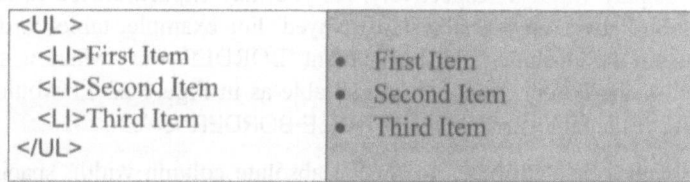

Figure 22-10 Unordered list

Tables

In HTML, a table is described as one or more rows of data. A table can also have a caption and column headers. The latter is essentially a row as well and is treated as such. Header data, however, is declared differently as we expect that its visualisation will distinguish it from table data. The following tags are therefore provided:

- <TABLE> and </TABLE>: to start and end a table

- <TR> and </TR>: to start and end a row within a table

- <TD> and </TD>: to start and end a table data within a row

- <TH> and </TH>: to start and end a column header within a row (the header row)

- <CAPTION> and </CAPTION>: to start and end a caption for the table

Figure 22-11 shows how these tags are combined and what it would look like when displayed. Note that column headers appear as a row of the table, but are specified using <TH> rather than <TD>. This is so that they are displayed with different emphasis to distinguish them from rows of data.

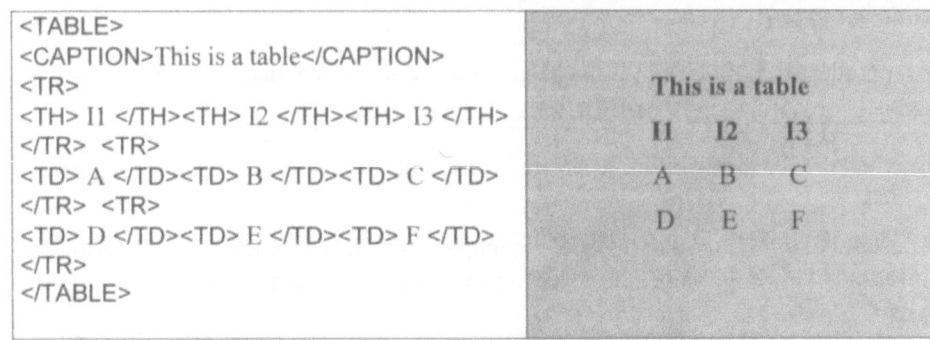

```
<TABLE>
<CAPTION>This is a table</CAPTION>
<TR>
<TH> I1 </TH><TH> I2 </TH><TH> I3 </TH>
</TR> <TR>
<TD> A </TD><TD> B </TD><TD> C </TD>
</TR> <TR>
<TD> D </TD><TD> E </TD><TD> F </TD>
</TR>
</TABLE>
```

Figure 22-11 Basic table definition and display

The basic table is typically presented with rows and data equally spaced down and across the display window respectively. As you may expect, attributes are available for finer control over how a table is displayed. For example, table borders may be specified using the attribute-value assignment 'BORDER = w', where w specifies the pixel width of the border. Thus, the same table as in Figure 22-11 would look as in Figure 22-12 if the table started with "<TABLE BORDER=3>".

There are many other attributes to set the absolute column width, spacing between columns, table alignment relative to surrounding text, data alignment within cells, background colour, etc. Their details are unimportant for our purposes and, in any case, users often leave it to browsers to calculate table cell sizes and positions.

This is a table

I1	I2	I3
A	B	C
D	E	F

Figure 22-12 Table with borders

22.4 Inline Objects

An HTML document would not be a multimedia document if it only handles text. Other media objects are introduced as so-called inline objects. These objects exist as files that are separate from an HTML document and are included at appropriate points using special tags. Inclusion is logical, ie. references to files are made rather than merging their contents into the HTML document. They are accessed and interpreted only when the document is visualised (see Figure 22-13). Note therefore that these media objects can be shared or re-used by many HTML documents, and if an object is updated, all documents referring to it will immediately see the new version. An

HTML document is thus still only an ASCII file but it describes a (virtual) multimedia document.

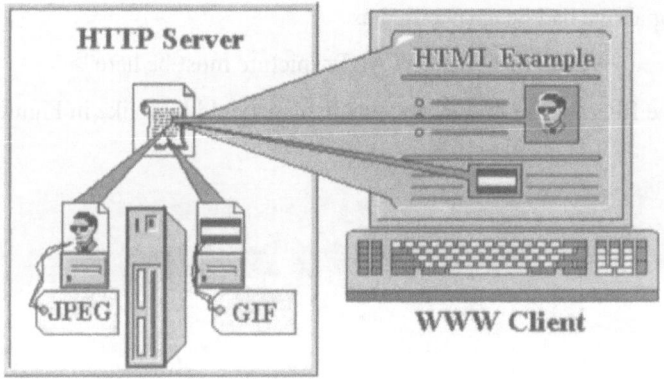

Figure 22-13 Inline objects

Images

Images may be included in HTML documents as inline objects. Browsers will typically support a number of image formats but the main ones used are GIF and JPEG. As communication bandwidths are still limited, the high compression ratio afforded by JPEG is best for pictures that need true 24-bit colour representations. However, the good compression JPEG provides comes at a cost — the compression is "lossy", ie. some aspects of the original picture are lost in the compression process, resulting generally in some degradation of picture quality when it is uncompressed and viewed. But for most pictures, the degradation is not very noticeable and is generally considered a good trade-off for faster communication of pictures over networks. For smaller images such as graphical icons, however, non-lossy GIF images may be better.

An image is included using the tag

<IMG SRC="file name">

This is illustrated in Figure 22-14.

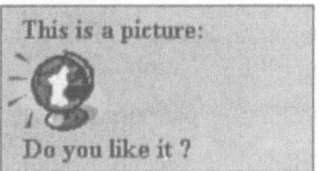

```
<B>This is a picture: </B><BR>
<IMG SRC="x.gif">
<B> Do you like it ?</B>
```

Figure 22-14 Inserting an image

HTML also anticipates that specified images sometimes cannot be displayed (eg. the browser or the hardware cannot handle graphics, the specified file no longer exists, etc) and allows the user to specify an alternate text to display in such cases. Thus, if the image tag above had been specified as

<IMG SRC="x.gif" ALT="picture must be here">

and the image file can't be found, say, the display would look like in Figure 22-15 (a).

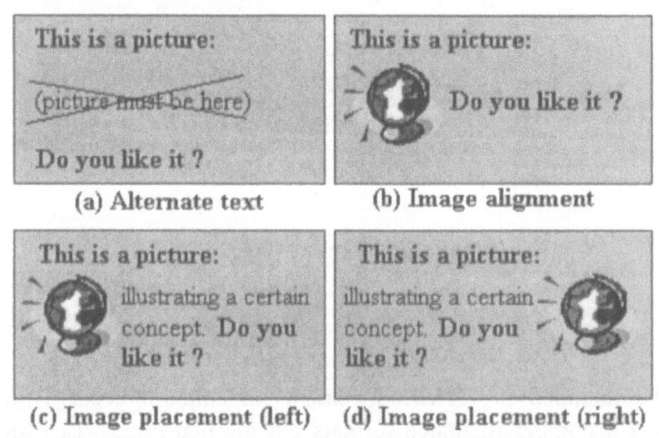

(a) Alternate text   (b) Image alignment

(c) Image placement (left)   (d) Image placement (right)

Figure 22-15 Various effects of image inclusion

Note that in Figure 22-14, image inclusion does not force a carriage return/linefeed - an explicit <BR> had to be specified to force the following text to the next line. Without it, the text (or whatever item follows the image) would follow on to the right of the image. There is therefore the question of how they should be aligned to one another. By default, they are aligned on their bottom edges. More generally, the alignment may be specified using the ALIGN attribute:

- ALIGN=BOTTOM: align bottom edges of objects (default)

- ALIGN=MIDDLE: align to middle of objects

- ALIGN=TOP: align top edges of objects

Figure 22-15 (b) shows the effect of MIDDLE alignment.

Users also have the choice of placing the image to the right or left of the display area using the same ALIGN attribute:

- ALIGN=LEFT: place image to the left

- ALIGN=RIGHT: placeimage to the right

In these cases, surrounding text (if any) will "flow around" the image. Thus, the following HTML fragment would produce the display in Figure 22-15 (c):

```
<B>This is a picture: </B><BR>
illustrating a certain concept.
<IMG SRC="x.gif" ALIGN=LEFT>
<B> Do you like it ?</B>
```

As with tables, a border may be specified around the image using the BORDER attribute. Replacing the IMG tag above with

```
<IMG SRC="x.gif" ALIGN=RIGHT >
```

would produce the display in Figure 22-15 (d).

Other External Files

Generally, any external file of any type may be included. To cope with this, browsers are usually written to allow 'plug-in' software handlers for different file types. This also facilitates the handling of any future media form — we need only write the software handlers for such media files and plug them into existing browsers. When such a file is accessed, the browser's job is to fetch it from the server, create a window within the current display and use the corresponding plug-in to visualise it (see Figure 22-16).

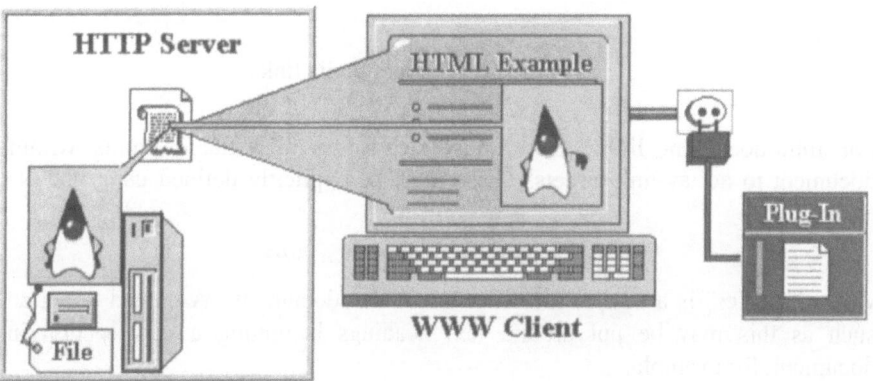

Figure 22-16 Handling external files using plug-in software

Such files are included using the tag:

```
<EMBED SRC="file name" WIDTH=w  HEIGHT=h>
```

The WIDTH and HEIGHT specifies the window size within which the plug-in software will visualise the contents of the specified file. When a plug-in software is added to a browser, it is associated with a particular file extension or a set of possible extensions. Thus the right plug-in to use can be determined by inspecting the file extension in the file name.

Note that this facility of HTML, together with browsers that can be extended with plug-ins, provide an excellent platform for customising web applications.

22.5 References to other Documents

As mentioned earlier, a (virtual) multimedia document becomes a hypermedia document with the addition of hypertext-style links. Links specified in HTML allows the browser to navigate to either a new point in the same document or to a different document (see Figure 22-17). Links are introduced using the anchor tag <A> (and </A>). Different anchor types are distinguished by attributes in the tag.

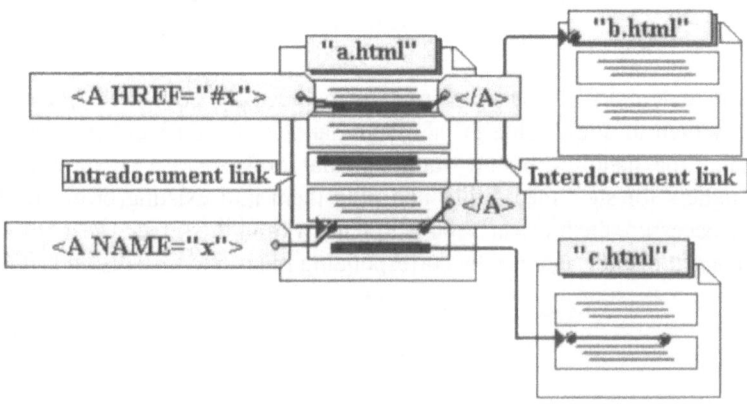

Figure 22-17 Hypermedia links

For intra-document links, there must clearly be identifiable points within the document to act as link targets. These must be explicitly defined using the NAME attribute:

<A NAME="marker"> ... </A>

where "marker" is a unique identifier within the document. A named target anchor such as this may be put around text headings beginning a new section in the document, for example.

Link sources are specified as anchors with the HREF attribute:

<A HREF="target anchor"> ... </A>

where "target anchor" specifies the link destination. Link sources are put around objects that we wish to highlight for user selection, ie. such objects will be visualised differently from surrounding objects, emphasising it as a user-selectable link source (users typically point-and-click to select links).

To specify an internal link destination, "target anchor" is written as "#marker". The '#' identifies the target as internal and 'marker' is of course a unique identifier introduced using the NAME attribute somewhere in the document (see Figure 22-18).

To specify an external link destination, "target anchor" must specify the file name of an HTML file, eg.

<A HREF="document.html"> ...

The search for the named file defaults to the current server. If the destination document in fact resides on another machine, a URL may be specified, eg.

<A HREF="http://www.unimas.my/IST.html">

It is also possible to jump to a named point within an external document by appending the "#marker" to the document reference, eg. HREF="document.html#marker".

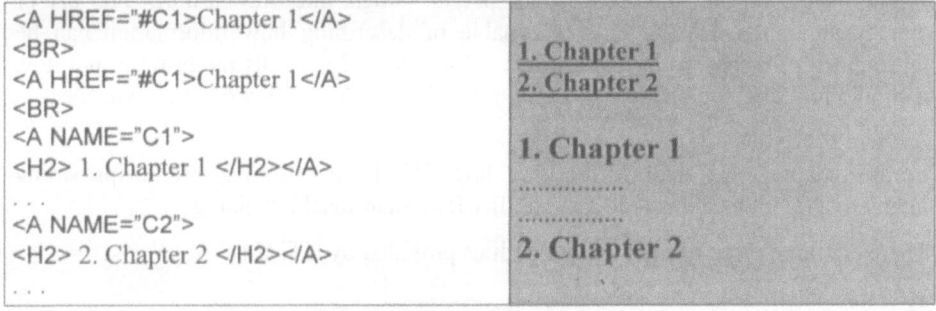

Figure 22-18 Internal links

23. Interaction over the WWW

23.1 Introduction

Pages on the Web, as we saw in Chapter 22, are written in a language called HTML - a universal platform-independent document formatting language. An HTML document consists simply of the text with tags that tell a web browser how the text should appear on the screen, or to do specific things, like draw a horizontal bar or display an image. HTML thus is capable of describing how information can be represented or displayed by the browser. More precisely, it tells the browser not how it should look, but which style to apply, much in the same way we use a style sheet in a word processor.

In this chapter, we shall further see how HTML is also capable of providing interactive facilities to provide a possibility for a man-machine dialog

There are three types of interactive facilities provided by HTML:

a) Links

b) Scripts

c) Applets

Links

It is all very well to be able to create a web page with headings, bars and pictures. However, the most important feature of a page is links. In the simplest case, the author of a particular HTML document may include links or references that point to other documents.

A user thus "selects" a link from the browser page, by doing a mouse click on the highlighted text for example, and the document associated with that link is accessed.

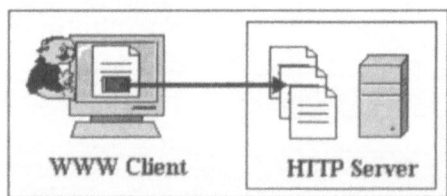

Figure 23-1 Simple link to another reference

Thus the link tells the browser where to go when it is clicked on, and looks like:

```
<a href="http//www.abcd.com/">Click Here</a>
```

The URL (the text in the quotes) can point anywhere on the Internet. The actual clickable link on the page is the text between the start and the end of the tag, e.g. "Click Here" in the example above. Even a picture can be a clickable button.

Scripts

Secondly, a more sophisticated interaction between a user viewing a document (client site) and a special program (normally called a *script*) running on a server site can be provided by HTML. Scripts are a way that a web server can process information and return the results to the client browser. Scripts could be used, for example, to search a database or to display the current time.

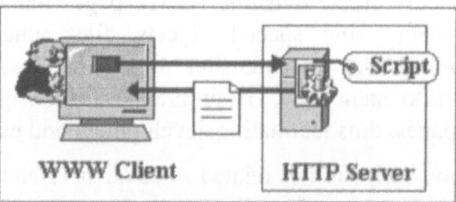

Figure 23-2 Interaction via scripts

As we know, HTML has special tags that are interpreted as interactive elements (e.g. input fields, push buttons, hot areas, etc.) by a client. Whenever such an interactive element is activated, the client connects to the server and sends the parameters via HTTP protocol. The script would have to be put in the scripts directory on the web server. The server then executes the script and responds with a dynamically generated text or HTML document. This can be done, for example, by including lines at the start of the script that specify the content type, as in:

```
#! /usr/local/bin/perl
print "Content-type: text/html\n\n";
```

Scripting is based around CGI - the Common Gateway Interface. CGI is simply a way of allowing web pages to communicate with server-resident programs for information processing. The CGI script is written in an appropriate programming language, such as PERL. Essentially, it is just a set of shared environment variables and a method of parameter passing that acts as a platform-independent "gateway" between the WWW and the server itself, as shown in the code below:

```
if ($ENV{'REQUEST_METHOD'} eq "get")
{ $buffer = $ENV{'QUERY_STRING'}; }
else { read(STDIN, $buffer, $ENV{'CONTENT_LENGTH'}); }
print "<html><head>\n"
```

Moreover, scripts written with a special language called JavaScript can be embedded directly into HTML pages much in the same way as "normal" HTML tags as in the following example:

```
<HEAD><TITLE>Sample Document</TITLE>
<SCRIPT>
function update(form)  {
        alert ("Updating Form...")
}  </SCRIPT>
```

The script is interpreted by the browser completely at runtime without any additional communication with an HTML server.

Some effects that are now possible with JavaScript were some time ago only possible with CGI scripts. As the name implies, JavaScript is a scripting language. It allows for the easy creation of nice effects without having to bother about real programming. For example, one can quickly create dynamic HTML pages that process user input and maintain persistent data using special objects, files, and relational databases. JavaScript is thus more like an extension to HTML than a separate computer language. In contrast to standard CGI programs, JavaScript source is integrated directly into HTML pages, thus facilitating development and easy maintenance

Despite the name, JavaScript is not related to Java. It is Netscape's cross-platform, object-based scripting language for client and server applications that allow the creation of applications that run over the Internet.

Applets

Additionally, the Java platform also provides live, interactive content on the WWW, with just-in-time software access that is readily available on all operating systems. *Applications* and *applets* are the most common Java programs.

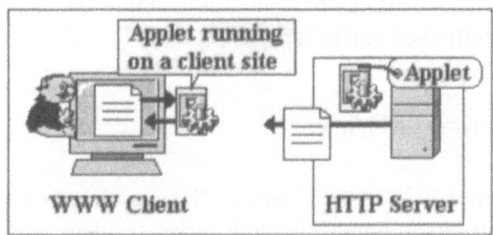

Figure 23-3 Interaction via applets

Applications are standalone programs, such as the HotJava browser, that execute independently of a browser and run directly on the Java platform. Applets are similar to applications, but they do not run standalone. Instead, applets comply to a set of conventions that lets them run within a Java-compatible browser on the WWW client.

Thus a WWW client can fetch an applet, say an animation applet, from a server site and run it locally to provide any kind of interaction that is needed.

There is in fact a lot more that can be done with web pages -- some of which involves complex scripts and programs to produce special effects and more sophisticated interactions. We shall explore some of these below.

23.2 HTML Forms

In today's multi-platform world, there is a need for platform-independent applications. One would not be required to write code for generating input windows, buttons or boxes nor code for handling the text in the window etc. It would be good if we just describe the way we want the interface to be and get our favourite web browser to work on generating the code to get the data. One such way is to use HTML "forms".

The form will obtain some form of useful information from the end user through the browser interface, and subsequently a program will perform some form of computation on that information. At the end of it, the results are written into yet another HTML document, which again is accessible through the web browser. It thus provides a mechanism whereby the viewer of a web page can enter and return information (i.e. parameters) to the web server.

HTML forms may be thought of a collection of variable names, such as Username, Age, Sex, etc. Each of these variables is associated to a text field or a selection area. When the user enters information into any text field, or makes a selection from the options present on the form, a value is assigned to the associated variable name. This value along with the variable name is subsequently passed to a special program that then processes it (for example, to update a database).

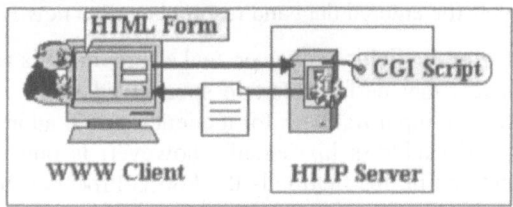

Figure 23-4 Processing forms

The web server processes this information by executing a CGI script, as shown in Figure 23-4 above. The script processes the parameters and returns as its results a text stream representing another HTML page.

A form is introduced by the tag <FORM> and terminated by the inverse tag <FORM>. The attributes of the <FORM> tag includes METHOD and ACTION. For example:

```
<FORM METHOD=POST ACTION=http://host/cgi-bin/script_name">
   </FORM>
```

METHOD specifies which technical protocol the web server will use to pass the form data to the program that processes it, and ACTION tells the server exactly which program that is.

After the form has been filled in, the entered data is sent to the named CGI script for processing. The script is confined to being in the cgi-bin directory or nominee. The exact location of the cgi-bin directory is defined by the web administrator.

A form field to request the user to enter *text* that is to be sent to the CGI script is introduced by the following tag:

```
<INPUT TYPE="text" NAME= "name of CGI script parameter"
SIZE="width of the input area">
```

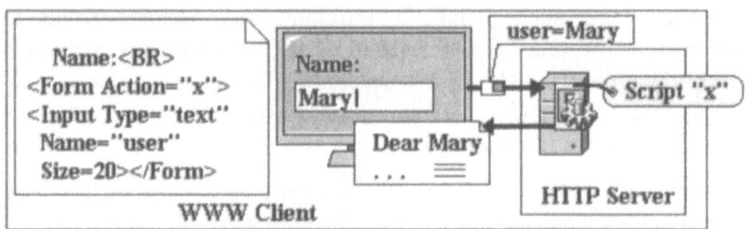

Figure 23-5 Getting an input text

Note that the input data is sent to the CGI script in the form

"Name of the parameter" = "Entered Value"

The CGI script processes the entered data and responds with a new HTML document

Any name may be used for the fields. However, make sure that it is not any of the pre-defined Forms parameters that perform certain specialized tasks. For example, one common error is to have an input field ask for a client's e-mail address, and using the variable email to store the address in. "email", however, is one of the predefined parameters. A value entered in this field tells the Forms Processor to send the form's results to that address, which is usually not what is the author intends.

A form to request a *password* or any secret text to be entered is:

```
<INPUT TYPE="password" NAME="name of CGI script parameter"
SIZE=width of the input area>
```

Instead of displaying the input, it displays ******* where the characters would go. It must be noted that this is not secure, unless the data is encrypted before being sent over the Internet. Even if it is encrypted, the encryption may still be broken.

If a particular form contains *multiple elements*, the following tag is used to pass the submission of the input data to the CGI script:

```
<INPUT TYPE= "submit" NAME="parameter" VALUE="Value if pressed">
```

The button when pressed will send, in addition to any information entered in the form, the message "parameter"= "Value if pressed".

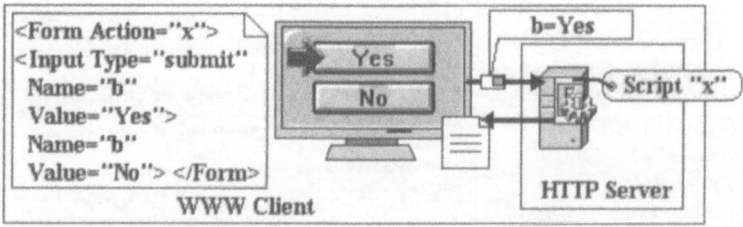

Figure 23-6 Form with multiple elements

Note that there may be several of these input tags within a form. The VALUE attribute identifies which button, i.e. <INPUT> has been selected. When the user clicks the "submit" button, the browser collects the values of each of the input fields and sends them to the web server identified in the ACTION keyword of the FORM open tag. The web server then passes that data to the program identified in the ACTION, using the METHOD specified.

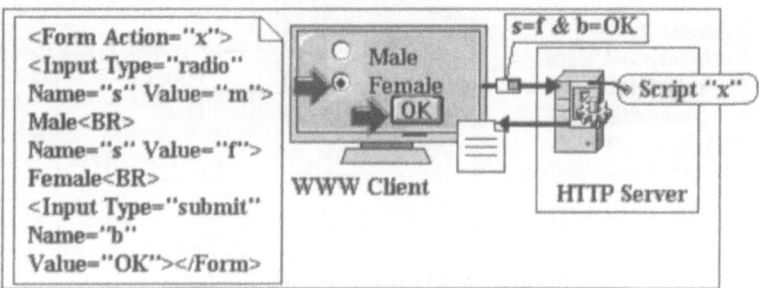

Figure 23-7 Form with radio buttons

A form to request the user to select from one of a series of *radio buttons* uses the following tag:

```
<INPUT TYPE>="radio" NAME="parameter" VALUE="Value if selected">
```

This will display little round buttons to click to make a choice and are good when one needs to give options, like Yes and No, and limiting the user to choose just one option.

A form to request the user to select one or more *check boxes* uses the following tag:

```
<INPUT TYPE="checkbox" NAME="parameter"
  VALUE="Value if selected">
```

Instead of giving the end user a round radio button for only one choice, this displays several square boxes that allow for more than one choice.

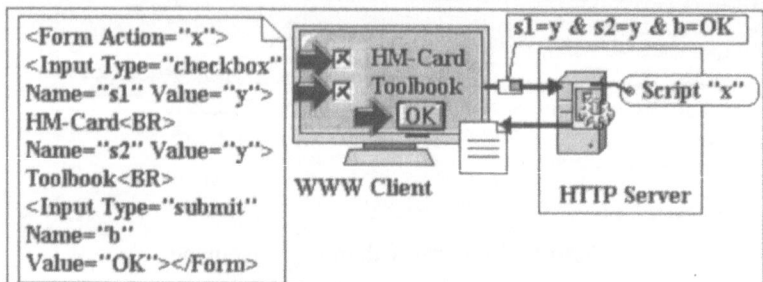

Figure 23-8 Form with check boxes

A form to allow the user to select an item from a *pop-up list* uses the <SELECT> tag. The <SELECT> tag encloses the tag <OPTION> which names a value in the pop-up list.

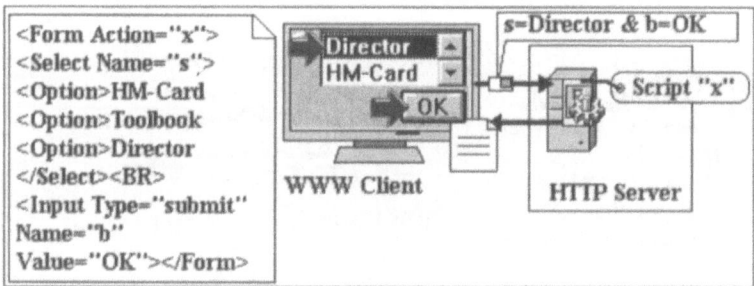

Figure 23-9 Form with a pop-up list

A form may, alternatively, use an *image* in place of the "submit" tag. This provides equivalent functionality. An image map is an image that, when clicked on, sends all the data that has been entered into the form plus the position, i.e. the x, y coordinates, clicked on to a CGI script.

Figure 23-10 Using an image as a submit or navigation button

An image map is defined by the following tag:

```
<INPUT NAME= "variable" TYPE="IMAGE" SRC= "picture">
```

A common use of an image map is to create customised buttons or regions in an image that allow a user to navigate to a new document.

The protocol used to communicate with a CGI script is stateless, i.e. no information is remembered about the transaction. To preserve state information for later recovery, a hidden field in a form can be created which can hold state information.

A *hidden field* is defined by the following tag:

```
<INPUT TYPE="hidden" NAME="variable" VALUE="value">
```

This is not seen by the user. Normally, hidden fields are used by CGI scripts to identify a particular user and recover state information about the user's session.

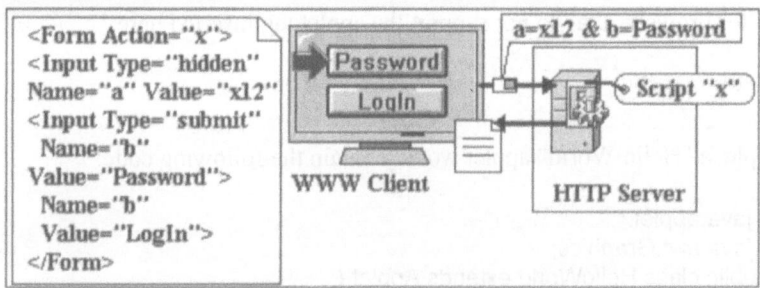

Figure 23-11 Using a hidden field

Of course several of these HTML form tags can be combined together to produce a form that requests several pieces of data.

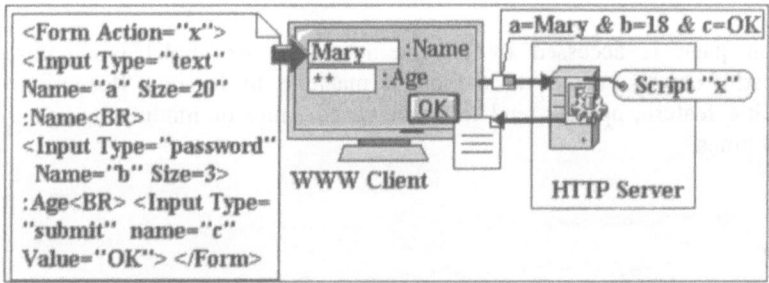

Figure 23-12 Combining various tags in a single form

Thus forms are a convenient means of getting user input. They can be used to provide questionnaires for immediate online feedback from users, order forms for products, or request for information. The information can then be sent to an e-mail address or directed to a database. Input is sent from the browser to the server with the help of a CGI for subsequent translation.

23.3 JAVA Applets

The Java language can be used to create applets that are small programs embedded in HTML pages to be subsequently run through a browser. The <applet> tag is embedded in a web page and names the program to be run. It is an extension to the HTML language and if there are browsers that do not support Java applets, the particular section will simply be ignored by the browser.

The applet tag must at the very least include the name of the Java class file to be included and its size as shown below:

```
<applet code="DemoX.class" height=100 width=300>

/*Text for browsers that do not support the applet tag inserted here.*/

</applet>
```

For example, a "Hello World" applet would contain the following code:

```
import java.applet.*;
import java.awt.Graphics;
    public class HelloWorld extends Applet {
  public void init() {
            resize(60, 15);
        }
        public void paint(Graphics g) {
            g.drawString("Hello world...", 10, 0);
        } }
```

When that page is accessed by an Internet user, the applet is automatically downloaded from the server to the client machine to be run. Because of this downloading feature, applets tend to be designed small or modular to avoid long download times.

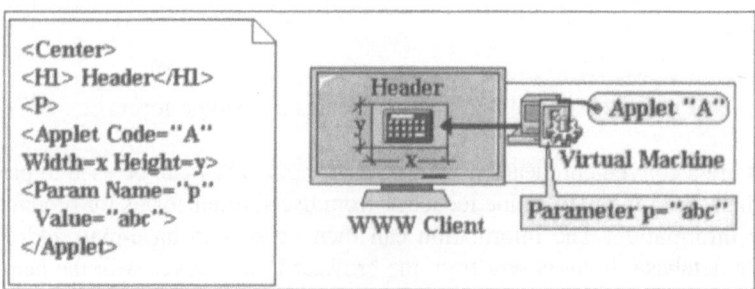

Figure 23-13 Embedding applets in an HTML document

Whenever a browser encounters an applet tag, it is rendered as follows:

* A rectangular space defined by the width and height parameters is reserved on the screen.

* A new virtual machine is activated and the reserved space is allocated for such a machine to be used as a virtual display window

* The code is rendered by the virtual machine using the parameters predefined by the applet tag

The same technique is often used to incorporate multimedia material developed with a standalone multimedia authoring system into WWW documents. A special applet (so-called "viewer") is developed for each particular authoring system. Files produced with WYSIWYG authoring systems are referred to as parameters of the Viewer applet. The viewer applet displays such files within the rectangular area allocated on a Web page.

For security reasons, applets have restrictions placed on them to ensure that nothing inappropriate or harmful through the network is done on client machines. They cannot, for example, read or write files on the user's machine without the explicit consent of that user. Similarly, applets cannot call or run any program on the user's machine.

23.4 Publishing and Searching Documents

Once the HTML documents are created, just like paper-based books or documents, they must be "published" to make sure that people can read or access them. HTML documents have to be posted on a server that is on the Internet. One the document is saved on a server, it has a unique Internet address, known as the uniform resource locator, or URL. Internet browsers use this address to locate the website on the server and render it on a local computer.

Figure 23-14 Publishing the HTML document

It is also important to get the website listed in the various WWW search services, like Yahoo, AltaVista, Lycos, Excite, etc. The web search guide is an interactive tool to help people locate information available via the WWW.

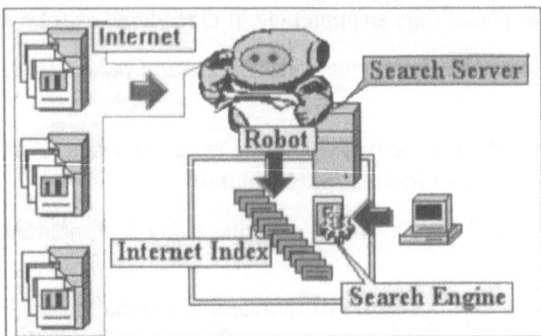

Figure 23-15 Search components

Search servers consist of two elements:

1. A program that roams the area to be searched, collecting data and links to more data. Information is gathered from document titles, descriptions, meta tags, category/topic, author, source, date, full text/abstract, location, etc. The range, type and quality of indexing vary a great deal. The programs follow a set of rules to gather such information from the web sites visited and are variously known as *Robots*, *Spiders* or *Crawlers*.

2. A search agent (Search Engine) – a software package that allows you to enter search terms/queries, checks the index, retrieves matches, and organises the data for follow-on searches if necessary.

What gets indexed are usually the web pages (title, author or the fulltext/abstract), web multimedia files (images, sounds, etc.) and USENET (see below) news articles. Many search services also provide access to non-web databases that contain contact information, financial data, maps, etc. Contents of documents in non-HTML format, contents of sites requiring registration, commercial databases like Dialog or online catalog records like OPAC do not however get indexed by these general search engines.

23.5 E-Mails and News

Network *news* is an electronic bulletin board system that is accessible via the Internet. The information or "articles" that make up the "news" are written by people interested in the topic. Articles are posted to the newsgroup so that others can read, reply and comment on them.

This collection of public discussion groups is accessed daily by millions of people worldwide. The news network started in 1979 as a means to share information about Unix. It became popular because, being text-based, it was quick. It was also convenient, world-wide and self-governing. Today, there are over 20,000 newsgroups that cover a wide range of topics with free-flow messages and serve as important sources for up-to-date information (and misinformation too), Some newsgroups are devoted to current events and headlines. However, network news usually describes topical discussion groups, not "the news" in the traditional sense.

Figure 23-16 Newsgroups

Network news works on the client/server principle. A client program enables the user to interact with a server in order to access information and services on the server computer.

Most newsgroups exist on a network called USENET. USENET is a network which is one component of the whole Internet "network of networks". The network news system is based on NNTP, Network News Transfer Protocol. NNTP is part of the TCP/IP suite of protocols. NTTP is a protocol, or set of rules, that enables news group articles to move smoothly through the Internet.

Electronic mail or *e-mail* is a quick, convenient, efficient and cheap way to communicate with other individuals or groups on the network. It is the most popular and pervasive Internet service.

To use e-mail, the user first uses an e-mail system (such as Eudora or Internet mail) to compose and send a message. Internet mail servers require routing information so that the e-mail can be delivered to the recipient, in much the same way one cannot post a letter via the post office without a recipient's address. An e-mail address is based on a username (which identifies the sender/recipient) and the Internet domain (which identifies the cyber location of the user). It is thus of the form:

username@internet_address

For example, mary@companyx.com or bill@schooly.edu.

The message is sent to a remote mailbox. It can be further retrieved from the mailbox and read by the addressee.

23.6 Other Interactions

The WWW has transformed rapidly from an R&D and academic environment to a commercial environment. Greater commercial interests and development continue to support its growth. Some of the upcoming trends in web interaction include the emergence of push media and database-driven publications.

Push media, as the name implies, "shoves" information at subscribers and in the process tax the resources of the Internet itself (and local networks too). Examples of such Web push tools are PointCast, BackWeb and Intermind.

Unlike "pull media" which requires a user to be actively engaged in finding/selecting information (like visiting a website page or searching an online catalog), push media finds the user. After making the initial contact, the user will be passive recipients of news articles, mail (some junk ones), magazine subscriptions, etc.

When information need to be updated often, hand-coded web pages can be expensive and difficult to maintain. *Database-driven* publications are increasingly being used to manage content and create both static and dynamic web pages. Many subscription-based online magazines and newspapers use databases to create both web pages and print publications. With databases, other subscription services are also possible, such as, customizing content for specific audiences and individuals, and tracking user activity. Thus organizations can provide up-to-date information quite readily.

24. Second Generation Hypermedia I

24.1 Introduction

Hypermedia systems based solely on the Node-Link model suffer from a number of shortcomings. They include:

a) Maintaining link associations is tedious

b) Links, by virtue of being physically embedded, break the integrity of document contents

c) Links are not context-dependent, leading to

  i) user disorientation ("lost in hyperspace" syndrome)

  ii) limited, often unsatisfactory, re-use of hypermedia resources

Second-Generation Hypermedia Systems, in contrast,

a) can define and browse hypermedia composites (collections of nodes and links)

b) separate links from document contents, thus preserving document integrity

c) support links with attributes

d) maintain referential integrity of links (automatic maintenance of the hyperweb)

An important consequence of these capabilities is that the same set of nodes may be re-used in different contexts, ie. to support different user needs. It offers, therefore, greater extensibility and tailorability.

The *Hyperwave*, earlier known as *Hyper-G*, server software is one of the most powerful distributed hypermedia technologies currently available that incorporates all of the features of second-generation hypermedia. In this and the next chapter, we will explore in some depth the Hyperwave approach to hypermedia.

24.2 Metainformation

To do more serious search on the Web (beyond just random "surfing"), we need to have searchable attributes attached to each document. For example, we may attach to a document, its title, author, keywords, update time, etc, including even the concepts and relationships contained in a document. Thus, we really would like to keep "meta information" - information about information.

Let us illustrate the purpose of meta information by using an analogy about taking and keeping photographs. Having taken photographs, you would normally want to put them into a photo album. To help you remember the events or occasion when the photographs were taken, you may write down the date when a particular picture was taken, who is in the picture, and where this picture was snapped. Information that describes the photographs is the meta information that can help you recollect the memories as you look again at the photographs perhaps two years later. Equally important too, the meta information could be used should you wish to organize your entire photograph collection by date or by place, for example. Later on, should you want to search the collection based on some attribute value (say, to find photographs taken at "Place X"), then the search can be conducted more efficiently.

You can similarly do this with Hyperwave. In addition to the actual document itself, you can add meta information attributes that describe the kind of information the document contains. Thus you can use meta information for powerful searching. You can look for a document that contains the word "PC" that was authored by "Author X", and that was inserted into the server after "Date Y". You can also use these attributes for other applications in a way that automates some tasks. For example, you may deposit an announcement with an expiration date. When this expiration date is due, the computer system removes the expired document automatically.

Likewise, managing a calendar of events is simplified. In a calendar of events, there is typically a list of dates, and for each date, there is a reference to some pertinent document showing what is happening on that date. The problem is when, the date say, March 9th changes to March 10th. To have to manually remember to update the list and remove the expired document is rather tedious. A system with stored meta information however can do such a task automatically.

24.3 Collections

The Hyperwave data model extends the Node-Link model with an information structuring facility orthogonal to hyperlinking. More specifically, Hyperwave introduces the notion of a *collection* of objects. A Hyperwave collection is a composite object, comprising documents and/or other collections. It is analogous to folders or directories in a file system whose contents are files and/or other folders or directories. The Hyperwave collection therefore describes a hierarchy of collections. The basis of this recursive definition is of course a document or an empty collection, in much the same way that files or empty directories form the leaves of a hierarchical file system.

Every Hyperwave server has one root collection - that which is the root of the hierarchy.

Subsequently:

a) every document or collection must be a member of at least one other collection, generically referred to as the parent collection (except, of course, the root collection which has no parent)

b) while a document or collection can be a member of more than one collection, the collection hierarchy must be cycle-free

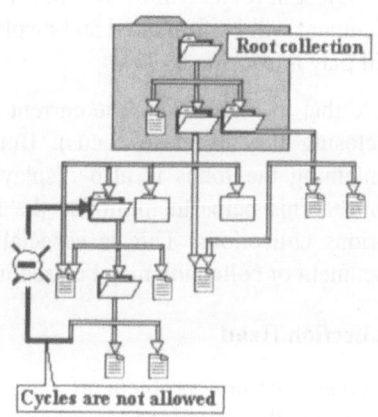

Thus, a Hyperwave collection hierarchy is more accurately described as a directed acyclic graph (see Figure 24-1). Note the significance of allowing a document or collection to have more than one parent: different contexts can be defined to suit the needs of different users while still benefitting from sharing media objects.

A Hyperwave collection is used for a number of purposes:

Figure 24-1 Hyperwave Collection

1. As a means of navigating through available information.

2. As a means of establishing the context of the current focus.

The collection can be visualised in ways that allow a user to select a member object (document or another collection) to be the "current focus". Depending on the browser and the hardware platform it runs on, a collection may be visualised as a menu of member objects that users select using a keyboard (as in navigating the file system in a Unix shell or MS-DOS shell), or a graphics display directly manipulated through a mouse (as in the Windows Explorer GUI to the Windows file system), etc.

Figure 24-2 illustrates a sample GUI visualisation. Users of the Windows Explorer GUI will immediately appreciate the similarity and the kind of interactivity it allows.

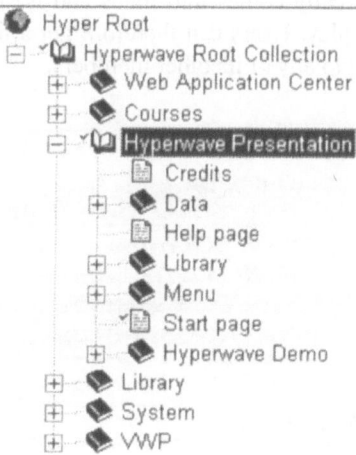

Figure 24-2 Possible visualization a collection hierarchy

An object in focus will be visualised in ways that are object-dependent, eg. an HTML document will be formatted and displayed in a window or sub-window, a music object will play music, etc.

Note that in Figure 24-2 the current focus is highlighted (in this case by a rectangle enclosing the object in focus). But as the surrounding portion of the hierarchy containing the focus is also displayed, its context may be easily determined at a glance. This helps to minimise the feeling of being lost as users navigate through various collections. This is especially significant in light of the fact that a given document or collection may be used in different contexts, as mentioned earlier.

Collection Head

Another common problem of navigating a hyperspace is that users often cannot determine the relevance or otherwise of a document until it is retrieved and its contents viewed. Even with an explicit display of the logical structure of information, the short titles of collections or documents are often not good indicators of their relevance to the user.

To help alleviate this problem, a Hyperwave collection may also have a document designated as the *collection head*. If such a document exists, it would be automatically visualised when the collection is accessed (ie. navigated to), together with the hierarchy display. Authors may therefore use this facility to create a (multimedia) synopsis of the collection's contents to help a user decide its relevance.

Figure 24-3 shows a possible visualisation of a collection and its designated head. We assume the collection accessed is the one entitled "IICM Information Server". Accessing it causes the display of the hierarchy to reveal its members (represented by titled icons). Additionally, because the collection has a head entitled "Welcome to IICM (Head)", it automatically comes into focus and is simultaneously visualised in the bottom half of the display. Users can therefore get a better idea of the collection contents before navigating to any of its other members.

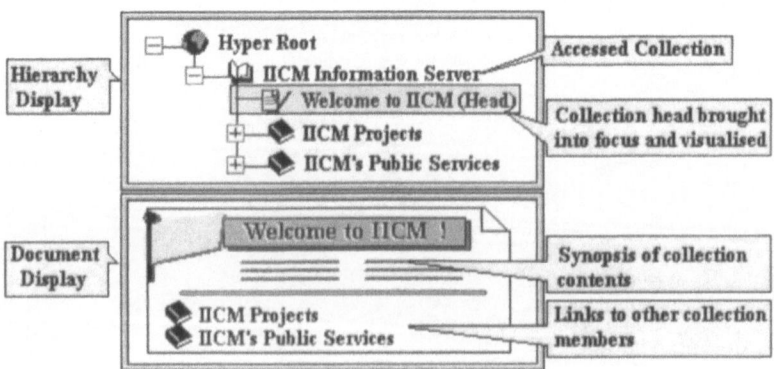

Figure 24-3 Possible visualisation of a collection with a head document

Additionally, the head may also provide links to other members of the collection. While this is redundant in a way, it provides users with alternative navigation mechanisms: use the hierarchy or use the links in the collection head. Note that if links are used for navigation, the hierarchy display will still be updated to reflect the context of the current focus.

A collection head that visualises links to all other sibling members in the collection is called a *full* collection head. It is, however, the author's responsibility to ensure that a full collection head really contains all necessary links (the nature of links in Hyperwave will be discussed later).

Maintaining Collections

In the node - link model, the idea of collections is loosely approximated by the concept of a 'home page'. A home page contains links to other pages, from which more pages become accessible, and so on. Thus a university, say, may have a home page that contains links to other pages describing its faculties, which in turn have links to pages describing academic programmes, staff, facilities, and so on. The university home page itself may of course be part of a bigger collection, say, a home page on universities in a particular country. In other words, related collections of information are implemented through links[1]. This also means that when a new node is to be added to a collection, some existing node in the collection must also be edited to create a link to it - otherwise it will not be part of the collection.

A Hyperwave collection, in contrast, is a structuring mechanism orthogonal to links. Related information may be grouped into a collection independently of links to/from them, ie. adding a new node to a collection does not require the creation of a link to it from some other node in the collection. The added node is immediately accessible through collection hierarchy navigation. Links to/from the new node may be added later and, as we shall see, in a way that supports multiple usage contexts while preserving its logical .

Similarly, the deletion of a node in the node-link model requires updating nodes that link to it. In fact, this poses a major problem: how do we know which nodes point to the one we are deleting? Given that first-generation links are unidirectional, the only way to be sure is to check every node in the web! This is clearly impractical since nodes may be anywhere in the world and, even if we could determine the documents in question, they could reside on machines to which we have no write access. In practice, therefore, the first-generation web community accepts the fact that a link active today may become a dangling link tomorrow.

In contrast, when deleting a node from a Hyperwave collection, the system automatically maintains the integrity of both the collection hierarchy and global links, with no additional effort needed on the part of the user. If the node also belongs to another collection, deletion does not affect its presence there. In other words, a node is

---

[1] Collection boundaries are fuzzy, however, since any inter-collection relationship is also represented by the same link mechanism.

only physically deleted when it is removed from every collection that contains it. As for links, let us just assert for now that dangling links will not occur as a result of the deletion (how this is possible will be discussed in section 25.3).

Thus, from the user's point of view, maintaining a logical collection of information is far easier in Hyperwave. Insertion and deletion of nodes are one-step processes for the user - much of the work in maintaining the integrity of collections and links is automatically performed by the system.

24.4 Sequences

While links let users freely navigate an information space, some collections of information are still better presented in linear order. For example, it is probably best for a new student to first work through a set of lessons in some predetermined order before navigating more freely among them. Of course, we can use links to organise things into a linear order. But recognising the frequent need for such linear structures, Hyperwave directly supports a special type of collection called a *sequence*.

In object-oriented terms, a sequence is a subclass of the collection data class, ie. it is still basically a collection, but with the added property that a sort order is imposed on its members. It remains therefore a structuring mechanism different from and independent of links. The sort order of members is specified as an attribute of the sequence, which will typically specify sorting based on attributes of member elements, eg. date of creation, alphabetical order of element title, etc. Alternatively, each member of a sequence can have a sequence number attribute.

A sequence imposes a constraint in the visualisation of members. Specifically, visualisation must begin with the first member of a sequence. Subsequently, navigation within the sequence is restricted to the 'Next', 'Previous', 'First' or 'Last' operations, respectively focusing and visualising the next, previous, first or last member in the sequence's sort order. Of course, a user may exit a sequence using the 'Exit' operation at any time[2].

This is illustrated in Figure 24-4. Note that a sequence creates in effect virtual bi-directional links between its members. This is why, from any member, we can only navigate to the previous or next member in the sort order. Navigation to the first or last element may be viewed as repeating previous or next operations, respectively, until the first or last element is reached. Of course, this constraint may be manifested in the user interface in various ways. The figure shows one possible manifestation: a navigation bar with clickable icons for the allowed operations. Thus, with the state of browsing as shown here, selection of 'Next' will visualise the member "3", 'Previous' the member "1", 'First' the member "1" and 'Last' the member "5".

---

[2] Since a sequence is orthogonal to links, alternative navigation structures not subject to sequence navigation constraints may of course be defined over the same elements. Direct access to individual elements may also be effected by setting up a parallel collection (with a full collection head) that shares the sequence elements.

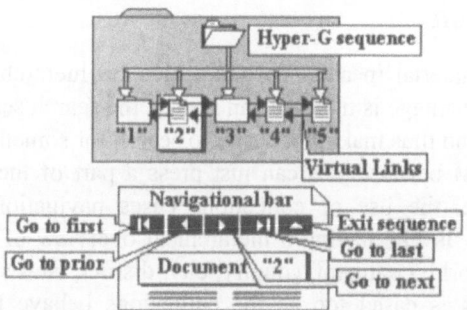

Figure 24-4 Sequence Visualisation

Note that the virtual links between sequence members are dynamically generated. Thus, if document "2" above was deleted, the virtual structure of the sequence automatically becomes:

$$\text{"1"} \leftrightarrow \text{"3"} \leftrightarrow \text{"4"} \leftrightarrow \text{"5"}$$

Similarly, addition of a new member will insert it in the appropriate position as dictated by the user-specified sort order for the collection. The system guarantees that the sequence will always be in a consistent state.

The provision of this special class of collections greatly simplifies the creation and maintenance of linear information structures. Also significant is that the integrity of such structures is dynamically maintained, ie. changes due to insertions and deletions can happen even during browsing. Being able to specify implicit sort orders is also a very powerful feature. In all, it regularises the form and handling of linear information, facilitating a more consistent browsing interface (eg. a standard navigation bar) and a more uniform behaviour.

The node - link model, in contrast, will require that authors manually establish and maintain the consistency of links whenever documents are inserted or deleted. Changes, therefore, cannot be done on-the-fly. Moreover, different authors may implement linear structures differently, eg. some may use uni-directional links, others may use bi-directional links, and yet others may link elements into a circular list, etc. The lack of a standard definition of a linear structure leads also to different presentation metaphors that are likely to confuse end-users.

We have casually talked about collections and elements above as possessing *attributes*. This is in fact another distinguishing feature of nodes *and* links in second-generation systems, ie. they are best treated as objects that, in addition to the information they carry, have attributes describing them. Some are system-defined attributes such as creation date, document type, etc., but users can also define custom attributes. The details are treated elsewhere in the book - it suffices to note here that such attributes, or *metadata*, are themselves searchable in Hyperwave (and in second-generation systems, in general). As we saw above, the sort order may be specified on the objects' metadata.

24.5 Conclusion

Grouping related material in advance into collection hierarchies has many obvious advantages. One advantage is that you can restrict the search scope to a collection and its subcollections, and thus making it easier to search for something. It is also easier to produce a CD-ROM because you can just press a part of the database on the CD-ROM. Furthermore, the use of collections eases navigation because having the document hierarchy is like having a hierarchical overview of geographical maps of different scales - world, continent, country, city, district, etc - along with a local map. Data administration is eased too as the collections behave like directories in file systems.

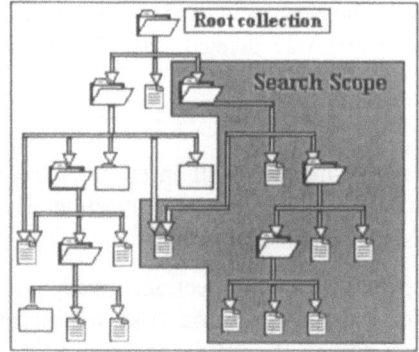

Figure 24-5 Restricting the search scope

The most important advantage of the collection hierarchy is that much link editing disappears as the system takes over many of the chores. Consider the following example.

A company keeps a list of its employees and this is kept in alphabetical order. Normally this is implemented as a list of the key field (say the name), where each entry in this list points to a document containing the detailed information of the employee. See Figure 24-6(a).

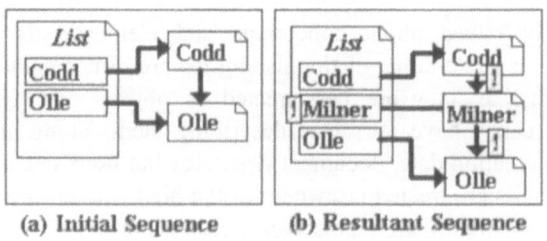

(a) Initial Sequence   (b) Resultant Sequence

Figure 24-6 Link maintenance

A new employee joins the company. Firstly, his employee document is created. Depending on the value of his key field (his name), an entry is created to be inserted into the list of key fields. Existing links would have to be "adjusted" to accommodate this new entry whilst maintaining the alphabetical ordering. For example, in the illustration (Figure 24-6 (b)) above, we would like to insert "Milner". The link between "Codd" and "Olle" is severed. Three new links between "List-Milner", "Codd-Milner" and "Milner-Olle" are created. This seems a tedious link maintenance job for the author or data administrator who has to manually establish and maintain the consistency of links whenever documents are added or deleted.

Compare this situation if the document is to be inserted into a Hyperwave collection. Here, if one were to insert the new document into a "sequence" (as discussed in section 24.4 above) where the sort order of members is specified as an attribute of the collection, then the newly created document is automatically accessible in the right order without any manual link creation or editing. Thus the maintenance job of the information provider is greatly reduced.

Another important advantage of composites in general and of Hyperwave collections, in particular, is the ability to customize the hyperweb. Again, let us illustrate this with an example as follows:

We have 6 educational modules, A to F, and we have three users with different learning profiles. We want to supply them with different modules according to their preferences. For example, User 1 would like Modules A, B, E and F whilst User 2 would like Modules D, B and C; and so on.

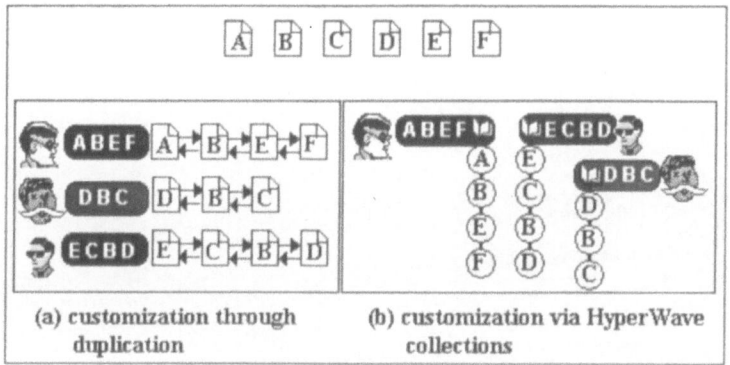

| (a) customization through
duplication | (b) customization via HyperWave
collections |

Figure 24-7 Customization

The only way to do this in ordinary WWW is to actually copy these modules a number of times and link them manually according to the individual needs of the users. See Figure 24-7 (a) above.

An obvious solution in Hyperwave is the use of separate collections. We can, for example, use a blue, red and green collection. We then copy these modules into those collections. However, we do not copy in the sense of duplicating the same modules many times. Instead, we just add a reference to the module. This is called "virtual copying". These three collections do not really contain the modules but instead have pointers to the modules (as shown in Figure 24-7 (b) above).

Thus in Hyperwave, the main documents or structural elements can be seen as self-contained, reusable hypermedia components, similar to procedures in programming languages.

25. Second Generation Hypermedia II

25.1 Introduction

Previously we have defined the following properties of Second Generation Hypermedia Systems:

- Ability to store and work with a metainformation
- Ability to define and browse hypermedia composites (collections of nodes and links)
- Automatic maintenance of the hyperweb
- Global typed links separated from a document's contents
- Automatic support of the referential integrity
- Extensibility and tailorability (i.e. customization of a hyperweb to suit the needs of a particular user)

We have discussed, in particular, the first three of the above. In this chapter we shall discuss the remaining three issues as they have been implemented in Hyperwave.

25.2 HyperLinks

WWW stores links directly in source documents as so-called "anchors". The *source anchor* is the visible representation of the link from which one can follow from (click on the highlighted area) to go to the connected document, which in turn is represented by the *destination anchor*. The anchors may appear anywhere in the document. In text documents for example, they are created in HTML by using a HREF reference to a URL. Thus, first-generation WWW links are:

- Type- or *attribute-free*, in that no meta-information (e.g author, access rights, keywords, type, date, etc) is kept
- *Unidirectional*, in that one can go from the source anchor to the destination, but not vice-versa
- *Embedded*, in that the link is stored directly in the HTML document itself and relies on the actual physical location of the document, that is the URL. Thus when the destination document is removed or re-located, the reference to it is no longer valid ("dangling") and the document cannot be fetched.

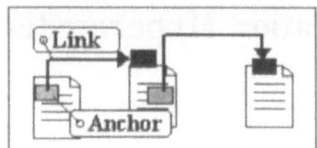

Figure 25-1 Simple link to another reference

Unlike WWW, Hyperwave stores links that are separate from the documents themselves in a *database*. A link is modeled by a source anchor, attached to the source document on one side and to a destination anchor or a whole destination document on the other. The destination anchors allow the making of links to selected portions of a document (for instance, a paragraph of a text document, a fraction of a large map, a few bars of a piece of music).

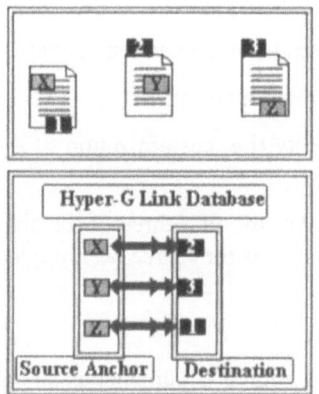

Figure 25-2 Separate link database

Links are separated from documents have the following advantages (over storing links directly in the source documents):

- Links are *bidirectional*. This implies that it is possible to find the source document from the destination and so you can navigate not only forwards, but also backwards from the destination to source. More interestingly is that you can generate link maps that show both incoming and outgoing links around a certain document (see Figure 25-3)

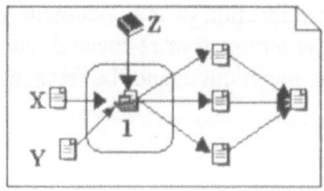

Figure 25-3 Link map showing both incoming and outgoing links

- The bidirectional links can guarantee *link consistency*. For example, if a document is removed, links pointing to it are removed as well. In Hyperwave, they are actually tagged as "open", i.e. the link is not visible to the end-user, but visible/known to the document owner. When the document is re-instated, the link is made visible again to the end-user.

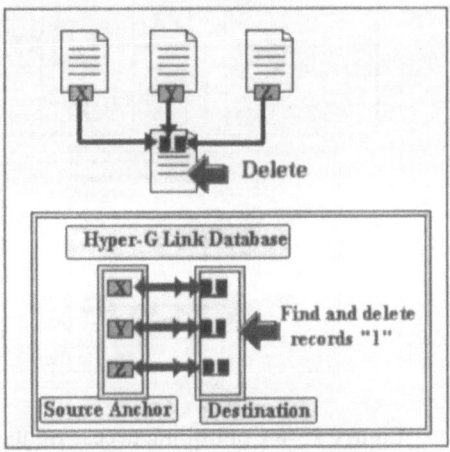

Figure 25-4 "Removing" links of a deleted document

- Links are realized as *objects* that contain characteristics or attributes (most importantly, the anchor's Position and the LinkType). They may be assigned keywords and are searchable. For example, "Find all links with keyword 'C' attached".

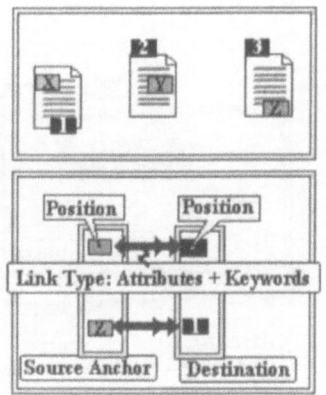

Figure 25-5 Link attributes

- Links may be assigned individual *access* permissions. This means that certain links in a document may only be visible (accessible) to certain users or user groups.

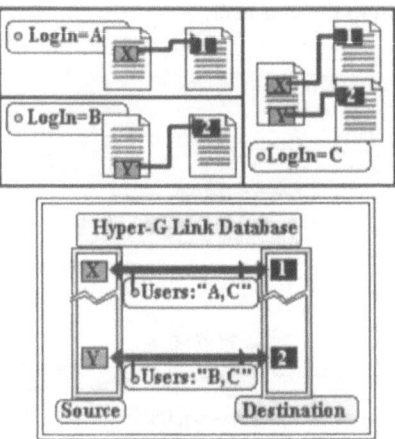

Figure 25-6 Controlling access rights

- *All types* of documents may be made to link with each other because the anchor positions are stored separately from the document itself. For example, one can deal with links in MPEG video streams without a need to modify or extend the MPEG standard. When showing the movie, the movie player receives both the MPEG stream and the associated anchor objects, and shows both.

- Creating and manipulating links do not require modification of the documents the link is attached to. Creating interactive links is thus easier.

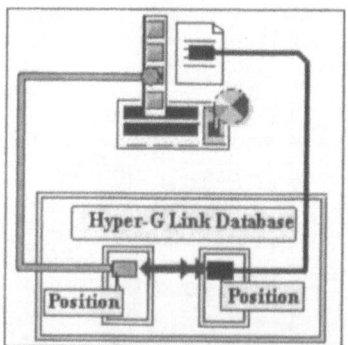

Figure 25-7 Linking read-only documents

However, it also means that creating a link to or from a document does not require a write permission for the document. This is useful for attaching links to *read-only* documents. For example, data on CD-ROMs or other servers to which the server cannot write. Automatic link generation is further simplified.

A simple decision to separate links from the document's contents can bring about many advantageous features, one of the most important being the automatic support of link consistency for referential integrity.

We next look at other features that can help customise a hyperweb.

25.3 Alternative Cluster

One of Hyperwave's structuring facilities is the *alternative cluster* (cluster, for short). In a cluster, one can combine documents with the same or similar content but different appearances. For example, different explanations (text, audio, video) of documents in different languages, etc.

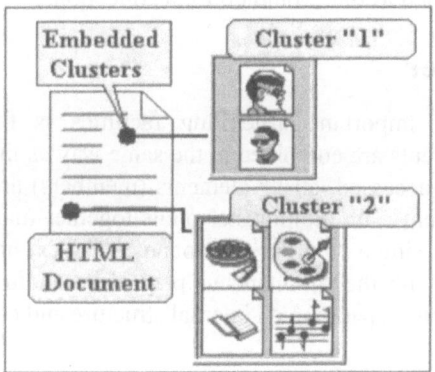

Figure 25-8 Embedded clusters

Clusters can be referred to or embedded as ordinary HTML documents or media objects. Only one of such cluster members is dynamically selected whenever the document is presented to a client. To select a cluster object, the system uses special information defining a particular user's profile or preferences.

It may also be the case that the same contents must be presented in different languages or that a certain media type must be mapped into another type because the former cannot be visualised by a particular hardware/software configuration or cannot be perceived by a particular user.

A multilingual document can consist of a cluster that comprises some language-independent objects and some language-dependent objects of the same document type. When the cluster is displayed, all the language-independent members are displayed and, depending on the language the user chooses, one of each type of the language-dependent document is displayed. Any document with more than one title is regarded as language-independent. For example, a picture may have one title in English and another in German. Or, one title could be in "lay" language and the other in an "expert" language.

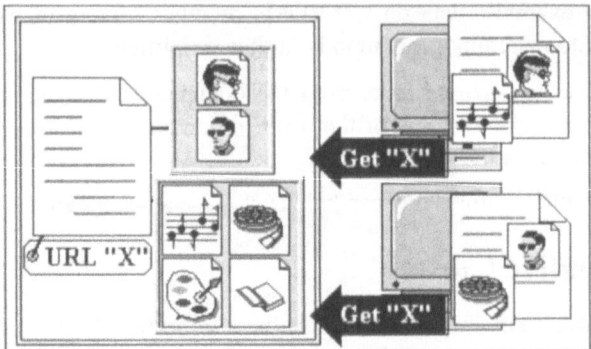

Figure 25-9 Only one cluster member gets selected

Individual clusters are easily created using a Hyperwave client. Once created, documents can be inserted as one would do for a collection.

25.4 MultiCluster

Another Hyperwave's important structuring facilities is the multicluster. In a multicluster, all documents are combined in the same way as in an alternative cluster. Once a multicluster is accessed, all its elements (members) are shown together as a new composite document. The multicluster pools together many single media items and presents them as a single "multimedia document". Text and images can then be shown together along with the simultaneous play of an audio track Thus pages can consist of small elements, separating an internal structure and content.

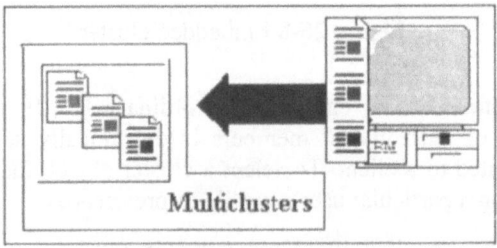

Figure 25-10 Single multimedia document from a multicluster

Suppose we have a repository of small documents (D1 – D6, in this particular case). We are selecting now four documents: D2, D3, D5 and D6 to concoct a new document. We form now a new document just by selecting the four documents in the multicluster. This is very useful for many applications (see Figure 25-11).

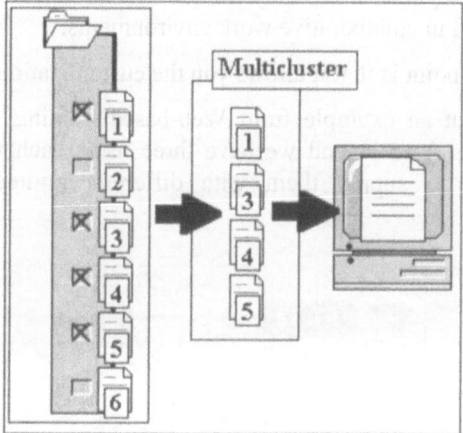

Figure 25-11 Generating a new document in a multicluster

25.5 Conclusion

The Web is fast evolving. Second-generation systems such as Hyperwave certainly has far advanced features compared to the simple, flat, node-link models of the prevailing first generation system. Compared to the first generation system, Hyperwave data is structured (into collections, clusters and sequences). It has meta-information attached, its data is cleanly separated from the user interface, and its links are kept in a separate object-oriented link database.

Let us conclude by looking at how we are able to customize a hyperweb to suit our needs because the second-generation features give us greater extensibility and tailorability.

Links in Hyperwave, as we know, are not embedded in the documents. If links are embedded, they cannot be removed automatically from other documents because you have not authored that other document. By keeping the links in a separate database, you can also add links to documents that do not belong to you.

For example, sometimes, you find a document on the Web and you want to make a private remark to that document like a yellow sticker in real life. Note however, the document does not belong to you and the author barely would allow you to modify the source HTML text. In Hyperwave, you can do that by adding your own links emanating from a document authored by some other person. Whenever you return to that document, you will see the anchor made before.

The anchor can be only visible to the author (private link). If the link is visible to a whole user group, the members of that group can create new links to this particular note.

The other feature we have seen is also about links having attributes which can keep information about the title, author, access rights, modification dates etc. This allows link filtering, i.e. certain links should be only visible to certain persons. It also allows you to, for example, distinguish between links that point to footnotes from other links.

It can allow you to say "show me only the documents that were modified in the last week". This is useful in collaborative work environments.

The most important point is that it allows you the customization of material.

Let us look again at an example from Web-based training. Suppose we have six educational modules A to F, and we have three users each with different learning profiles. We want to supply them with different modules according to their preferences.

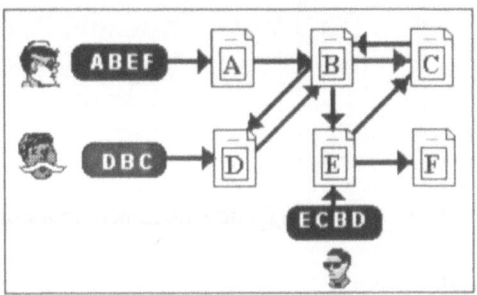

Figure 25-12 Different users and individualized links

There exists a number of ways of solving this problem. Thus for example, we can define three user groups: "ABEF", "DBC" and "ECBD". For each user group, we define a set of links.

Now you can see what happens. If a user from the user group "ABEF" logs in, only the "A-B-E-F" links are visible. If a user from the user group "DBC" logs in, only the "D-B-C" links are visible. And so on.

The advantage of this solution is that no copying of modules is done, and if we have to make a correction/modification in one module, the correction will have to be done only once.

There are many other possible, exciting, customizable applications not thought of before that can now be developed with the power of second-generation hypermedia systems.

26. HM-Data Model

26.1 Introduction

A database, in the general sense of the term, is a set of data we create and maintain for reference and analysis. In a technical sense of the term, a database imposes certain well-defined structures and operations over the data set so that creating, finding, analysing, updating and maintaining the consistency of data is made as easy and as efficient as possible, particularly for very large data sets. In both senses, hypermedia is a database.

More specifically, hypermedia is a form of database, just as a relational, or a network, or an object-oriented database is. It is distinguished from other forms by the basic structuring of data into nodes and links, and by the operation of link navigation. It can perhaps be further characterised by the multimedia nature of the nodes it handles[1]. It is not, however, competing to replace other forms - in fact, it can and does coexist with them, providing collectively a richer information environment than otherwise afforded to users.

As a data model, hypermedia is still evolving. In preceding chapters, we have examined the basic Node - Link model and the Hyperwave model. We continue in this chapter with examining another model which, like the Hyperwave model, is a second-generation model. It shares therefore many similarities with the Hyperwave model, particularly the organisation of information into collections and the separation of links from document contents. But there are also differences, as we shall see, that differentiates it from the Hyperwave model.

The model, called the HM-Data Model, views the database as comprising *multimedia pages*. These are roughly what we have earlier referred to as multimedia documents. A multimedia page can be a complex unit in itself, combining text, graphics, images, sound, video streams, etc., and possessing a behaviour when visualised. This behaviour, in addition to presenting multimedia information, can also include sophisticated user interaction facilities (to capture and analyse user inputs). For example, a sophisticated page may have choice points and, depending on user inputs, different material may be presented.

---

[1] Commercial DBMSs, however, have recognised the need to handle multimedia data and have provided for binary data fields. Database creators can use these fields to hold any form of digital media. So the distinction that hypermedia databases handle multimedia information may no longer be true in principle, although in practice the hypermedia form is still the preferred form when dealing with multimedia data.

The HM-Data Model, however, is less concerned with the internals of a page than it is with how a set of pages is organised. In the following, therefore, we will consider multimedia pages as atomic, ie. as the basic indivisible chunks of multimedia data to be organised. We will examine instead the use of quite a novel method of hyperlinking to structure such information chunks into hypermedia databases.

26.2 Data Structures

A database, according to the HM-Data Model, consists of *Structured Collections* (S-collections or just collections, for short). Quite simply, an S-collection encapsulates *members* over which some *internal structure* is defined. This structure is in fact a link structure expressing the relationships or associations between members. A member is either a page or another S-collection. One member in an S-collection is chosen and designated by the user as its *head*. Additionally, an S-collection may have an associated page called its *label* or *content* (see Figure 26-1). Every S-collection is of course uniquely identified.

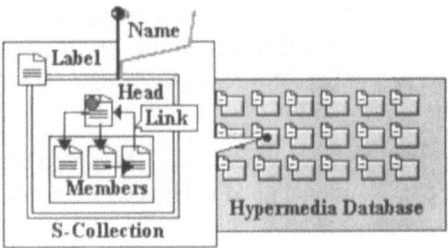

Figure 26-1 Structured collections

There are clearly similarities between an S-collection and a Hyperwave collection. Every S-collection, however, has an internal link topology. In contrast, Hyperwave collections do not impose any link structure between members except for sequence collections. Furthermore, S-collections support a number of other link topologies besides sequences (see below).

Despite the use of the term '*head*', an S-collection head is actually quite different to a Hyperwave collection head. Because every S-collection has a link topology, its visualisation must begin with some designated member - and this is the head. A Hyperwave collection, in contrast, need not have a head and may be visualised even without one. If present, it serves to provide a synopsis of the collection's contents. In S-collections, contents synopsis is provided by the label page. Thus, A Hyperwave collection head is more akin to an S-collection label.

Also, as a consequence of possessing a link topology, the operations for viewing any S-collection are more structured. In contrast, Hyperwave constraints viewing operations (viz. next, previous, etc), only in the case of sequences.

26.3 Browsing

We may think of an S-collection as an opaque container. So if we are outside the container, its members will not be visible to us. To see what's inside it, we must enter it. Of course, we can only be inside one container - the current container - at any given time. But once inside, we will be able to visit its members by navigating its link topology (see Figure 26-2).

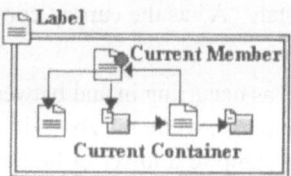

Figure 26-2 S-collection as a container

A member we visit in the current container may be a page or another S-collection. If a page, it will be visualised in some appropriate way - typically involving the presentation of the page's media objects on the computer display and/or sound system. If an S-collection, its label (which is a page, by definition) will be visualised.

The most recently visited member of the current container is the current member. Access to other members from the current member is determined by the container's link structure, ie. only links emanating from the current member can be selected. All such links are typically visualised as anchors on the current display (these may be icons, hot-words, push-buttons, etc). Navigation within the current container therefore is from member to member as allowed by its link topology.

Note that visiting (ie. navigating to) an S-collection does *not* enter it, even though its label is visualised. The point of the label, as mentioned earlier, is to present a synopsis of the collection to allow us to decide whether or not we want to enter it. If no label is present (labels are not mandatory), the head plays that role instead, but we are still outside the collection. To enter it, we must explicitly use the *Zoom-In* operation. Zooming into an S-collection makes it the new current container, its head the new current member and all links emanating from the current member accessible.

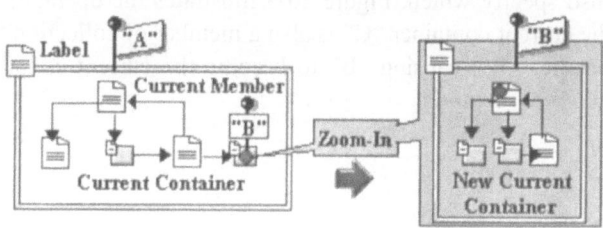

Figure 26-3 The Zoom-In operation

Figure 26-3 illustrates the operation. Prior to zooming in, "A" is the current container and "B" the current member. Applying the zoom-in operation on "B" makes it the current container, its head "X" the current member, and all the links emanating from "X" accessible. Navigation after zooming in is restricted to the links in the current container, or zooming into the current member (if it is a collection) or *zooming out* of the current collection. The zoom-out operation is of course the complement of zoom-in. Its effect is to restore the current container and the current member to the state immediately prior to the most recent zoom-in. Thus, a zoom-out operation for the situation Figure 26-3 will reinstate "A" as the current container and "B" as the current member.

Navigation may thus be viewed as occurring in and between "planes". Link navigation within an S-collection is in one plane, while the zoom-in and zoom-out operations are orthogonal to this and effects a jump to a lower or higher plane. This is illustrated in Figure 26-4.

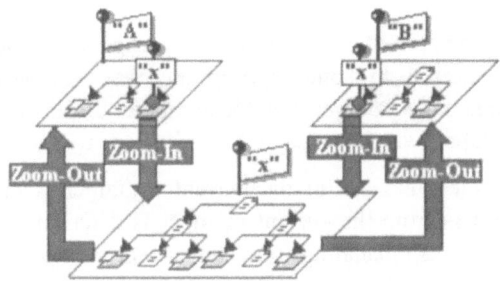

Figure 26-4 Navigation "Planes"

Note also that an S-collection may be a member of more than one other S-collection, ie. collections may be re-used just as with Hyperwave collections. A zoom-out operation, however, will return to the plane from which it was reached. Thus, if "x" was zoomed in from "B", zooming out gets back to "B" and not "A". This preserves therefore the context of viewing an S-collection.

One other orthogonal navigation operation is defined in the model: the *Zoom-Up* operation. This operation effects a jump from the current container to another that also contains the current member. As there may be more than one such container, the operation must also specify which. Figure 26-5 illustrates the operation. The current member "x" in the current container "C" is also a member of collection "A" and "B". The zoom-up specifies "B", causing "B" to become the current container with "x" remaining as the current member.

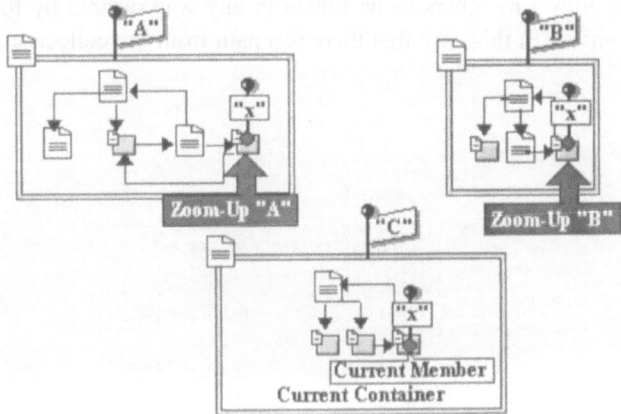

Figure 26-5 The Zoom-Up Operation

The zoom-up operation is its own complement. Thus, in the above example, the jump back to "C" after a zoom-up to "B" is a zoom-up to "C"! Perhaps more accurately, we can view the operation as a lateral jump amongst collections that contain the current member (the term "zoom-up", therefore, may not be entirely appropriate!). This may appear a rather odd type of navigation to provide, but in effect it changes the context (ie. the container) of the current member. It is not difficult to extend the operation to "cycle through" all the contexts of the current member. This could be used by authors, for example, to browse through the contexts of a given S-collection that he/she wishes to re-use, just to see how it has been re-used so far.

26.4 Data Classes

In the HM-Data Model, a particular S-collection is an instance of one of four predefined types of S-collections:

1. Folder,

2. Envelope,

3. Menu, and

4. Freelinks

Each type or data class defines a particular link topology which constrains the way members can be linked to one another. Additionally, the integrity of the links in any of these types will be automatically maintained.

Figure 26-6 illustrates the link topology of each type:

- the Folder connects each member in a bidirectional circular list

- the Envelope links each member to every other member

- the Menu connects the collection head to every other member using bidirectional links

- the Freelinks allows members to be linked in any way desired by the author; the author must ensure in this case that there is a path from the collection head to each member

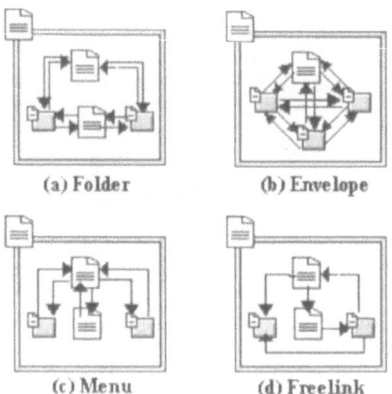

(a) Folder   (b) Envelope

(c) Menu   (d) Freelink

Figure 26-6 Classes of S-Collections

Comparing these to Hyperwave collections, we can see that the Hyperwave sequence collection roughly corresponds to the Folder type, but the latter is a circular list. Of course, all the topologies above can be defined in Hyperwave using links, but they must be manually created. In contrast, the HM-Data Model supports the automatic creation of links for all types, except for the Freelinks type (see next section). Hyper-G, however, allows links to be defined between nodes from different collections while the HM-Data Model does not.

26.5 Illustrative Example

Consider, for instance, an HM-Card hypermedia database containing a large amount of computer-based educational material, where users can browse particular courses represented in hypermedia form. To be more specific, let us assume that we have a number of computer based courses prepared in the form of S-collections: say "Course#1" and "Course#2" in Figure 26-7.

Each course has a title page as its label and a number of members corresponding to chapters of the course. If a course, say Course#1, refers to another course, say, Course#2, the course referred to has to be inserted into the same S-collection as a member (see Figure 26-7). A chapter consists of primitive pages and refers to other courses or chapters.

It should be noted that if particular chapters and/or pages are relevant to the contents of a number of courses, the corresponding S-collections may be re-used without any extra overhead (see, for instance, S-collection "Chapter-B"). S-collection "Author-X" has a short description about the author as its head and the author's courses (S-collection "Course#1", S-collection "Course#2", etc.) as members.

The above discussion has indicated how primitive chunks (i.e. "pages") may be gathered into more complex structures (in this case, "chapters"). The property of the HM-Data Model that an S-collection may belong to many other S-collections, even recursively, provides all the necessary power to deal with more complex situations. Note the recursive membership of documents "Course#1" and "Author-X" in this example. Such recursive membership elegantly handles the common situation where a user needs to be able to access information about "Course#1" while browsing information about "Author-X" *and* vice versa. Moreover, if a certain chapter ("Chapter-B") refers to another course ("Course#3"), then the S-collection "Chapter-B" can be extended with the relevant member.

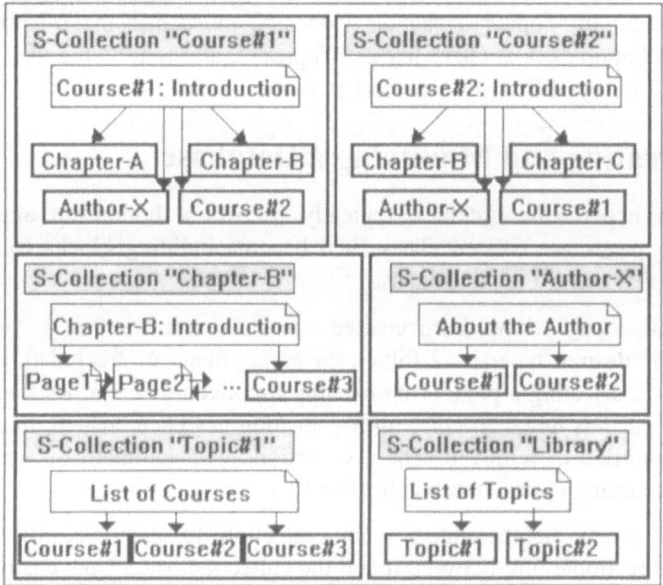

Figure 26-7 A sample hypermedia database

To conclude our example, the S-collections representing courses might be inserted into S-collections dealing with particular topics (say, "Topic#1", "Topic#2" etc.). Finally, one could combine all the topic S-collections into an S-collection "Library of Courseware".

To understand the basic properties of this model, let us simulate the steps of a typical user session. Suppose the user accesses the S-collection "Library of Courseware" (see Figure 26-7) in some way. The label of the S-collection displays information about the contents of the S-collection. Suppose also that the user "opens" the S-collection "Library of Courseware" and activates the link to the S-collection "Topic#1" within the "Library of Courseware". The S-collection "Topic#1" becomes the current member, and the chunk of multimedia information defined as its label is displayed. Note that the navigational paradigm associated with the current document "Library of Courseware" is still active. The user has the possibility to access another topic by clicking on it. After selecting a particular topic, the user can "open" this S-collection. Once an S-collection is "opened" the user obtains (i.e., can follow) links encapsulated within it (perhaps a menu of courses).

Each choice from the menu results in the presentation of the label of the corresponding S-collection. If the user has selected and entered the S-collection "Course#1" and then selected the S-collection "Chapter-B", the abstract of the chapter is visualised ("Chapter-B" is the current member) and links to other members (i.e., to other chapters) become available. The user can either read the current chapter (i.e., open the S-collection) or browse other chapters. Clicking on button "ZOOM OUT" returns the user to S-collection "Topic#1". Now clicking on another member of "Topic#1" (say, on "Course#2") visualises that member's label, clicking on button "ZOOM OUT" leaves "Topic#1", and returns the user to the S-collection "Library of Courseware", and so forth.

26.6 Creating and Modifying a Database

Building a hypermedia database typically follows a bottom-up approach. First, multimedia pages are created. They then become building blocks for complex S-collections that constitute the database.

Assuming that pages have been created, an author creates a new S-collection by selecting the desired type (ie. a folder, envelope, menu or freelinks), assigning it a unique name, selecting a page or an existing S-collection as its head, and optionally selecting a page as its label. Once an S-collection has been created, members can be inserted, modified or removed. These operations will automatically update the link structure according to the chosen collection type.

Insertion of a new member into a menu collection, for example, will automatically create a bidirectional link between it and the collection head. Conversely, removing a member will remove its corresponding link to/from the head. Similar automatic creation and deletion of links apply to envelopes and folders. With folders, of course, we must also specify the insertion position in the circular list. The exception to all this is the freelinks collection, where the user must explicitly insert and/or remove links to create the desired link topology.

Links are second-generation, ie. separated from rather than embedded in the members. This is of course essential since a member can be re-used in another collection with a different link topology. Links may be visualised in a variety of ways and users, when adding or modifying a member, can typically elect how a source anchor is visualised. These may be hot-spots, hot-words, scrolling menu lists, icons, etc., depending on the particular implementation of the model.

It should be apparent now that the HM-Data Model is highly modular. Pages and collections can be created independently but at the same time can be re-used through a flexible nesting or containment mechanism. It greatly facilitates therefore multi-author development of hypermedia databases, involving principally:

a) creating pages (using some appropriate multimedia editor application)

b) creating S-collections of appropriate type (determining therefore their internal link structure)

c) re-using previously created pages and S-collections to define the contents of S-collections being created

d) storing new S-collections into the database (thus making them available for re-use in other S-collections)

Any S-collection can be modified at any time and, as mentioned above, internal link associations will be automatically updated as members are added/removed. Note, however, that removing a member does not actually delete it from the database. To delete an S-collection, we must do so explicitly. All collections containing the one being deleted will be updated accordingly (see Figure 26-8).

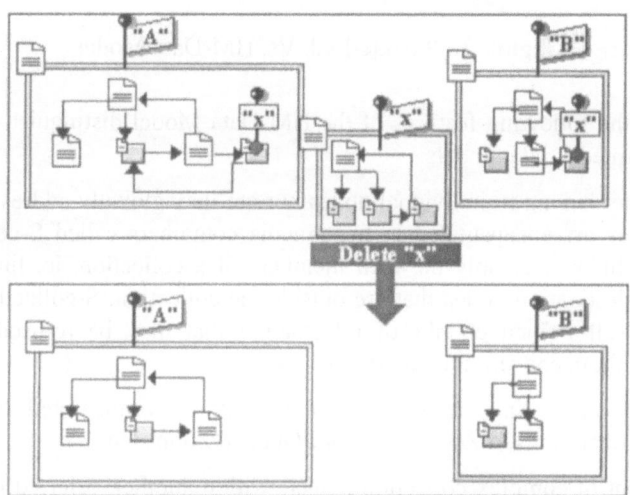

Figure 26-8 Impact of deletion on nested S-collections

Of course, similar to import/export facilities of many database systems, subsets (of pages and/or collections) of a database may be separately saved and used by another. In should be clear, however, that copies are actually made in these cases and that the separate databases are maintained independently, ie. changes made in one cannot be seen in the other.

26.7 Conclusion

The HM-Data Model essentially replaces the "spaghetti" view of the basic Node-Link model with more structured, independent but fully compatible hypermedia modules called S-Collections (see Figure 26-9). Such modules, in fact, closely resemble abstract data types discussed earlier: they encapsulate an internal structure, which may re-use other modules, and navigation operations. The types of modules - folder, menu, envelope and freelinks - are data classes with predefined public methods for navigation and private methods for maintaining internal link integrity. Every S-collection may therefore be viewed as instances of these classes, acquiring thereby all their capabilities/behaviour. This object-oriented view of the HM-Data Model uncovers the possibility of model extension through class inheritance and specialisation, and the prospect of an implementation that allows users to customise their own S-collection structure and behaviour while still remaining fully compatible with system-defined collections.

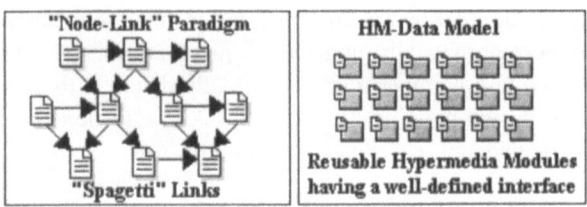

Figure 26-9 Node-Link Vs. HM-Data Model

In summary, the following features of the HM-Data Model distinguish it from other existing hypermedia data models:

a) Links neither belong to individual nodes nor are they globally addressable objects. Instead, they are encapsulated in hypermedia containers called S-collections. By definition, links exist only between members of a collection, ie. links cannot be created to destination nodes that are outside the collection. S-collections therefore represent well-defined chunks of information that may be re-used in different contexts without concern for superfluous links.

b) The restriction of links to local contexts only is compensated by orthogonal navigation operations of Zoom-In, Zoom-Out and Zoom-Up.

c) Containment of complex collection objects within another, referred to as "re-use" rather than "reference", is in line with object-oriented views and closer to the intended concept of sharing existing resources, particular in different contexts. The term "reference" too strongly suggests "jumping to another location" (with a fixed given context). "Re-use" on the other hand implies an (logical) embedding of the external object into the current context (switching between embedding contexts is via Zoom-Up).

d) Authoring is effected by memberwise inclusion of hypermedia chunks, as opposed to spaghetti linking of nodes in other models. Any S-collection can be included in any other. Recursive membership relations remain a possibility and will allow the modelling of arbitrarily complex hypermedia databases.

e) All operations are addressed to a particular data object (S-collection) and do not affect the link structure of other objects. This object-oriented character of the model presents new ways of supporting the logical integrity of hypermedia databases.

26.8 Further Reading

The classic book on Multimedia and Hypermedia is the one by Nielsen [Nielsen 1995]. A nice modern book on the same subject that is very worthwhile with both a good survey and novel ideas is [Lennon 1997], while [Gloor 1997] is emphasizing visualization aspects. Of the many books on HTML it is hard to choose the best one, but [Musciano and Kennedy 1997] is pretty good.

The notion of second generation WWW systems was first introduced in [Maurer 1996]: it is based on experiences with [Hyperwave]. On modern applications to teaching see [GENTLE]. For the HM - Data Model consult [Maurer and Scherbakov 1996] or the easy accessible [HM-Card].

References:

[GENTLE] http://www.iicm.edu/gentle.htm

[Gloor 1997] Gloor, P. *Elements of Hypermedia Design,* Birkhäuser (1997).

[HM-Card] http://www.iicm.edu/hmcard

[Hyperwave] http://www.hyperwave.com

[Lennon 1997] Lennon, J.A. *Hypermedia Systems and Applications: WWW and Beyond,* Springer (1997).

[Maurer 1996] Maurer, H. (Ed.) *Hyperwave: The Next Generation Web Solution,* Addison Wesley (1996).

[Maurer & Scherbakov 1996] Maurer, H. and Scherbakov, N. *Multimedia Authoring for Presentation and Education*, Addison Wesley (1996).

[Musciano & Kennedy 1997] Musciano, Ch. and Kennedy, B. *HTML- the Definitive Guide,* O'Reilly (1997).

[Nielsen 1995] Nielsen, J. *Multimedia and Hypermedia-The Internet and Beyond,* Academic Press (1995).

Springer
and the
environment

At Springer we firmly believe that an international science publisher has a special obligation to the environment, and our corporate policies consistently reflect this conviction.

We also expect our business partners – paper mills, printers, packaging manufacturers, etc. – to commit themselves to using materials and production processes that do not harm the environment. The paper in this book is made from low- or no-chlorine pulp and is acid free, in conformance with international standards for paper permanency.

Springer